Press Portrayals of Women Politicians, 1870s–2000s

Women in American Political History

Series Editors: Pam Parry and David R. Davies

Advisory Board

Maurine Beasley, Barbara G. Friedman, Karla K. Gower,
Janice Hume, Margot Opdycke Lamme, and Jane Marcellus

Women in American Political History focuses on influential women throughout the history of American politics. From the Colonial period through the Founding up to the present, women often have played significant and meaningful roles in politics, both directly and indirectly. Many of their contributions have been overlooked. This interdisciplinary series seeks to advance the dialogue concerning the role of women in politics in America and highlight their various contributions, including women who were elected and appointed to office and those who have wielded political power behind the scenes, such as first ladies, journalists, activists, and public relations practitioners. The series welcomes contributions from all methodologies and disciplines across the social sciences and humanities.

Recent Titles

Press Portrayals of Women Politicians, 1870s–2000s: From "Lunatic" Woodhull to "Polarizing" Palin, Teri Finneman, 2015.

Press Portrayals of Women Politicians, 1870s–2000s

From "Lunatic" Woodhull to "Polarizing" Palin

Teri Finneman, Ph.D.

LEXINGTON BOOKS

Lanham • Boulder • New York • London

Cover photos:

Top left: This illustration of Victoria Woodhull testifying before Congress that women should have the right to vote appeared in the February 4, 1871, issue of Frank Leslie's Illustrated Newspaper. Photo courtesy of the Library of Congress.
Top right: This portrait of Jeannette Rankin was created in 1916, the same year she became the first woman elected to Congress. Photo courtesy of the Library of Congress.
Bottom left: Photo courtesy of Margaret Chase Smith Library
Bottom right: Alaska Gov. Sarah Palin campaigns in Dover, New Hampshire, in fall 2008. Palin was the first woman chosen as a Republican vice presidential candidate. Photo courtesy of Roger H. Goun

Published by Lexington Books
An imprint of The Rowman & Littlefield Publishing Group, Inc.
4501 Forbes Boulevard, Suite 200, Lanham, Maryland 20706
www.rowman.com

Unit A, Whitacre Mews, 26-34 Stannary Street, London SE11 4AB

British Library Cataloguing in Publication Information Available

Library of Congress Cataloging-in-Publication Data
Names: Finneman, Teri Ann.
Title: Press portrayals of women politicians, 1870s–2000s : from "lunatic" Woodhull to "polarizing" Palin / Teri Finneman.
Description: Lanham : Lexington Books, 2015. | Series: Women in American political history | Includes bibliographical references and index.
Identifiers: LCCN 2015033978 | ISBN 9781498524247 (cloth : alkaline paper) | ISBN 9781498524254 (electronic)
Subjects: LCSH: Women politicians—Press coverage—United States—History. | Press and politics—United States—History. | Mass media—Political aspects—United States—History. | Sexism in political culture—United States—History. | Woodhull, Victoria C. (Victoria Claflin), 1838–1927—Public opinion. | Rankin, Jeannette, 1880–1973—Public opinion. | Smith, Margaret Chase, 1897–1995—Public opinion. | Palin, Sarah, 1964—-Public opinion. | Public opinion—United States—History. | Discourse analysis—Political aspects—United States.
Classification: LCC HQ1236.5.U6 F49 2015 | DDC 320.0820973—dc23 LC record available at http://lccn.loc.gov/2015033978

♾ ™ The paper used in this publication meets the minimum requirements of American National Standard for Information Sciences—Permanence of Paper for Printed Library Materials, ANSI/NISO Z39.48-1992.

Printed in the United States of America

To Yong Volz, my dissertation chairwoman,
and Ryan Thomas, my best research partner

Contents

Chapter 1

Politics, Power, and the Press

In 2008, Hillary Clinton stood before supporters of her failed bid for the Democratic presidential nomination and noted the progress her campaign made for women in politics:

> Although we weren't able to shatter that highest, hardest glass ceiling this time, thanks to you, it's got about 18 million cracks in it—and the light is shining through like never before, filling us all with the hope and the sure knowledge that the path will be a little easier next time. ("Transcript: Hillary Clinton Endorses Barack Obama" 2008)

She then praised the suffragists who paved the way for women to vote and noted that "children today will grow up taking for granted that an African-American or a woman can, yes, become the president of the United States." In 2015, Clinton again entered presidential politics in an attempt to become the nation's first female president, with *The New York Times* noting her bid could be "the first time a woman captures a major party's nomination" (Chozick 2015). However, Clinton is certainly not the first woman who has paved the way for women in politics or even the first woman in the United States to run for the presidency. For nearly 150 years, American women politicians have tried to shatter that "highest, hardest glass ceiling." Since Victoria Woodhull's groundbreaking run for the presidency in 1872, more than 100 women have vied for the nation's highest office with varying degrees of seriousness (Falk 2010; Havel 1996). The Center for American Women and Politics at Rutgers considers just 13 of these women to be of legitimate historical note (*Women Presidential and Vice Presidential Candidates* 2012), indicating the challenges and rarity of the endeavor. Women politicians also face challenges breaking into Congress, often referred to as the "old boys club" (Blake 2014).

1

Since Jeannette Rankin broke that barrier for women in 1916 with her election to the U.S. House, women have slowly gained national representation, particularly since the second wave of feminism in the 1960s. In 1979, women comprised just 3 percent of Congress compared to 18.5 percent in 2014 (*Women in Elective Office 2014* 2014). Yet, despite this growth, representation still falls far short of the nation's 50 percent female demographic.

Although women in politics continue to face challenges, the United States is clearly within reach of its first woman president, whether that be in 2016 or in an election soon after. This book explores the historical path to an American woman president by examining how political, feminist, and journalistic cultures across history have advanced and regressed the opportunities for women in politics from the 1870s to the 2000s. In particular, this book examines how these cultures influenced women politicians' media coverage, which provides tangible evidence of the reinforcement and negotiation of gender norms across time. As this book will illustrate, the American press has historically treated women political candidates differently due to their gender. Even though women in other countries have served as presidents and prime ministers, the U.S. media continue to question whether women here can hold the nation's top political post: "Still their ability to lead their country is questioned, still the media ask, can they really do it?" (Ross 2010, 99). This is problematic because the representation of women in news media, in particular, "send[s] important messages to the viewing, listening, and reading publics about women's place, women's role, and women's lives" (Byerly and Ross 2006, 40). Stereotypical and biased news coverage, therefore, can have a chilling effect on women who may have otherwise considered running for public office or can create unrealistic standards for those who do (Falk 2010; Ross 2010). This is contradictory to the news industry's purported belief in the role of media to enhance democracy "by providing an open forum of debate that reflects the diversity of society" (Curran 2005, 127).

Scholars have written at length about the existence of sexist media coverage and its societal implications (i.e. Falk 2013, 2010; McCabe 2012; Gill 2007; Anderson and Sheeler 2005; Braden 1996; Kahn 1996; Witt, Matthews, and Paget 1995). One has gone so far to say that "the media have been the bane of the political woman's existence" (Witt, Matthews, and Paget 1995, 184) since Rankin was elected to Congress in the early twentieth century. Women going back to Susan B. Anthony have complained about media coverage, but Anthony's line of thinking that "biased coverage was better than no coverage at all" (Braden 1996, 1) may very well still apply to women in politics today. There has been an unspoken rule that sexism should not be discussed due to the criticism that women receive for mentioning it, thereby trapping them in an endless cycle of sexist media coverage (Falk 2013). These women tend to be asked condescending questions and "often must field the same outworn gender-related questions that reporters asked a century ago" (Braden 1996, 144). For example, many have been asked, "Are you running as a woman?" (Witt, Matthews, and Paget 1995, 12), thereby putting the emphasis on their gender rather than their professional platform. In other words, women interested in political careers are typically framed "as women first and then, maybe, as politicians" (Ross 2010, 99). Other problems faced by these women include overcoming the "outsider" framing frequently selected by journalists in their coverage, as well as the unrealistically high expectations set by the media on their performance (Ross 2010). There are still stereotypes about women being emotional, lacking in leadership—particularly in areas like the military and finance—and being incapable of handling politics and motherhood at the same time (Falk 2010). Gendered news strategies and lackluster news coverage therefore make a female president "seem less normative and more difficult to achieve" (Falk 2010, 3). In addition, the trivialization of women candidates throughout history has resulted in "the absence of widespread political knowledge about the impressive and capable women who have lived political lives" (Falk 2010, 3). Therefore, although prominent male politicians are referenced, this book does not go into depth about their history or analyze their news coverage. Rather, this book seeks to remedy the absence of knowledge about political women pioneers and about women's political history in general.

The unique contribution of this book is its longitudinal and contextual approach to analyzing media coverage of national women politicians. The goal is to explain the discursive strategies used by mainstream newspaper reporters in their coverage of pioneering women in politics in order to understand how these strategies have and have not changed throughout history. In other words, what role has the press played in women's political history, and how has that role potentially changed from the era of the partisan press in the 1800s to the era of objective reporting in the 1900s to the era of infotainment and instant news in the 2000s? What aspects of these women's political campaigns have the press focused on or ignored? Has the press served as a supporter of the status quo or functioned as an agent of change in regard to women in politics? Answering these questions involves studying journalistic word choices (both what is said and what is not) and source choices in news articles. This book examines press coverage of Victoria Woodhull, the first woman to run for president in 1872; Jeannette Rankin, the first woman elected to Congress in 1916; Margaret Chase Smith, the first woman to receive a nomination for president at a major party's convention in 1964; and Sarah Palin, the first Republican woman selected as a vice presidential candidate in 2008. This book also describes "the implication of previous discursive positions on subsequent ones" (Carvalho 2008, 163). In other words, how is press coverage of one woman politician reflected in the coverage of her successors? What themes are apparent and continued throughout the history of newspaper coverage of pioneer women politicians? Does the press reference prior women politicians in its contemporary coverage and, if so, how? In addition, how have changing historical contexts influenced press coverage?

To answer these questions, this book analyzes the discourse, or word choices, used in press stories of the four women political pioneers noted above. This particular study is focused on *critical* discourse analysis, which has become a prominent framework for analyzing media texts (Carvalho 2008; Garrett and Bell 1998). Critical discourse analysis is "a theory and a method of analyzing the way that individuals and institutions use language" (Richardson 2007, 1). The concept "critical" involves "the use of rational thinking to question arguments or prevailing ideas" (Fairclough, Mulderring, and Wodak 2011, 358). In other words, this study aims to question prevailing ideas of how newspapers use language when writing about women politicians. This includes analyzing not only what is said in the media text but also what is *not* said, as critical examination of texts involves both strategies (Richardson 2007).

Critical scholars believe reality is created by social, economic, cultural, and gender structures, which both *influence* the people within them and *are influenced by* the people within them (Guba and Lincoln 1998, emphasis added). Therefore, to understand a past reality, examining its historical context is important. Critical researchers believe their work "can provide rich insight into human behavior" (Guba and Lincoln 1998, 197) through the interpretation of texts. For media scholars, this includes examining how the media select and construct knowledge, as well as the media's role in circulating dominant ideologies (Hardt 1998). By undertaking critical analysis, researchers hope to enlighten the public and prompt change to better society (Guba and Lincoln 1998; Hardt 1998).

Critical discourse analysis is important because of how influential discourse is in society (Fairclough, Mulderring, and Wodak 2011). Although the extent of discourse effects can be difficult to determine (Fairclough 2001), scholars argue that discourse does contribute to "the construction of social identities, social relations, and systems of knowledge and meaning" (Jorgensen and Phillips 2004, 67). Therefore, critical researchers are interested in examining what texts say about a society, the influence of texts on social relations, and the role of texts in social inequalities, including inequalities between men and women (Richardson 2007; Jorgensen and Phillips 2004). This involves bringing awareness to the argument that discourse contributes to "the reinforcement of unequal power relations" (Jorgensen and Phillips 2004, 88). The ultimate goal is to enhance democracy through more egalitarian discourse (Jorgensen and Phillips 2004), which—in the case of political news coverage—would entail using the same discursive strategies for women candidates as those used with men.

Studying journalism discourse in particular is important because of the broad reach it has throughout society. It is believed that media discourse has "a pervasive and powerful influence in social reproduction" (Fairclough 2001, 45) due to the scale of mass media and the accessibility of media texts to the general public. Similarly, media serve as "crucial presenters of culture, politics, and social life, shaping as well as reflecting how these are formed and expressed. Media 'discourse' is important both for what it reveals about a society and because it also contributes to the character of society" (Bell 1998, 64-65). In other words, analyzing media discourse provides further understanding of language norms, thus revealing what is viewed as acceptable by a particular society at a particular time (Garrett and Bell 1998). Media discourse can shape individuals' opinions not only about the world itself "but also of their *place* and *role* in the world" (Richardson 2007, 13, original emphasis). For the purpose of this book, this would mean the place and role of women, specifically in regard to politics. Although scholars debate the level of effect the media has on consumers, this study embraces the view that media can still influence "*what* you have opinions on" and "help shape social reality by shaping our *views* of social reality" (Richardson 2007, 13, original emphasis). As a result, it is important to take seriously the news media's choice of language.

To be clear, this does not suggest that discourse is a one-way street with journalists alone setting the agenda. Rather, there is a circular process wherein "social practices influence texts . . . and in turn texts help influence society via shaping the viewpoints of those who read or otherwise consume them" (Richardson 2007, 37). In other words, journalists are influenced by the societal norms and times in which they live, which then influences their word choices in their stories. The word choices in their stories then influence the consumers who read them. To better understand the societal context of the journalists whose work is analyzed in this book, a historical-diachronic discourse analysis approach is used. This approach is discussed in further detail next.

One of the gaps in critical discourse analysis research is longitudinal examination of how "the reporting of a particular story, theme, or issue develops over time" (Richardson 2010, 3). Analyzing single media texts offers little insight into journalistic practice since "the effects of media power are cumulative, working through the repetition of particular ways of handling causality and agency, particular ways of positioning the reader" (Fairclough 2001, 45). Therefore, it is important to study multiple media texts across time. In attempts to address this gap of longitudinal work, both Carvalho (2008) and Wodak (2001) promote a historical approach to discourse. This research uses the historical-diachronic discourse analysis approach promoted by Carvalho, who highlights the importance of understanding the historical and social contexts of the particular time(s) under review in a research study. In other words, simply analyzing media texts is not enough. One must also understand the time(s) from which the discourse came. Carvalho also argues that understanding the progression of complex issues in media texts over time "is one of the most important contributions to be made by social researchers" (Carvalho 2008, 164). This approach has proven to be useful for studying societal issues, such as sexism (Fairclough, Mulderring, and Wodak 2011).

Therefore, this book takes a qualitative historical-diachronic approach to examining press coverage of women politicians over time by analyzing the similarities and differences in discourse among the cases and incorporating a broad scope of historical context. Specifically, this context includes providing biographical information about each politician selected for study; context about her political era; context about the state of the media during her political era; context about the state of feminism during her political era; and then, of course, analysis of each woman's newspaper coverage. This contextual approach also coincides with strategies promoted by sociological and women's history scholars, thereby providing additional support for a longitudinal multi-case approach (i.e. Haydu 1998; Ragin 1987; DuBois et al. 1980).

Since this book places an emphasis on political, feminist, and media cultures, it is important to understand what is meant by each. Chapters 2 through 5 in this book provide more specific historical context, but a brief overview of the concepts is provided here.

The concept of political culture has interested historians and political scientists for at least 60 years (Formisano 2001). However, the concept has lacked a universal definition, a problem compounded by the number of scholars who have skirted the issue "by simply not bothering with any definition at all" (Formisano 2001, 394). The matter is further complicated when gender is added as a component. Women in the United States were not granted universal suffrage until 1920. Yet women most certainly were politically active in the years prior to winning the right to vote. So did U.S. women have their own political culture or not? It is useful to examine how other scholars have approached the concept. In his study of major political systems, Almond (1956) defined political culture as "a particular pattern of orientation to political action" (396). This is important as it allows political culture to go beyond formalized structures, such as political parties, thus allowing use of the concept for those disenfranchised or otherwise left out of mainstream political bureaucracies. Indeed, decades later, a scholar argued the definition should include "all struggles over power, not just those decided by elections. The women's movement, the struggles for racial justice and the rights of labor, conflicts for control of churches and voluntary organizations, even power struggles among members of the family" (Howe 1991, 1235–36). This inclusion of the women's movement as a political culture is a critical step. In addition, feminist historian Ellen DuBois contributes to the debate by noting that political culture goes beyond voting, "recognizing that the underlying values that characterized and distinguished the ways they thought about political life are fundamental" (Cott et al. 2003, 151). Therefore, a number of historians offer conceptualizations that allow for a separate women's political culture.

Yet there is some disagreement among scholars as to whether a separate women's political culture has ever existed in the United States. This book embraces the perspective of historian Paula Baker, who is known for creating "the signal piece of work in the history of political culture," specifically in regard to women's history (Cott et al. 2003, 151). Baker's 1984 work, "The Domestication of Politics," covers 1780 to 1920 and favors the existence of a separate women's political culture prior to suffrage. Therefore, Baker is an obvious starting point for examining what she refers to as the values, relationships, practices, and resistance to patriarchal dominance associated with women's political culture during pre-feminism and the first wave of feminism. Baker's perspective will be discussed in more depth in chapter 2. For now, it is necessary to explain *why* there is disagreement over women's political culture.

Women's historian Rebecca Edwards is among those to challenge the concept. She declares early in her 1997 book, *Angels in the Machinery,* that she found "no evidence of a separate 'women's political culture' in the Gilded Age" (Edwards 1997, 8). She continues by saying: "On the contrary, women who enlisted in a variety of political projects—even the most radical suffragists—repeatedly worked through party mechanisms and cooperated with male allies who shared their views" (Edwards 1997, 8). Edwards acknowledges that she is "defining politics narrowly" (Edwards 1997, 9), explaining that she does so because Americans in the nineteenth century defined politics as political parties and elections. Although certainly historians must be aware of the context of the times in which they are writing, they must also beware of the trap that Lerner (1975) and Baker (1984) warned about: only analyzing women through the lens of men. By accepting the patriarchal definition of politics, historians do a significant disservice by confining women's history to a hegemonic, male-approved framework that continues the cycle of belittling women's contributions and differences. Therefore, as previously noted, this research subscribes to Baker's approach that there was a separate women's political culture in the United States that differed from men's in structure, priorities, and limitations, at least until 1920, as will be outlined further in this book's chapters. However, a caveat is that, like many other historians' focus on women's political culture (Kerber 1988), this book focuses on a white, middle-class perspective that is not necessarily representative of diverse women's views due to the scope of this particular study. Another major concept in relation to women's history and of relevance to this book is feminism, which has been defined as "a political ideology [that] recognizes inequalities between women and men in a given class and attempts to equalize those relationships among propertied groups" (DuBois et al. 1980, 43). One scholar describes three conditions of feminism: an "opposition to sex hierarchy," a belief that "woman's condition is socially constructed," and a formation of group identity, or women seeing themselves as their own social group due to their sex (Cott 1987, 4–5). In other words, women identify with other women and believe that their status is determined by society, not by biology. These women also oppose gender inequality in its political, economic, and social forms, thereby making them feminists. The following chapters will delve further into feminism and the complicated relationship that women in national politics have had with the women's movement since the 1800s.

Finally, this book is interested in journalism culture. Although the alternative press has certainly played a role in broader journalistic culture, this book focuses on mainstream press culture and coverage due to its broader public reach. Culture generally consists of a set of ideas, practices, and artifacts (Hanitzsch 2007). This book examines artifacts (newspaper articles) in order to better understand practices of journalists and the ideals of a particular era that influenced those practices. Journalism culture can be further defined based on three concepts: institutional roles, epistemologies, and ethical ideologies (Hanitzsch 2007). This book focuses on aspects of the first. Institutional roles involve the responsibilities and contributions of the press, which are further broken down into interventionism, power distance, and market orientation (Hanitzsch 2007). Interventionism involves the extent of advocacy that journalists undertake in their work, while power distance refers to how close journalists are to those in power, such as government officials (Hanitzsch 2007). The spectrum of market orientation ranges from the press focusing on serving a democratic purpose to the press focusing on consumerism (Hanitzsch 2007). All of these areas will be examined in further depth in the remaining chapters.

Although this introduction has provided an overview of the framework of this book, one must keep in mind that "no single framework, no single factor, four-factor or eight-factor explanation can serve to contain all that the history of women is" (Lerner 1975, 12). In other words, "historians cannot comprehend all the variables bombarding a single event" (Appleby, Hunt, and Jacobs 1994, 253). Therefore, this book, like other history books, cannot cover every factor surrounding these women, their political careers, and their media coverage. However, while there is "no 'correct' interpretation of the past . . . the act of interpreting is itself a vicarious enlargement from which you can benefit" (Gaddis 2002, 10). Examining these women politicians' cases in further detail and having a better understanding of the past can provide more insight for the future.

Again, this book features four select women who made notable progress for women and politics in U.S. history: Victoria Woodhull, an Ohio native, was the first woman to run for president after earning the support of the Equal Rights Party in 1872; Jeannette Rankin, a Republican in name only from Montana, was the first woman elected to Congress in 1916; Margaret Chase Smith, a moderate Republican from Maine, was the first woman to be nominated for president at a major party's political convention in 1964; and Sarah Palin, a conservative Republican from Alaska, was the first Republican woman vice presidential candidate in 2008. These cases were chosen for a few reasons. First, regardless of whether she won or lost, each woman made pioneering strides for women and politics. Each broke a barrier for women in presidential or congressional elections, thereby paving the way for future women in politics at the national level. As a result, all four garnered significant press attention, allowing for ample news stories to analyze. In addition, the cases selected are "informative cases" as they are expected to "represent the phenomenon under study quite clearly" (Swanborn 2010, 52). Because the women were all political pioneers, it was suspected that they faced at least some of the same discursive treatment in the press, allowing for analysis of both similarities and differences. Although some may argue that four cases are not adequate for a thorough analysis, case studies allow for "the detailed examination of an aspect of a historical episode to develop or test historical explanations that may be generalizable to other events" (George and Bennett 2005, 5). Therefore, the patterns found in press coverage of each woman were expected to inform the coverage trends of her successors, which was indeed the case. In addition, the variance in political persuasions of the selected women added a layer of richness in order to consider whether political affiliation made a difference in coverage.

Finally, the historical time of each woman was also taken into consideration when selecting cases. These cases cover approximately 45-year increments in order to understand the changes (or lack thereof) in journalistic and political cultures and how that may have influenced newspaper coverage of pioneer women politicians over time. The years of these cases also align with pre-feminism, the first wave of feminism, the second wave of feminism, and the third wave of feminism to analyze how the environment for women at a particular time may have also influenced media coverage. This is why Sarah Palin was selected for analysis rather than Geraldine Ferraro, although chapter 6 does touch upon Ferraro's media coverage. Palin offered an opportunity to examine more recent contexts of journalism, feminism, and politics in order to understand their influence on a recent pioneering run. It is also useful to explain Rankin's inclusion in this book since, unlike the others, she was not on a presidential ticket. Rankin offers an opportunity to examine what historical factors were present when a woman broke a glass ceiling in national politics. In other words, it's important to understand if there were differences in press coverage or other historical contexts that made it possible for a woman to win a major political office 100 years ago. Certainly a number of historical women politicians could have been chosen for analysis. The women ultimately chosen were selected as representative cases of particular times. Taking into account the above context, this book is divided into five additional chapters.

Chapter 2 features Victoria Woodhull, whose run for president forced the press to take notice of rising political women after the Civil War. This chapter examines how the press formulated an early prototype image of female political figures during the 1872 presidential election, a time when media were still largely partisan and when women's political culture largely focused on improving home life. Not surprisingly, Woodhull's media coverage was blatantly negative and filled with attacks on both her political views and her personal life to the point of vilifying her. This chapter focuses on the initial discursive strategies to delegitimize a woman politician.

Chapter 3 features Jeanette Rankin, the only woman in this analysis who won her pioneering race. As the first woman elected to Congress, Rankin served as a powerful symbol that the universal suffrage movement was nearing victory. This chapter examines how the press covered the campaign of a woman politician who would win a national office for the first time during the 1916 election cycle. Rankin's race came at a time when newspapers were transitioning between subjective and objective reporting and when women were realizing they needed state and national representation to advance their platforms. Rankin's news coverage provides evidence of the power of discourse when the media legitimates a campaign. However, new gendered discursive strategies also emerged in Rankin's media coverage that would prove problematic for future women politicians.

Chapter 4 features Margaret Chase Smith, the first woman nominated for the presidency at a major party's convention. This chapter examines how the press covered the campaign of a woman politician in 1964 during a time when newspapers were largely complaisant to the status quo and when views of gender roles were again rigid. The historical context of the time, Smith's differing campaign strategy, and voters' attitudes that a woman president was a concept for the future all played significant roles in the ultimate dooming and trivialization of her candidacy. Gendered stereotypes, gendered news frames, and double binds for women were all evident in Smith's news coverage, indicating not just a continuation of gendered discursive strategies in the press but a growth in this discourse.

Chapter 5 features Sarah Palin, the first Republican woman vice presidential candidate. This chapter examines how the press covered Palin during the 2008 presidential election, a time when journalists were cynical of government and focused on personal characteristics of candidates. Palin was framed as a political celebrity and her news coverage provides evidence of a compounding of gendered discursive strategies to delegitimize women candidates, as evidenced by its similarities with Woodhull's, Rankin's, and Smith's news coverage. Yet, significantly, Palin's coverage included one notable difference, which illustrates that acceptance of these gendered strategies may finally be eroding.

Chapter 6 recaps the main points of this book and analyzes the similarities and differences in the press coverage of the four women featured in this study. Putting the four cases together, the chapter discusses how the media discourse of political women was initiated, modified, ramified, and crystalized from the 1870s to the 2000s. The chapter also includes brief examination of media coverage of other notable women politicians: Geraldine Ferraro, Elizabeth Dole, Nancy Pelosi, and Hillary Clinton. The chapter concludes with discussion of the political, journalistic, and scholarly implications of this book's findings and suggestions for future research.

Finally, the Appendix explains the specific methodology used to conduct this study, including how the news articles for this research were found, the number of articles analyzed, sampling strategies, coding framework, and methodological limitations.

Figure 2.1   Victoria Woodhull was the First Woman to Run for President in the United States.
This 1872 Thomas Nast cartoon referring to Woodhull as "Mrs. Satan" ran in the February issue
of Harper's Weekly. *Source*: Photo courtesy of the Library of Congress.

Chapter 2

Media Vilification
of Victoria Woodhull

Upon her death in 1927, Victoria Woodhull was remembered in *The New York Times* as a "pioneer suffragist" and an "indomitable leader" to whom the younger generation "owes so much" ("Victoria Martin, Suffragist, Dies" 1927, 19). Yet the first woman to run for president in the United States was viewed much differently by her peers in 1872. A story in the *Arizona Sentinel* warned that: "No good man, no honest man, no conscientious man will stir a finger to aid any woman in the fulfillment of any purposes of which this Woodhull can be regarded as representative. Her connection with a movement damns that movement." ("The Women Going Wrong" 1872, 2). Although it is not surprising that an obituary would wax poetic, the startling difference in discursive tone used to describe the same person is intriguing. Just what was it about Victoria Woodhull that prompted such a harsh portrayal in the press? Was it simply the fact that she was a woman running for president—the first to attempt to override that patriarchal barrier in an era when women were not even allowed to vote—or was there more to it? How did the journalism culture of the era play a role in this sharp discourse?

In order to understand the context of her news coverage, this chapter begins with an overview of the biography of Woodhull to learn what motivated this pioneering woman to run for president in the first place and the path that led her to this historic moment in U.S. history. This includes discussion of her connection to Susan B. Anthony and Elizabeth Cady Stanton as well as to other famous nineteenth-century figures, such as railroad tycoon Cornelius Vanderbilt, preacher Henry Ward Beecher, and journalist Theodore Tilton. In other words, Woodhull was not a no-name third-party candidate but a connected figure well-known in the era's political scene, although clearly a controversial one at that. This chapter also touches upon the election of 1872 by outlining not only Woodhull's political platform but the main contest between Republican Civil War hero and current president Ulysses S. Grant and Liberal Republican/Democratic nominee and famous New York newspaper editor Horace Greeley. This historical background of politics, feminism, and journalism will enlighten the discursive analysis of newspaper coverage that comprises the second half of this chapter. This analysis ranges from Woodhull's official nomination for president by the Equal Rights Party in May 1872 to her political defeat as she sat in a jail cell in November 1872. Before we can discuss why the nation's first female presidential candidate spent Election Day in jail, however, we must first understand Woodhull's "royal" beginning.

NAMED AFTER A QUEEN

Victoria Claflin Woodhull's mother knew her daughter was destined for greatness even before her seventh child was born, based on dreams and visions she had during her pregnancy (Underhill 1995). Born September 23, 1838, in Homer, Ohio, the infant was named after England's new monarch, Queen Victoria. Referred to by a biographer as "a rare jewel in a quarrelsome and indolent family that was considered the town trash" (Gabriel 1998, 7), Woodhull's unstable and unusual childhood was instrumental in her eventual rise to fame. Raised with little schooling but convinced by her eccentric mother that her intelligence came from "heavenly spirits" preparing her for "a special destiny" (Underhill 1995, 19), Woodhull was soon telling her own stories of visions and trances. She and her younger sister Tennessee, also known as Tennie, began working as mediums/clairvoyants during their childhood, a profession that would lead to both wealth and mockery in the press in the coming years. The business failures of their father, Reuben "Buck" Claflin, were another significant aspect of Woodhull's childhood. Although forced with her siblings to endure his alcoholic rages, Woodhull believed her father's stories that the family had "lost its rightful place in the world" (Underhill 1995, 20). She and Tennie would spend their adulthood focused on acquiring wealth and trying to gain the prosperity that they felt was taken from them (Underhill 1995). Finally, an illness at 14 proved to be the last leg in the stool of childhood influences that set up Woodhull for her future in politics. The doctor summoned to care for her, Canning Woodhull, was twice her age and full of tales of his prominent background. The pair married soon after her 15th birthday, but it didn't take long for Victoria Woodhull to realize her new husband not only lied about his background but also was prone to drunkenness and womanizing (Gabriel 1998; Underhill 1995). This disastrous relationship during a time when women had little choice but to stay in unhappy marriages would later contribute to her strong views about women's rights and her future as the "woman's rights [presidential] candidate" ("Untitled" 1872b, 1). However, those strong views would also be skewered by the press during her presidential campaign, as will be described further shortly. Without a stable husband to support their family, Woodhull resumed work as a clairvoyant (Underhill 1995). For women, clairvoyance was a rare opportunity to have a voice and work outside the home (Gabriel 1998). At the same time, however, the profession had its detractors and was often considered a synonym for prostitution (Gabriel 1998), hence why the press was so critical of it. Woodhull's work in clairvoyance is important to point out for a few reasons. She met her second husband, Colonel James Blood, a Civil War veteran and spiritualist, when he sought out her guidance in 1864. Soon after, Blood and Woodhull left their spouses and formed their own family with Woodhull's two young children (Underhill 1995). However, Woodhull retained her original married name, which is why she was still referred to as "Mrs. Woodhull" in the press. Blood's support during the next decade was important to her political career, yet her second marriage would also be a point of controversy in the press during her presidential campaign.

Woodhull's rise to political prominence began when she led her family to New York City in 1868 in search of new opportunity after states began clamping down and implementing fines on mediums (Underhill 1995). Aware that the aging Cornelius Vanderbilt sought clairvoyants, Woodhull and Tennie were determined to financially benefit from the railroad tycoon (Underhill 1995). The millionaire's generosity became a critical factor in Woodhull's rise in politics.

Prominence in New York

The romantic relationship that formed between 22-year-old Tennie Claflin and 74-year-old Cornelius Vanderbilt was clearly a factor in the richest man in America maintaining an interest in the two sisters, contributing to their rise in prominence in the late 1860s and early 1870s. In September 1869, Woodhull played the stock market and walked away with a fortune thanks to advice from Vanderbilt (Gabriel 1998). With his financial support, the sisters opened their own brokerage firm on Wall Street in early 1870, becoming the first women ever to do so and garnering Woodhull valuable publicity (Underhill 1995). The *Charleston* (S.C.) *Daily News* ran a front-page blurb from the *New York Evening Express* about the groundbreaking business move that described the sisters as "very affable and agreeable in their manners," but the reporter questioned whether "the 'female feature' is an advertising sensation" of some sort ("Women in the Stock Market" 1870, 1). *The New York Times* also covered the opening and wrote that the firm "was thronged from early morning until late at night by a crowd of curiosity hunters, who gazed at the females and besieged them with questions" ("Wall Street Aroused" 1870, 8). At the same time, the *Times* noted "there was a strong popular feeling against the persons . . . because of their antecedents." The story discussed the sisters' past as clairvoyants and magnetic physicians, writing that work ended when their powers were "exhausted or discovered to be all humbug." This "strong popular feeling" had not faded by the time Woodhull embarked on her presidential campaign.

Despite the skeptical and negative press that came with her pioneering business move, attention from the media was exactly what Woodhull wanted. The prior year, Woodhull's interest in the suffrage movement arose when she attended the first National Female Suffrage Convention in Washington, D.C. (Gabriel 1998). Surrounded by upper middle-class women who were better educated and better connected, Woodhull "was a nobody" (Underhill 1995, 55). So when her Wall Street firm became national news, the suffragists took notice (Underhill 1995). Buoyed by the newfound attention and the women's rights possibilities, Woodhull announced in the *New York Herald* on April 2, 1870, that she was running for president, saying she was a woman of action, not just talk (Underhill 1995). She had come to realize that advocating suffrage wasn't enough and that the "fight for equality started not in the voting booth, but in the bedroom, where polite society refused to go" (Gabriel 1998, 38). Her unhappy first marriage and her conversations with other women who had experienced domestic problems had taught her that women deserved the same economic and social freedoms as men: "She held that anything less than a revolution in domestic relations—taking away a husband's ownership of his wife—would not change women's status in society" (Gabriel 1998, 38). Her presidential announcement quickly made its way around the country as newspapers in Tennessee, Illinois, Vermont, and Pennsylvania were among those to publish the news (*Nashville Union and American*, April 3, 1870, 1; *The Cairo Daily Bulletin*, April 6, 1870, 2; *The Evening Telegraph*, April 4, 1870, 5; *Burlington Weekly Free Press*, April 8, 1870, 2). Woodhull's announcement came at an interesting time for women. To understand 1872, however, one must first back up and examine women's political culture more broadly.

Women's Political Culture

Although there were women interested in politics before the mid-1800s, a separate women's political culture in the United States developed in the mid-nineteenth century due to two major political developments (Baker 1984). The first was a change in political practices for white men. As states increasingly changed rules connecting property ownership with suffrage, more and more white men earned the right to vote. White women then realized that "their disfranchisement was based solely on sex" (Baker 1984, 629). In addition, the new influx of white male voters contributed to the growth of political parties, further separating men and women by creating a men's political sphere. Elections and other political events were typically held in bars and barber shops, that is, places that men frequented. As a result, women began forming their own organizations and creating their own political sphere (Baker 1984). The second major political change to influence the creation of women's political culture was the rise of abolitionism. Women played a significant role in anti-slavery organizations by raising money, contributing information to mass media, and getting involved in public life (Lerner 1975). Abolition efforts "taught women how to turn women's rights into a political movement" (Baker 1984, 634), thereby offering a valuable learning opportunity for women.

With these outside factors influencing women to become politically involved, examining the values associated with women during the nineteenth century is important to understanding the foundation of women's political culture. Both suffragists and anti-suffragists believed women's place was in the home, where they "exercised moral influence and insured national virtue and social order" (Baker 1984, 620). This role for women was viewed as acceptable by men, who therefore raised "little visible opposition" over the political activities of women's organizations aimed at improving family and community life and morality: "Women's moral nature gave them a reason for public action, and, since they did not have the vote, such action was considered 'above' politics" (Baker 1984, 631). Motherhood in particular was seen as a critical component of women's political culture. Women were expected to raise "civic-minded, virtuous sons" who would ensure "the survival of the republic" (Baker 1984, 625). To achieve this goal, women argued that they needed more educational opportunities and participation in public life, which thereby resulted in "translating moral authority into political influence" (Baker 1984, 625).

The early years of women's political culture therefore focused on local volunteer efforts focused on moral and social reform issues that gave women a source of power and feelings of public contribution (Baker 1984). In particular, the formation of the Woman's Christian Temperance Union in 1873 and the temperance movement became a powerful political ground for women as it "engaged more women than any other nineteenth-century cause and shows how women could translate a narrow demand into a political movement with wide concerns" (Baker 1984, 637). In a time when women were reliant on men for financial support and had few or no options in an unhappy marriage, a number of women favored prohibition since they viewed alcohol as the root of their family problems (Freeman 2000). This shared sense of purpose and involvement in women's organizations allowed women to gain "political skills, a sense of consciousness as women, and feelings of competence and self-worth" (Baker 1984, 621). While these developments served as a foundation for the ultimate success of suffrage in 1920, they also help explain attitudes of some of the women *against* suffrage in the late nineteenth century. Anti-suffragists believed suffrage and equality with men would "undercut female political culture" and take away the "glorification of separate spheres" that gave women a special status and power in public life (Baker 1984, 634). Men and women in the late nineteenth century viewed women as "more spiritual and morally pure than men" (Edwards 1997, 5). Anti-suffragists argued that voting would "make women partisan and unwomanly" (Kraditor 1965, 225). Meanwhile, suffragists believed the qualities that made women unique were needed in the mainstream political culture of voting and holding office (Baker 1984). They claimed that voting would "enable their unchangeable womanliness to undo the evil that men had wrought through their sordid parties" (Kraditor 1965, 226). The rise of this political culture for women thereby provides the historical setting in which Woodhull became the first woman to run for president in 1872 but also explains the challenges she faced by doing so at the time.

Of particular relevance to Woodhull's story is her connection to the formal women's movement, which will be discussed more throughout this chapter. It is significant to note a few other important factors that occurred beforehand, however. In 1869, women in Wyoming territory had been granted the right to vote. In addition, the nation had recently ratified the 15th Amendment giving black people the right to vote, prompting discussion that women should also fall under the constitutional change. However, divisions within the suffragist movement complicated its progress as there was not one encompassing ideology for movement supporters (Kraditor 1965). At the national level in 1869, Elizabeth Cady Stanton and Susan B. Anthony launched their own women's rights organization, the National Woman Suffrage Association, in response to congressional Republicans refusing to include women's suffrage in the 15th Amendment (Kraditor 1965). A competing American Woman Suffrage Association formed shortly thereafter. There were personal and political differences between the two organizations. For the national association, suffrage was one component of a broader agenda for advancing women's equality. These women focused on national changes and often lobbied Congress (Woloch 2002). Meanwhile, the more popular American association took a more conservative stance and focused on winning suffrage in states (Woloch 2002). Nonetheless, both organizations drew further attention to women's rights, and Woodhull hoped the election of 1872 would "force the country to face up to the 'woman question' " (Underhill 1995, 78). The fact that Woodhull would only be 34 years old on Election Day and would fail to meet the constitutional mandate for a president to be at least 35 was of no concern to her. Interestingly, it also would not be of concern to the press, as it was not brought up in her press coverage. What would soon become major concerns, however, were her mother and a journalistic culture all too ready to criticize public figures.

THE 1870s PRESS

A month after announcing her presidential aspirations, Woodhull, her second husband, and Tennie launched a newspaper, *Woodhull & Claflin's Weekly,* to support her campaign and to advocate for women's rights. During the Civil War, "Americans had become addicted to newspapers" and, by the 1870s, "the press had become a dominant force in the national dialogue" (Gabriel 1998, 58). During the decade, the number of newspapers in the nation nearly doubled due in part to the expanding West, economic gains in the South, and a general popularity of newspapers (Mott 1962). Other factors that influenced industry growth included a more educated public, better infrastructure for delivering newspapers, a decline in subscription prices, and increased revenue from advertising (Rutenbeck 1995). New York City especially was a newspaper town with 150 publications by 1870 as technological changes made it easier to mass produce papers (Snay 2011). Each paper had its own personality/advocacy determined by the editor/publisher and/or political party behind it (Gabriel 1998). Many newspapers doubled in size from four pages to eight, thereby offering more content to the public as well (Rutenbeck 1995). Scholars disagree, however, on the influence behind the content. Some note that most newspapers remained partisan by the end of the decade, although an increasing number had distanced themselves from partisan control (Mott 1962). Others argue that independent newspapers outnumbered partisan papers by the end of the 1870s as some editors sought to distance themselves from political corruption and believed independence would lead to more revenue opportunities (Rutenbeck 1995). Then there is the middle-of-the-road approach that notes there were a growing number of independent newspapers, particularly in metro areas, but that "independence did not mean 'neutrality'" as editors continued to express opinions (Sloan 2011, 204; see also Rutenbeck 1995). Regardless of the precise numbers, it is evident that newspapers in the 1870s were in a period of transition between partisan and independent control, although politically slanted content remained in both.

There were other signs that the press was in transition. By the 1870s, at least some journalists began to view their jobs as a profession, thus beginning the gradual process of professionalization (Banning 1998). Editors came to believe that news content played a bigger role in attracting readers and influencing public opinion than editorial content (Sloan 2011). Event-oriented news and human interest stories were given more emphasis to entice the public to buy the paper (Barnhurst and Nerone 2009). However, when reporters covered events, they focused primarily on the crowd, not the speaker or speech itself (Ryfe 2006). Furthermore, reporters often used first-person accounts written in chronological order that aimed to create a conversation with readers, thereby making the reporter a witness or participant in the event as opposed to a detached observer (Ryfe 2006).

During this time, journalists were overwhelmingly men. Suffrage newspapers were in the early stages, giving women their own outlets to voice their views. In 1868, Anthony and Stanton launched *The Revolution.* Suffragist Lucy Stone became editor of *The Woman's Journal* in 1870, and Abigail Scott Duniway ran *The New Northwest* in Oregon starting in 1871, to name a few (Bradley 2005; Beasley and Gibbons 2003). In 1870, only 35 women worked as journalists, comprising 0.6 percent of the industry (Sloan 2011). By the end of the decade, the number rose to about 300, but numbers were still staggeringly low (Chambers, Steiner, and Fleming 2004), making Woodhull's newspaper career a rare move for women and another one of her pioneering efforts.

By now a popular figure, Woodhull received newspaper coverage when she launched her paper. An article in the *Delaware* (Ohio) *Gazette* noted that Woodhull's paper would support her candidacy, advocate suffrage, "and play the mischief generally" ("Untitled" 1870, 2). The writer suspected the effort was a ploy to get more attention for Woodhull's Wall Street firm. The *Memphis Daily Appeal*, however, was impressed: "Its editorial is full of spicy reading matter . . . we do not know when we have so much enjoyed a newspaper. Its mode of treating things is so novel and refreshing when compared with the ordinary run of 'woman's rights' literature" ("Woman's Rights" 1870, 4). What was also notable about Woodhull's new venture is that it introduced her to Stephen Pearl Andrews, a radical reformer who would write for her paper and influence her political views. Most notably, he promoted the idea of "free love," or the right of individuals (particularly women) to determine their personal lives without government interference or public scorn, a concept that would soon become a buzzworthy component of her political platform (Underhill 1995).

As Woodhull continued her advocacy for women, she achieved another pioneering moment when she became the first woman to testify before a congressional committee in January 1871. Although she failed to convince Congress that the 14th and 15th amendments gave women the right to vote, Woodhull helped electrify the women's movement with this monumental publicity (Underhill 1995). By now, "she had outstripped in celebrity and political influence the suffragists whose attention she had struggled to win" (Underhill 1995, 115). Her efforts secured her a place on the stage at the next suffrage convention in May 1871 between renowned suffragists Stanton and Lucretia Mott (Underhill 1995). Even the more reserved Anthony had to acknowledge Woodhull's assistance to the mission, despite Anthony's concerns over Woodhull's colorful character and broader reform goals (Underhill 1995). Although their relationship would soon fracture, Anthony was initially "reinvigorated by the spunk, energy, and clear political strategizing of this young woman" (Barry 1988, 235).

Woodhull used the public opportunity of the suffrage convention to enhance her advocacy beyond women's rights and to push for reforms in labor, railroad policy, taxes, prisons, and civil service in a platform believed to have been written by radical reformer and newspaper employee Andrews (Underhill 1995). Now with support from prominent suffragists, Woodhull surely left the convention feeling positive about her political future (Underhill 1995). Within days, however, her empire slowly began to crumble.

On May 15, 1871, Woodhull's mother filed a complaint with police alleging that her daughter's husband wanted to kill her. There is no evidence that Colonel Blood was abusive to his eccentric mother-in-law (Underhill 1995). Yet the accusation and accompanying court testimony were disastrous for Woodhull's already precarious reputation as family private affairs soon were blazoned in the press. Among the revelations were that Woodhull's first husband lived with her and her second husband (as did other family members) and that she may not have been legally divorced when she married Blood (Underhill 1995). Hoping the public would sympathize with her family struggle, Woodhull instead discovered she "had become a figure of fun" (Underhill 1995, 140). Now in damage control, Woodhull wrote a letter to *The New York Times* to try to explain her situation. In the May 22, 1871, letter headlined "Mrs. Woodhull and Her Critics," Woodhull explained that her first husband was ill and incapable of taking care of himself. She believed it was her duty to care for him, of which her current husband approved. Woodhull noted that "various editors have stigmatized me as a living example of immorality and unchastity" (5). She accepted that she was a public figure and open to criticism, but vowed she would not "be made the scapegoat of sacrifice, to be offered up as a victim to society" by hypocrites. Those condemning her for practicing free love were among those secretly practicing it themselves, Woodhull wrote in her first public hinting of the affair between renowned preacher Henry Ward Beecher and the wife of noted journalist Theodore Tilton. However, Woodhull's attempts to defend herself through the promotion of free love sealed her connection to the controversial concept more often associated with promiscuity than equality (Underhill 1995; Gabriel 1998). It also connected her to Tilton and Beecher, which would ultimately end her political career.

ELECTION OF 1872

In the coming months, Woodhull traveled to various states to lecture her beliefs and promote her campaign while her newspaper kept the promotion up in New York City. In the January 13, 1872, issue of *Woodhull & Claflin's Weekly*, the newspaper stated that "we have endeavored to apply the principle of freedom and equality to all," reminding readers that it was "the only paper open to the free discussion of all subjects, even the most radical, as well as that class of subjects mostly ignored by all other journals" (8). That class of subjects included marriage and sexuality. In addition to writing original material, the *Weekly* reprinted articles about Woodhull that appeared in other newspapers.

In May 1872, Woodhull was back at the annual suffrage convention and ready for her big moment. In Apollo Hall in New York City, she "called the delegates to a revolution—political and social, educational and industrial, economic and sexual" (Underhill 1995, 4). As Woodhull increasingly took over the convention, Anthony grew furious and ordered the lights of the convention hall shut off (Barry 1988; Underhill 1995), signaling quite clearly her break with Woodhull and her controversies. Yet Woodhull would create her own faction and left the convention with what she wanted: the nomination for the presidency from the new Equal Rights Party (Underhill 1995). Press coverage of this event will be examined later in this chapter since it was a notable component of her presidential campaign coverage. Controversial but still determined, Woodhull now had the party backing she wanted going into the election of 1872.

Even without her personal controversies, Woodhull—and any other candidate—stood no chance of ousting a Civil War hero from the White House. Still, Ulysses S. Grant had his own share of controversies while he attempted to lead a nation still wounded from the debilitating war. In the early 1870s, Americans were still debating Reconstruction and the appropriate treatment of the South: "The political, social, and economic challenges were enormous . . . the North had to secure the fruits of its victory while reintegrating the former states of the Confederacy into the Union" (Snay 2011, 158). At the same time, the start of the Gilded Age was creating expanded industrialization, leading to increased inequality between the wealthy and the poor (Snay 2011). By 1870, more than one-fourth of the nation's population lived in an urban area (Husband and O'Loughlin 2004). The growth in the working class led to a rise in the labor movement, while the rich benefited from New York City's financial center and the recent doubling of railroad tracks (Snay 2011). Although the railroad bosses were viewed as greedy and corrupt, the transportation altered the nation with its ability to deliver food and products (Husband and O'Loughlin 2004, 49). Industrialization had a significant impact on women of the era. With many goods now being made in factories instead of the home, women's roles were changing. The home now became a place where "women were to nurture their harried husbands, educate their children, and compensate for a spiritually impoverished world outside of the home" (Husband and O'Loughlin 2004, 100). As noted previously, the concept of separate spheres for men and women became standard. Along with this came "often heavy-handed condemnation of the so-called unnatural women who entered the public sphere" (Husband and O'Loughlin 2004, 100), offering insight into why Woodhull was ostracized in and out of the press for her numerous public activities.

Grant's major political challenger for the presidency, New York newspaper editor Horace Greeley, was among those opposing women's rights, believing that giving women the right to vote and hold office would "corrupt" them (Snay 2011, 174; see also Barry 1988). Born in 1811 in New Hampshire, Greeley is best known for his work at *The Tribune*, which he started in 1841. The longtime editor's prominence was such that "every school boy, every grandmother of Christendom had learned much of Horace Greeley" even before he sought the presidency (Ingersoll 1873, 484). His newspaper was said to have the "greatest influence upon public opinion of any journal in the country" during the Civil War (Fahrney 1936, 1). Throughout his career, Greeley attempted politics with mostly failed results. Still, his increasing criticism of Grant's first term and the handling of Reconstruction, the economy, and fiscal policy—along with accusations of corruption within the administration—prompted Greeley to join the presidential race (Van Deusen 1953; Maihafer 1998). He became the candidate for both the Liberal Republicans and the Democrats, yet the strength of Grant's supporters and widespread ridicule proved problematic. Like Woodhull, who was referred to as "Mrs. Satan" (Gabriel 1998), Greeley's candidacy was mocked by prominent cartoonist Thomas Nast (Ingersoll 1873). Although admired as a newspaperman and philosopher, Greeley had a reputation for being "peculiar" and a flip-flopper, and his campaign was "mostly treated with laughter" (Maihafer 1998, 238).

Meanwhile, Grant was still riding his popularity as a war hero and, as president, as an advocate for peace. Some had promoted him for president as early as 1864 as a challenger to Lincoln, a prospect that Grant quickly overruled (Smith 2001). Following the war, Grant remained a presidential adviser and assisted with Reconstruction. Discontent with President Andrew Johnson was evident from his impeachment proceedings, however, thereby opening the door for Grant to win the presidency in 1868 on the simple platform that he desired peace (Smith 2001). During his first term, Grant oversaw Reconstruction and the ratification of the 15th Amendment giving blacks the right to vote while also dealing with the Ku Klux Klan, Indian relations, foreign relations with Britain, and an economy faced with a swelling national debt due to the war (Smith 2001). As for his stance on women, Grant invited Woodhull to the White House when she was in town lobbying Congress and purportedly told her that he supported the suffrage movement. However, no action followed their discussion (Underhill 1995). A number of Grant biographers don't mention Woodhull or women's rights at all and simply discuss Greeley in reference to the election of 1872 (Bunting III 2004; Smith 2001; McFeely 1981; Hesseltine 1935). Grant continued to be viewed as the candidate "for peace and for order" who was "safe and dependable" (McFeely 1981, 383).

   With a better understanding of the context of the times, an analysis of how the press portrayed Woodhull during her official campaign from May to November 1872 is now pertinent. First, a brief explanation of the data within the news stories analyzed is provided.

WOODHULL'S NEWSPAPER TRENDS

A table comparing the newspaper trends of all four women analyzed in this book can be found in the Appendix (see Table A.1). The analysis of Woodhull's news coverage involved 279 newspaper articles from 31 states and the District of Columbia between May 1 and November 7, 1872. This allowed for examination of articles from Woodhull's official presidential nomination by the Equal Rights Party in May through two days after Election Day in order to capture postelection reaction. Before examining the major themes found in the stories, a few structural issues are of note. For instance, articles about Woodhull were more likely to be found on the second page of the newspapers; one-fourth of them were on the front page. One must keep in mind, however, that newspapers were often four to eight pages during this time, thereby offering editors fewer placement options than they have today. Woodhull more often made the front page in May, when she secured the party nomination, than the other months, although—based on her first week of November coverage—it's likely her arrest coverage for that entire month would top the May front-page tally.

   There were not any visuals of Woodhull included in the newspapers analyzed, although this is due to the journalistic customs of the era to publish a text-heavy product as opposed to any agenda against Woodhull specifically. Similarly, it is not surprising that more than three-fourths of the articles about her were briefs (a handful of paragraphs or less) instead of full stories since newspapers of the era often ran very short snippets of news. Another structural aspect of interest is that more than three-fourths of the framing power in the Woodhull articles came from journalists, followed by Woodhull and her supporters, and then a small percentage from people who opposed her candidacy. Framing power was determined based upon what sources discussed Woodhull in each article. Since newspapers were still in the pre-stages of professionalization, journalists clearly drove the discursive agenda. While it is interesting to note that Woodhull and her supporters were quoted more in articles about her than were sources opposing her candidacy, this does not mean that Woodhull had a positive edge in the press. Although there were a number of articles that simply stated basic facts about her campaign, as will be described below, the widespread bias against her by the journalists writing about her was readily apparent. The below analysis explores this further as there were three main themes that emerged in the Woodhull stories. The first theme examines discourse related to Woodhull and her connection to the women's rights movement of the time. The second examines discourse related to Woodhull's politics. Finally, the third examines discourse related to Woodhull's personal traits. These themes have similarities with the framework established by Rainbow Murray in her book, *Cracking the Highest Glass Ceiling: A Global Comparison of Women's Campaigns for Executive Office.* Murray defines gender stereotypes in a political context as "pervasive attitudes about men and women within politics" related to "gender roles and attributes, which may be damaging to women candidates" (Murray 2010, 7–8). She focuses on three concepts within gender stereotypes: ideology, issues, and personal traits. How these stereotypes impacted Woodhull is explored next.

WOODHULL AND THE WOMEN'S MOVEMENT

The articles about Woodhull's connection to the women's rights movement can be divided into three main subcategories: those that highlight the friction between her and the mainstream movement, those neutral or positive about her as a women's rights candidate, and those critical of her as a women's rights candidate. Each is examined in further detail below.

Division in Their Ranks

The press detected the friction between Woodhull and Anthony in early May 1872 and let the public know about it. The *Boston Post* was among the first to carry news on the matter with the headline "Mrs. Woodhull on a Rampage" (May 7, 1872, 2), a colorful word choice certainly intended to discredit her and make her seem unstable and emotional. This type of headline was also catchy for consumers and illustrative of the press's subjectivity at the time. The article noted that Woodhull had not only verbally "attacked" the government and Greeley in a speech at a women's labor reform convention but had also "censured bitterly Miss Anthony as a deserter from a cause she had pledged herself heart and soul with not long ago" (May 7, 1872, 2). Two days later, the *Evening Star* in Washington, D.C., ran the same article (May 9, 1872, 1), although with the headline "The Widow Woodhull Furious," stating the information came from the *New York Standard*. Although the article notes that Woodhull gave "a long address," only these short (and controversial) portions of her speech are reported, and without additional context. This strategy is indicative of the journalism of the time to focus more broadly on the hype around a speech than the speech itself, yet in Woodhull's case this practice served to legitimate the view that she was troublesome and simplified her overall political message.

A *New York Times* story about the annual suffrage convention that opened days later provided this same troublemaker framing for Woodhull. The article noted the convention attendees were "the leaders, the woman suffragists purely, and the party headed by Victoria Woodhull" (May 10, 1872, 8). In other words, Woodhull was outside of the mainstream, with the discourse hinting that she was illegitimate. The story says a Woodhull supporter was "received with loud and continued hissing" (May 10, 1872, 8) after speaking against the National Woman Suffrage Association's platform and suggesting a broader discussion of social issues. Following the session's adjournment, Woodhull's supporters were reported to have cheered for free speech and free discussion. Therefore, it is clear in multiple places in the story that Woodhull and her supporters are challengers outside of the dominant membership, seemingly unpopular and rambunctious at that. This aligns with Murray's (2010) gender stereotypes ideology concept of women political candidates being viewed as overly liberal. Interestingly, the rift that occurred between Woodhull and Anthony during the convention is downplayed in the story as merely a disagreement regarding the location of the next session. The story only vaguely notes that Woodhull "came forward and delivered a few vehement remarks" (May 10, 1872, 8) and makes no mention of Anthony shutting the lights off on Woodhull's speech. *The New York Times*' mostly bland treatment of this event closely follows the journalistic conventions of the age to write in chronological order, to include observation of the crowd, and to skip coverage of actual speeches. Yet this journalistic practice also oversimplified the event, giving Anthony and her ideological faction the advantage.

However, rival newspaper *The New York Herald* provided a more direct account of the event by declaring "at last the great row between the two woman's rights factions, so long threatened and so often promised, has begun" (May 11, 1872, 10) in the lead of a lengthy story about the convention proceedings. Woodhull's side is referred to as "the rebels," which also discursively serves to legitimize Anthony's side by indicating Woodhull is outside the norm. Although the writer points to the "stampede of the rank and file to the side of Woodhull," indicating her rebellion has support, the framing that began the article does not do any favors to these women who are trying to build serious legitimacy with the general public. Rather, they come off as quarrelsome women who can't even agree on their own issues. Although it's true there were disagreements and different factions, male political parties have also long had disagreements over issues (see Horace Greeley running as a Liberal Republican against Republican Grant). Therefore, the *Herald's* declaration that "no one living may prophecy where it [the women's quarrel] will end" is overly dramatic and emotional. However, conflict has long been considered a news value by journalists and a means for selling newspapers (Vos and Finneman 2014). Indeed, late nineteenth-century news strategies involved "emphasizing events, dwelling on individual personalities, and using drama to lure readers" (Dicken-Garcia 1989, 89). Woodhull did not tend to benefit from this type of framing.

One other interesting bit worthy of note in the *Herald* is a separate story that quotes Anthony as saying "she proposed to advocate no particular man or party but any candidate who would pledge himself to support woman suffrage" during the upcoming election (May 11, 1872, 10). Although Woodhull is not mentioned in the article, readers of the era could surely read between the lines to see that Anthony was not supporting Woodhull's presidential bid. This is particularly clear not only because this story appeared below another article about Woodhull receiving the presidential nomination from the Equal Rights Party, but also because of Anthony's sole choice of male pronouns. She did not even leave a window of opportunity open for a Woodhull endorsement with her decision to say "no particular man" and "himself" instead of "man or woman" and "himself or herself." In this case, both Anthony's discourse and her lack of discourse served to illegitimate Woodhull as a presidential contender.

Other newspapers offered brief notices of the internal friction. *The Charleston* (S.C.) *Daily News* ran an article stating "the agitators for female rights, however, are not all agreed" and that Anthony and Stanton "do not hesitate to express their contempt for the Woodhull machine and its presidential nomination" (May 14, 1872, 1). Referring to the suffragists as "agitators" has its own negative connotation, but the disapproval of the two most prominent suffragists was a discursive move clearly aimed at delegitimizing Woodhull. The *Weekly Louisianan* also noted the separation between Woodhull and Anthony (May 25, 1872, 1) as did *The New Northwest* in Oregon: "there is a division in their ranks which the late nomination [of Woodhull] will doubtless tend to widen" (June 7, 1872, 4). It's notable to mention that *The New Northwest* had a female suffragist publisher yet the newspaper ran articles critical of Woodhull, as will be explained in more depth throughout this analysis. This particular article, however, makes it clear that Woodhull is a divisive figure who is responsible for at least some of the suffragists' problems. This theme was evident in coverage from South Carolina to Louisiana to Oregon— Woodhull was problematic with an ideology too liberal for the mainstream.

The Women's Rights Candidate

Not all of Woodhull's coverage in relation to the women's rights movement was negative. A number of newspapers ran very short briefs that simply stated Woodhull was the woman's suffrage or the woman's rights presidential candidate and included no other commentary (see *Sunbury* (Pa.) *American,* May 11, 1872, 2; *Orleans County* (Vt.) *Monitor,* May 20, 1872, 2; *Memphis* (Tenn.) *Daily Appeal,* May 21, 1872, 2; *Western Reserve Chronicle* (Ohio), May 29, 1872, 2; *The Opelousas* (La.) *Courier,* July 13, 1872, 1). In addition to this neutral coverage, Woodhull also received some positive commentary in the press. In an interview with *The New Northwest,* Greeley is quoted as saying that Woodhull "seems to command money" and "is the only advocate of woman suffrage of any political importance" (June 7, 1872, 2), with this outside viewpoint briefly equalizing her candidacy. A few weeks later, the New York *Sun* called her "the irrepressible champion of women's rights and candidate for the presidency" (July 17, 1872, 3). The *Public Ledger* in Memphis referred to Woodhull and her sister as "the great guns of the women's rights movement" and said their expected lectures in Memphis were sure to draw crowds (October 2, 1872, 2). However, this type of coverage was few and far between, thereby indicating few newspapers were willing to show support for Woodhull in relation to women's rights and discursively legitimize her candidacy. Aware that she was controversial, editors of the time also perhaps did not want to potentially lose customers in the competitive environment by legitimating her campaign.

The Notorious Woodhull Woman

With positive articles hard to come by, it's not surprising there were a number of negative articles about Woodhull as the women's rights candidate. In what served as a reminder to readers that the women suffragists couldn't vote, *The Cairo* (Ill.) *Daily Bulletin* said Woodhull would likely only get three votes in the whole country: from her mentor Andrews, her husband, and perhaps her biographer Tilton (May 15, 1872, 2), indicating Woodhull had zero legitimate support. Other newspapers also enjoyed mocking Woodhull. *The Centre Reporter* in Pennsylvania ran a story from New York about the suffragist convention that was said to be written "for the amusement of the readers" and had the headline "A Pitiable Spectacle" (May 24, 1872, 3). Suffrage paper *The New Northwest* carried a story from the *New York Herald* with a similar tone. The reporter wrote that "while we do not wish to belittle anything so intimately woven with the future of the human race, we wish to enjoy its incidents to the full extent" (June 7, 1872, 4). Reporting on the women's rights advocates provided "amusement which is inexhaustible," the reporter wrote (June 7, 1872, 4). Rather than realize the historical importance of the first woman presidential candidate, these newspapers—even a suffrage paper—found Woodhull and women's politics laughable and told readers they should find this humorous, too, thereby justifying the current status quo of male-dominated politics and illustrating advocacy of this on the part of the press. This belittlement was the precedent set for coverage of women political candidates. How this precedent played out into the future will be examined further throughout this book.

The negative coverage of Woodhull does not end here, however. Another negative story about the convention that ran in the Democratic *Centre Reporter*, but was originally written by the *New York Express*, noted that "lewd and debauched women were mingled in one shocking, profane mass" and that it was not surprising that Woodhull was nominated "considering the crowd she is the leader of" (May 24, 1872, 3). Clearly the reporter was simplifying Woodhull's supporters and aiming to evoke an emotional response with the word choices of "lewd and debauched." This served to build upon prior views of Woodhull as an immoral and promiscuous woman and attempted to downplay her historical achievement. *The Hickman Courier* in Kentucky referred to her as "the notorious Woodhull woman" (May 25, 1872, 1). Days later, *The Tiffin Tribune* in Ohio wrote that candidates like Woodhull and Greeley wouldn't be heard of again until after the election results in November "show how badly they have been defeated" (May 30, 1872, 1). The *Tribune* was a Republican paper, so it makes sense that it would favor Grant, but the negative coverage there and in the Democratic *Courier* and *Centre Reporter* illustrates there was bipartisan dislike of Woodhull and her candidacy. Indeed, even the black press took aim at Woodhull. *The Weekly Louisianan* carried an article from *The Independent* (presumably a New York newspaper) that said convention delegates insulted Frederick Douglass by selecting him as Woodhull's running mate. The story further noted that "the wildest and most ridiculous speeches were made to a crowd of a hundred or two spectators, advocating every political and financial vagary" (May 25, 1872, 1). *The New Northwest* wrote of the "vast army of wives and mothers in this nation who do not indorse [sic] the social views of Mrs. Woodhull" (June 7, 1872, 2), again indicating a woman's newspaper wasn't even willing to support and build the credibility of one of its own during a notable moment in women's history.

Woodhull herself spoke out against the negativity surrounding her, particularly in regard to how other women treated her. The New York *Sun* quoted her discussing "the disgraceful treatment" that she and her sister received from fellow women:

> They have vilified us long enough and patience has ceased to be a virtue . . . We have endeavored to show the world what a woman can do by industry and honesty and yet we are daily maligned and insulted. By whom? By women! It is too much. I can't stand it, and I won't. (August 24, 1872, 4)

It is noteworthy that *The Sun* gave Woodhull a platform to fight back. Since so many of the articles studied for this analysis were briefs, readers across the nation weren't provided with much more than shallow, simplified coverage of Woodhull and much was focused on delegitimizing her candidacy. With this review of Woodhull's ties to the women's movement complete, it is now useful to analyze the articles focused on her politics and platform.

WOODHULL AND POLITICS

Woodhull actually did receive some positive political coverage, but most of it was sharply critical. The analysis of this coverage begins with her more favorable coverage.

Shake the World

In *The New Northwest,* Elizabeth Cady Stanton wrote a complimentary article that said Woodhull's "speeches and writings on all the great questions of national life are beyond anything yet produced by man or woman on our platform" (May 3, 1872, 1). This article appeared before Woodhull and Anthony's public falling out, but it is noteworthy to see Stanton standing up for Woodhull and legitimizing her as a political figure. The *Boston Post* also commented on Woodhull's platform, noting that she "flings a very broad banner to the breeze" (June 6, 1872, 1). The paper further opined that

> It is such an astounding event in politics for a candidate to volunteer opinions on topics outside the commonplace and comparatively ignoble matters pertaining to revenue, representation, law and taxation that the soaring eloquence and the wide scope of Mrs. Woodhull's manifesto deservedly attract attention. (June 6, 1872, 1)

Although the *Boston Post* questioned whether any party could accept "the new Woodhull Constitution," the newspaper did not doubt her sincerity: "of [the] earnestness of Mrs. Woodhull, we are not left in doubt. She proposes to 'shake the world,' and we know of no more desirable object to whose attainment she can direct her energies. The world needs shaking sadly" (May 13, 1872, 2). Not only was Woodhull's *candidacy* groundbreaking, but these articles make clear that her *campaign strategy* was as well. She wanted to talk about a variety of topics that did not get attention but she felt were important to discuss. The *Boston Post* at least agreed that the status quo was insufficient and Woodhull was legitimate to push its boundaries.

As far as her specific goals, *The Sun* in New York and the *Newport* (R.I.) *Daily News* were among the newspapers that described the platform of Woodhull's Equal Rights Party in more detail. This platform included support for a new Constitution, a national code of civil and commercial law, the abolishment of monopolies, one system of money and currency, direct and equal taxation, the abolishment of war, uniform compensation for labor, abolishment of capital punishment, help for the unemployed, and free trade with all nations (*The Sun*, May 11, 1872, 1; *Newport Daily News*, May 13, 1872, 2). *The New York Times* also included details of her platform in a story originally carried in the *Boston Pilot* that contained large portions of Tilton's biography of her. This article included Woodhull's belief that the government should abolish the gold standard and issue its own money with a fixed and permanent value (September 14, 1872, 3). Of course the article also mentioned Woodhull's free love platform and belief that "marriage is of the heart and not of the law, that when love ends, marriage should end with it" (September 14, 1872, 3). The story ends on a snide editorial note, a strategy aimed at telling readers that Woodhull was not to be taken seriously. Still, readers were at least provided with a full-length story largely provided from Tilton's favorable point of view and offered more than a simplified brief's worth of content, even if the intent was to provide entertainment.

However, it was not typical for Woodhull's platform to receive much room in the papers. As previously noted, much of her campaign coverage entailed briefs, not full stories. This was not necessarily a pointed move against Woodhull since short articles were part of the broader journalistic practice of the era. Still, it meant the public was limited as to what it knew about her candidacy. A few positive articles focused on the reaction of crowds to Woodhull. *The Sun* in New York wrote that Woodhull's convention speech "was greeted with a perfect tumult of applause and shouts of delight" and that, after she was chosen as the presidential nominee, "for [a] full five minutes, cheer after cheer rent the air. Women waved their handkerchiefs and wept, men shouted themselves hoarse" (May 11, 1872, 1). The *New York Herald* wrote that the audience "again rose and cheered as if their lungs would break" when Woodhull was nominated (May 11, 1872, 10). The *Nashville Union and American*'s article said Woodhull's remarks "were greeted with a tumult of applause" (May 12, 1872, 1). Although Woodhull's politics and personal character were heavily criticized, as will be discussed further below, at least a few newspapers noted that she had more support than was publicly evident. Although sources aren't directly quoted, the crowds serve as evidence that Woodhull's candidacy was legitimate to at least some people. The *Washington Standard* in Washington Territory ran an article quoting one woman who said Woodhull "represented the sentiment which thousands would endorse if they dared give utterance" (June 22, 1872, 2). Similarly, the *New York Herald* hinted that many women would side with Woodhull but "dare not do so openly as they are unfortunately saddled with husbands, fathers, and brothers who might kick at the further spread of this terrible heresy" (May 11, 1872, 10). In other words, Woodhull likely had more support than was believed at the time, but people were too afraid to challenge the views of the status quo and to speak out in favor of her to bring credibility to her campaign.

The nation's strong patriarchal grip made it difficult not only for women candidates but for their supporters to have a voice without facing disapproval both in and out of the press. In a nation where women were still treated like property and had little voice, the positive support Woodhull did receive is remarkable.

The Satanic Ticket

Despite the sprinkling of positive stories, however, it was more common for Woodhull to be raked over the coals in the press in regard to her candidacy. The *Bloomington* (Ill.) *Daily Leader* was among the early critics of her presidential nomination, referring to her and Spotted Tail (an Indian tribal chief incorrectly reported as her running mate) as "the Satanic ticket" (May 13, 1872, 2), a strategy aimed at generating an emotional response and attacking Woodhull's credibility. What is ironic is that the newspaper could have been criticized right back for incorrectly naming her vice presidential partner. Frederick Douglass won the nomination (although not with his consent), not Spotted Tail. Still, going so far as to refer to Woodhull as satanic was a brutal discursive move. Other journalists also sought to come up with clever word choices to belittle Woodhull's credibility, with one article in *The Charleston* (S.C.) *Daily News* calling Woodhull's party the "odds and ends party" (May 18, 1872, 1) and another article referring to Woodhull as an "enemy of matrimony" (July 16, 1872, 3). Newspapers in Tennessee, South Carolina, Pennsylvania, and Kansas were among those that ran this brief about Woodhull's nominating convention:

> She prophesied that from this convention would go forth a power which would shake the world. She denounced political parties and the Constitution and declared that on our country's centennial, a new Constitution would take the place of the present blood-stained document. [*Nashville Union and American,*

May 12, 1872, 1; see also *Knoxville* (Tenn.) *Daily Chronicle*, May 12, 1872, 1;
The Daily Phoenix (S.C.), May 12, 1872, 3; *Memphis Daily Appeal*, May 12,
1872, 2; *The Columbian* (Pa.), May 17, 1872, 2; *The Athens* (Tenn.) *Post*, May
17, 1872, 3; *The Wichita* (Kan.) *City Eagle*, May 24, 1872, 2]

The journalist's choice to boil down Woodhull's speech and use the words
"prophesied," "a power," "denounced," and "blood-stained" was certainly
intended to feed into the public's stereotype of Woodhull and delegitimize
her. The prophesy and power discourse no doubt was meant to remind readers
of her controversial past as a clairvoyant, while references to denouncement
and blood make her seem animalistic. This contrasts with the framing of
Woodhull in an article that appeared in *The Hickman* (Ky.) *Courier* during
the same time frame. The article describes Woodhull's acceptance speech
and frames her as heartfelt as she thanked her supporters for the honor of the
nomination and said she "must have borne a place in your very hearts indeed"
(May 25, 1872, 1). Although Woodhull was a complex woman, it's almost
hard to believe that the prophesy brief and the gratitude brief were about the
same person. This is illustrative of the varying advocacy within the press at
the time.

Other examples of critical Woodhull press coverage include the *Lamoille
Newsdealer* in Vermont running an article stating Woodhull's "crazy con-
gregation have [sic] nominated the creature for the presidency" (May 22,
1872, 2), again using animalistic discourse. A number of papers ran tongue-
in-cheek briefs that referred to Woodhull as the "goddess of liberty" (*Eaton*
(Ohio) *Weekly Democrat*, May 23, 1872, 4; *Andrew County* (Mo.) *Republican*, May 24, 1872, 4; *Jasper* (Ind.) *Weekly Courier*, May 24, 1872, 2; *The
True Northerner* (Mich.), May 24, 1872, 2). In addition, *The Wheeling* (W.V.)
Daily Intelligencer published an article about "the nastiness of taking castor
oil" and noted "one's gorge rises at it as if it were one of Mrs. Woodhull's
lectures" (July 12, 1872, 1), word choices intended to prompt a negative
reaction from readers. This type of discourse again ties into the belittlement
theme noted earlier, with Woodhull viewed as a "figure of fun."

Along the same lines, framing Woodhull as a joke was common among
the articles discussing her candidacy, again illustrating the subjectivity of
the press at the time and its apparent attempt to appeal to consumers. An
article in *The Donaldson Chief* in Louisiana said, "It remains to be seen
how many people will be 'taken in' by the huge joke perpetuated for the
'National Reform Convention'" (May 18, 1872, 2). *The Charleston* (S.C.)
Daily News said spectators at Woodhull's nominating convention "did not
know that the thing was a broad farce" and was solely to bring attention to her
newspaper and brokerage firm (May 14, 1872, 1). A number of newspapers
took advantage of Spotted Tail's near nomination and ran briefs stating that

he "indignantly denies that he authorized the association of his name with that of Victoria C. Woodhull." Spotted Tail is quoted as saying, "Woodhull! Squaw! Ugh! Me no run!" (*Holmes County* (Ohio) *Republican*, June 6, 1872, 2; *The Democratic Press* (Ohio), June 6, 1872, 4; *The Holt County* (Missouri) *Sentinel*, June 7, 1872, 2; *The Ottawa* (Ill.) *Free Trader*, June 22, 1872, 7). The story that an Indian didn't want anything to do with Woodhull likely provided amusement to the nation's primarily white readers and served to legitimize the sentiment against Woodhull.

The *Nashville Union and American* also ran a story referring to Woodhull's nomination as a "farce" and noted that a number of her supporters were "long-haired men and short-haired women" (May 18, 1872, 1), an insult in an era when the opposite was standard. Not only that, but the reporter noted that mediums were present at the convention, as well as "a quack doctor, an astrologer . . . several female preachers, several Communists, [and] a number of darkies" (May 18, 1872, 1). Further, the reporter claims that he saw a lunatic "who must have been released from the asylum for the occasion, and there were not a few others who looked very much like him" (May 18, 1872, 1). Associating Woodhull with a number of populations looked down upon at the time was a clear discursive effort to discredit her among mainstream society. Other newspapers also used discourse aimed at generating an emotional reaction and to justify a status quo that did not include Woodhull and her views. For the suffrage paper *The New Northwest*, this meant pointing out that Woodhull had "extreme and erroneous views on the marriage and other social questions" that were "a source of weakness to the cause," meaning suffrage. The paper declared it was glad that Woodhull had left the mainstream movement (May 31, 1872, 2), an ideological discursive move to illustrate Woodhull was liberal and outside the boundaries considered legitimate.

The beginning of this chapter noted that *The Arizona Sentinel* was among those to run particularly harsh stories about Woodhull. One writer at the paper clearly disliked Woodhull and her platform, referring to her as "a stench in the nostrils of all virtuous women and pure men" and noting "her ideas are not merely preposterous; they are revoltingly indecent and nasty" (*The Arizona Sentinel*, June 29, 1872, 2). The *Sentinel's* headline of "Women Going Wrong" serves to defend the status quo as does the commentary that the nation would be on its way to ruin before it would adopt Woodhull's platform, illustrating strong advocacy on behalf of the newspaper. Suffragists were advised to cut the cord from Woodhull's platform or "go to the bottom with it" (June 29, 1872, 2). *The Pacific Commercial Advertiser* in Hawaii also ran choice words about Woodhull's candidacy: "encouraging such women even to aspire to high positions is disgraceful to American institutions and an insult to the true women of the country" (August 17, 1872, 4). In Pennsylvania, an article in *The Elk County Advocate* described one of Woodhull's free love lectures as "obscene" and said "the good sense and moral sensibility of the entire nation were grossly outraged" (November 7, 1872). The viciousness of some of the attacks on Woodhull is startling and illustrates how determined opponents were to maintain the hegemonic status quo and to appeal to the emotions of readers to ensure Woodhull did not gain credibility. Her candidacy was clearly viewed as a threat that elicited strong commentary from around the country—and this doesn't yet include the discursive attacks on her personally as is discussed next.

WOODHULL'S PERSONAL TRAITS

Because the prior discussion has already presented a clear picture of Woodhull's discursive treatment by the press, this section will attempt to be concise so as to not become too redundant. However, it is worth noting discourse about Woodhull's personal traits, and this is also an opportunity to explain how Woodhull ended up in jail on Election Day and the press reaction to that. As with the prior sections, this analysis will discuss both positive and negative discursive approaches toward Woodhull.

A Grand, Brave Woman

As previously noted, Stanton wrote a complimentary article about Woodhull that appeared in *The New Northwest* in Oregon shortly before Woodhull's fallout with Anthony. It is worthwhile to examine this text closer. Stanton wrote that she knew some people disliked the suffragists' ties to Woodhull, but she pointed to Woodhull's congressional testimony, "an honor conferred on no other woman in the nation before," and how Congress recognized Woodhull "as the leader of the woman suffrage movement in this country" (May 3, 1872, 1). Stanton asked, "Shall we ignore a champion like this?" Even if the scandal talk about Woodhull were true, "though it is false," Stanton asked, "Shall we not welcome her to the better place she desires to hold?" (May 3, 1872, 1). She called Woodhull "a grand, brave woman, radical alike in political, religious, and social principles" and said that she "blush[es] for humanity" when she thinks of the "merciless and continued persecution of that little woman by the entire press of this nation" (May 3, 1872, 1). What is noteworthy is that Woodhull's controversial personal life in New York was apparently well-known on the other end of the country and that "the entire press of this nation" took an interest in her, indicating her prominence in the political scene at this time. The fact that Stanton would risk her own reputation to defend Woodhull and try to legitimize her speaks volumes of both their relationship and Woodhull's perceived importance to the movement. Since this article appeared in a suffragist-backed publication, Stanton was clearly trying to sway those friendly to the cause to unite behind the woman who had done much for it despite the skepticism over Woodhull's personal life. More specifically, Stanton is attempting to emotionally appeal to Christian readers with her pleas to essentially save the fallen woman who wants to redeem herself yet continues to face persecution. Undoubtedly, Stanton, who was the first woman to run for Congress in 1866 (Ginzberg 2009), felt a kindred spirit with Woodhull.

A few other articles that take a positive spin on Woodhull's personal self are also noteworthy to mention. *The Orangeburg* (S.C.) *News* ran an article from the *Springfield* (Mass.) *Republican* that described Woodhull's manner as "graceful and refined" (May 18, 1872, 1). Most notably, however, the journalist wrote that "however we may oppose her opinions as expressed from the platform, we shall not assail her personal character without ample grounds" (May 18, 1872, 1). Although this is a backhanded compliment, it is interesting that an attempt was made to keep the focus on the politics instead of the personal and to try to promote more objectivity in reporting to a certain extent. The *Kokomo Howard County* (Ind.) *Republican* also gave Woodhull a compliment of sorts by noting "whatever the personal character of Mrs. Woodhull may be, of one thing we are assured, that she is earnest working for the bettering of the condition of her sex" (November 1, 1872, 2). This is significant as there was little discourse about Woodhull bettering the culture of women and politics. This commentary, along with Stanton's advocacy, was a rare journalistic challenge to gender and political norms in Woodhull's campaign coverage, thereby planting the seed for further challenges in the future.

Perhaps the biggest personal cheerleader of Woodhull, for a time anyway, was her biographer Tilton. Snippets of his biography appeared in *The New York Times* and illustrated his attempts to put a positive spin on her personal life. Tilton wrote of her "spiritual visitants" and how one prophesied that she would "become the ruler of her people" (September 14, 1872, 11). Tilton addresses one of Woodhull's biggest controversies—living with both her ex-husband and her current husband—by praising the "nobility of her moral judgments" for helping her "wretched wreck" of an ex-husband. Tilton further notes that "no slander ever fell on any human soul with greater injustice" than that of Woodhull (September 14, 1872, 11). Although Tilton is clearly trying to humanize and justify Woodhull in an attempt to turn public opinion, this discourse also served as a reminder of her controversial personal life, which the press was all too happy to criticize.

A Fit Subject for a Lunatic Asylum

The press found a number of colorful ways to mock Woodhull personally. *The Charleston* (S.C.) *Daily News* was particularly unique with its criticism of Woodhull's spiritualist beliefs and an article noted that both Grant and Greeley would be helpless against "the invisible powers of the air, the witches, demons, goblins, ghosts, vampires and sorcerers who are about to rally for Woodhull and the Black Douglass" (May 18, 1872, 1). Another odd article appeared in the *Nashville Union and American* and told of a saloon owner who bought wolves and named them after Woodhull and Douglass to create a side show. Reportedly, "the citizens of this city go every evening to see him enter the cage of these trick wolves" (June 27, 1872, 4). *The Pacific Commercial Advertiser* in Hawaii said Woodhull's election to the presidency "would most probably bring to her its chief charm in the better opportunity and greater freedom it would give her in selecting as many husbands and as often as she pleased, from the crowds that would hover around her" (August 17, 1872, 4). Again, these were discursive strategies to use humor to mock Woodhull's candidacy and decrease her credibility among voters, offering simplified discourse—a caricature—of who she was. This also served to entertain consumers, who therefore may have been more likely to be loyal to the newspapers.

But the two biggest personal issues that the press grabbed onto during the 1872 campaign season were Woodhull's financial troubles and her arrest just days before the election. In August, the press caught wind of court proceedings during which Woodhull and Tennie testified that they were broke. Their brokerage firm suffered due not only to Woodhull's political career but also their high-risk strategies and the unstable market (Underhill 1995). During the summer, their newspaper had also ceased publication (Underhill 1995). Word spread from state to state that the women "do not own a dollar's worth of property," (i.e. *The New York Times,* August 28, 1872, 2; *Nashville Union and American,* August 28, 1872, 1; *Wheeling* (W.V.) *Daily Intelligencer,* August 28, 1872, 1; *Memphis Daily Appeal,* August 28, 1872, 1; *The Hickman* (Ky.) *Courier,* August 31, 1872, 4; *Eaton* (Ohio) *Weekly Democrat,* September 5, 1872, 4). *The Emporia* (Kan.) *News* added its own commentary to the news, noting "two more 'dead beats' are disposed of" (September 6, 1872, 2). This completely callous discourse is again indicative of the level of disdain against Woodhull by many in the press and the public. However, the before-mentioned relationship between Woodhull, Beecher, and Tilton that would ultimately bring her down was the biggest scoop the press would ever have on her.

Woodhull had known for some time that prestigious preacher Henry Ward Beecher was a secret advocate of free love. Beecher not only had an affair with her but also with Tilton's wife, and reportedly with others (Underhill 1995). Tired of the preacher's hypocrisy, his lack of public support for her, the public's vilification of her, and the double standard that men could have sexual freedom but women couldn't (Underhill 1995), Woodhull re-launched her newspaper in early November and exposed him (*Woodhull & Claflin's Weekly*, November 2, 1872). She apparently had verbally mentioned Beecher's adultery during a spiritualists' convention a few months prior since *The Daily Phoenix* in South Carolina ran an article saying she was "a fit subject for a lunatic asylum" for even suggesting such a thing (September 25, 1872, 3). However, the *Weekly's* publication of Beecher's dirty laundry set off a national frenzy that only grew when Woodhull, Tennie, and their associates were arrested November 2—three days before Election Day—on charges of mailing obscene literature. They would still be in jail on Election Day, stymieing any opportunity for Woodhull to attempt to vote.

Press coverage of their court case could fill a chapter on its own. Since this work is focused on Woodhull's campaign, not her jail time, just a few examples will be provided since the case does overlap with Election Day. While a number of newspapers stuck to fairly neutral explanations of the case (i.e. *The New York Times*, November 3, 1872, 1; *The Daily State Journal* in Virginia, November 5, 1872, 1; *The Knoxville* (Tenn.) *Daily Chronicle*, November 5, 1872, 1), some were clearly outraged by Woodhull's latest move. *The Wheeling* (W.V.) *Daily Intelligencer* ran a *New York Express* story that said the women's arrest was expected for publishing "the most atrocious charges that ever obtained currency in any community" (November 4, 1872, 1). *The Dixon Sun* in Illinois called Woodhull's newspaper "the vilest one that has ever come under out notice" and said her language "ought to blow the smut out of hell" (November 6, 1872, 5). *The Vermont Watchman and State Journal* hoped "those notorious and pestiferous women" with the "filthy newspaper" would be sent to the Sing Sing prison "in order that the community be spared the disgrace and shame of their further presence in its midst" (November 6, 1872, 2). The public and journalists refused to believe the story about Beecher was true and saw its publication as yet another inappropriate and scandalous move by Woodhull and her allies. The emotionally charged discourse was a vehement strategy to undermine her credibility and to attract consumers no doubt fascinated by the latest Woodhull news. After a long campaign filled with press attacks, Woodhull's political career ended in a blaze of discursive fury.

DISCUSSION

To use a cliché, Woodhull was clearly a woman ahead of her time. It's interesting that a number of the issues advocated by Woodhull that would "shake the world" in 1872 are commonplace today: minimum wage, the abolishment of the gold standard, unemployment benefits, free trade, and divorce laws, among them. Certainly to be a pioneer, one has to be a bit unusual and determined to rock the status quo. However, Woodhull's character and deviation from acceptable gender norms of her era were clearly too much for her contemporaries to handle and played a significant role in her negative press coverage. The context of the time worked both for and against her. In an era when blacks were suddenly given the right to vote, the push to also add in women's rights was perceived as too much for a nation grappling to find a return to normalcy. Yet the 15th Amendment was a critical political platform for suffragists to latch onto and Woodhull's congressional testimony gave her the credibility boost necessary to even launch a notable campaign. Although Woodhull's mother believed in the 1830s that her daughter would rise to fame, clearly the context of the 1870s was important for that to even be possible. The growth of New York City as a financial center to start a brokerage firm, the advances in technology that eased starting a newspaper, the changes for blacks, and the early stages of feminism all combined to give Woodhull the tools to become a national figure. Yet many of the changes were difficult for people of the time to handle and a defense of the status quo of gender relations kicked in. While one could point out that the vast majority of journalists at this time were men and therefore arguably more likely to defend male privilege, it is interesting (and discouraging) to see that even the suffragist paper *The New Northwest* with a woman publisher wrote and carried disparaging discourse about Woodhull during a groundbreaking time in women's history. Clearly, the broader journalism culture of the time played a significant role in Woodhull's vilification due to the press's acceptance of partisan and subjective discourse as well as the competitive atmosphere for attracting consumers.

The press viewed Woodhull as not only a "figure of fun" but also "satanic" and used its discursive power to belittle her candidacy and harshly condemn her political aspirations in an attempt to maintain the hegemonic status quo. Whether using emotional or simplifying discursive strategies, there clearly was a mass effort to delegitimize her candidacy. Although one could argue that this type of discourse is solely connected to Woodhull herself (and critics of her unusual character may argue she brought this type of coverage upon herself), the fact remains that this was the precedent set for covering women in politics. Further chapters in this book will determine if this precedent does indeed play out across time. However, the fact that a woman has yet to be elected president in the United States suggests that the negative initial precedent has indeed reverberated throughout history.

Although some news coverage in 1872 included comments from Woodhull and her supporters, journalists were clearly in control of the discursive framing of her candidacy and were responsible for the negativity. In the pre-yellow journalism era, emotional word choices of comparing Woodhull to castor oil, Satan, a lunatic, and a deadbeat were all meant to delegitimize any ground she had gained as a pioneer on Wall Street, a pioneer in the newspaper industry, a pioneer feminist, and a pioneer in politics. In addition, journalistic customs of the era to write briefs instead of stories often did not allow for the full context of her platform to reach the public, thereby allowing for a shallow stereotype of her candidacy to form. Even though Woodhull had no chance of beating Grant, her political propositions—beyond free love—did not receive much entrance in the marketplace of ideas as a result of these journalistic gatekeepers. Overall, these contemporary journalists played a significant role in condemning the credibility of a woman in politics.

Woodhull's news coverage provides evidence for the argument that the press serves as a defender of the status quo rather than as an agent of change, at least in relation to women's issues. Her coverage also reinforces the point of Richardson (2007) that journalists are influenced by the societal norms and times in which they live, which then influence the word choices in their stories and potentially attitudes of the reading public. The fact that journalists continued using language that framed Woodhull in a negative light in the months leading up to Election Day is indicative that the reading public overall found this acceptable or at least indicates that journalists felt no pressure to change discursive tactics.

It is interesting to ponder how the press would have framed a Susan B. Anthony or Elizabeth Cady Stanton presidential candidacy—in other words, someone challenging the norm yet not to the extreme of Woodhull. Would the press coverage have been as vicious? Perhaps. After all, other politicians also faced discursive mocking during a time when the partisan press still heavily reigned. However, one could also argue that a woman like Woodhull was needed in order to put a strong enough dent in the "glass ceiling" to speed the possibilities for women in the future. Even though Woodhull is largely forgotten today, her ardent challenge of gender norms during her time did attract some support and undoubtedly aided in the (albeit slow) evolution of attitudes toward women in politics.

The next chapter will jump in time nearly 45 years to see how the press covered another campaign of national importance: the election of the first woman to Congress in 1916. First, however, a brief epilogue of Woodhull's story is provided:

How many votes Woodhull received on Election Day is not clear due to the fact she was not listed as an official candidate on the ballot and instead was a write-in candidate (Gabriel 1998). Woodhull and her partners were eventually cleared of the obscene literature charges and attempted to move on with their lives. However, it was clear things would never be the same. By 1876, Woodhull no longer attracted the crowds she once did for her lectures. She also decided to close her newspaper again due to health and financial concerns (Gabriel 1998). With little left in common with her second husband, she filed for divorce from Blood. Vanderbilt died the following year, prompt-ing a family dispute over his will. His son William is said to have paid off Woodhull and Tennie so they would not testify in court, prompting the sisters and their family to leave for England where they would establish new lives (Gabriel 1998). Woodhull married wealthy British banker John Martin while Tennie married wealthy British businessman Francis Cook. Still, their long time in the controversial spotlight did not vanish with their move overseas, and the press continued to remind the public of it (Gabriel 1998). In an attempt to reinvent her life, Woodhull denied her past and blamed her second husband and Stephen Pearl Andrews for much of that period of her life. Yet twice more she hoped to have presidential aspirations only to see the efforts fail (Gabriel 1998). Her third marriage brought her a security and wealth that she had longed for, however, and in 1892, she and her daughter started another newspaper, *The Humanitarian*. Woodhull, who changed her name to Martin with her final marriage, lived in England until her death on June 9, 1927, at age 88.

Figure 3.1 Bain News Service Took this Photo of Jeannette Rankin in 1917, Just Months after She Became the First Woman Elected to Congress. *Source*: Photo courtesy of the Library of Congress.

Chapter 3

Media Legitimization
of Jeannette Rankin

Upon her election to Congress in 1916, Jeannette Rankin reportedly said, "I know I'll be the first woman member of Congress, but I won't be the last" (Neukom 1916, 6). Clearly aware that her groundbreaking achievement would benefit future women, Rankin had now become a national role model for women in politics. But why Rankin? Fifty years after Stanton became the first woman to run for Congress and nearly 45 years after Woodhull ran for president, why was it Rankin who broke that particular glass ceiling and won national office? Certainly the political pioneer was a hard worker who ran a smart campaign boosted by a political network. But Rankin's rise to the U.S. House of Representatives was clearly aided by a powerful trio: location, location, location. Rankin's physical, temporal, and socio political locations were critical factors as to why she saw victory and Stanton and Woodhull did not. Furthermore, they are indicative as to why Rankin enjoyed overwhelmingly positive and neutral campaign coverage, as will be explained throughout this chapter, while Woodhull did not.

Because examining Woodhull's background and time proved critical to understanding her press coverage, this chapter also begins with an overview of Rankin's life and how a single woman from Montana put the first crack in the political patriarchy of Washington, D.C. Like Woodhull, Rankin worked her way into a prominent position in the national suffrage movement while also facing criticism from leadership for her political ambition. Also like Woodhull, Rankin was a noted lecturer who sought more rights for women than just the right to vote. Both women also rose to prominence after careers in New York City. However, Rankin had critical capital on her side that Woodhull did not: a political culture influenced by progressivism, a woman's movement on the brink of national victory, and a journalistic culture beginning to professionalize.

Taking all of those factors into account, this analysis focuses on news coverage of Rankin's political career from June 1916 through her election that November. In addition to explaining the key discursive themes that emerge from Rankin's news coverage, this chapter also evaluates the discursive similarities and differences with Woodhull's coverage. First, however, a trip back to the old West is necessary as Rankin entered politics with a key secret weapon: Montana.

TERRITORIAL ROOTS

Born near Missoula on June 11, 1880, Rankin grew up surrounded by mining and logging prosperity in Montana Territory. Her father was one of the most successful businessmen in the area due to his ranching and lumber enterprises, creating a comfortable lifestyle for his family and providing Rankin with the financial resources to pursue the opportunities she did in adulthood (Smith 2002). The oldest of John and Olive Rankin's seven children, Rankin was a "lively" and "strong-minded" child whose parents encouraged individualism and imparted to their daughter "the freedom to think and act, [a] faith in her capability, and a sense of personal responsibility" (Smith 2002, 34, 39). These qualities would be crucial to her future as a groundbreaking politician, but they also served to end her career soon after it started, as will be explained later in this chapter. Living in Missoula, "where everyone had come from somewhere else," exposed Rankin to a variety of people, as well as to the benefits of hard work that led to progress and change (Smith 2002, 26). Her own parents were pioneers; her Canadian father had moved to Montana in 1869, and her mother arrived from New Hampshire in 1878 (Smith 2002). During Rankin's youth and early adult years, farming communities developed "literally by the hundreds" across Montana as even more pioneers headed West for opportunity (Malone and Roeder 1976, 189). Between 1880 and 1920, Montana's population exploded from 39,000 residents to nearly 550,000 (Census Bureau n.d.). This growth led to the creation of another congressional seat in 1916 and provided an opening for Rankin. Optimism for the future was high out West, and the new residents saw themselves as "advancing the cause of civilization;" for them, "growth was progress, and progress was good" (Malone and Roeder 1976, 189), a philosophy that benefited Rankin politically in the 1910s.

In 1898, however, Rankin was still uncertain about her future. She enrolled at Montana State University (now the University of Montana) and graduated in 1902 with a major in biology, but going to college was just something to do rather than a real interest for her (Smith 2002). She declined marriage offers, remaining single throughout her life, an unusual path at a time when

90 percent of women married (Smith 2000). Rankin spent her early adult years as a teacher and seamstress, joining the 5 million women who worked outside the home in similar careers at the turn of the century (Smith 2000). This was short-lived, however, as she quit working to care for her father during his illness (Smith 2002). After his death, she resumed care for her family and took two getaway trips to visit relatives that would put her on the path to her political future. She first traveled to the East Coast to visit her brother, Wellington, then a student at Harvard. During a side trip to New York City in 1905, Rankin was stunned by the inequality extremes between Fifth Avenue and the tenements (Smith 2002). She found similar problems during a visit to an uncle in San Francisco in 1907, leading her to briefly work at a local settlement house to help children. Determined to become a social worker in order to do more, Rankin enrolled in the New York School of Philanthropy in 1908 to receive training (Smith 2002). Rankin's time in New York also introduced her to the suffrage movement, a cause that fascinated her so much she would soon switch gears and go to work for the movement (Smith 2002). This was the beginning of Rankin's life in politics.

A SENSE OF PURPOSE

Now filled with a "sense of purpose" (Anderson 2002, 9), Rankin graduated in 1909 and found work as a children's social worker in Washington state. However, she found that suffrage work suited her better. Rankin believed that women needed the right to vote in order to generate laws beneficial to children and to spur other reform efforts (Smith 2002). In 1910, she played an active role in the suffrage movement's success in Washington and attracted the attention of suffrage leaders in the East (Anderson 2002). By 1911, Rankin was back in New York as a suffragist. In the past decade, both Anthony and Stanton had died, and new leadership had taken the reigns. Before exploring the state of suffrage and feminism in the 1910s, however, it is useful to chart the transition of the women's movement in the years following Woodhull's association with the cause.

The disconnect between the National Woman Suffrage Association and the American Woman Suffrage Association lasted two decades before the organizations agreed to merge in 1890 to create the National American Woman Suffrage Association (Hill 2006). By the 1890s, women had secured partial suffrage in 19 states (Hill 2006), which typically meant women were allowed to vote on local school issues (Baker 1984). Four states—Wyoming, Colorado, Utah, and Idaho—granted women full suffrage by the end of the century. (Washington Territory did so in 1883 but this was overturned by the Supreme Court in 1887) (Hill 2006). However, despite the combined power of the two suffrage groups, their cause gained little ground between 1890 and 1910 due to resistance from states and Congress (Freeman 2000).

Outside of the national women's associations, women found other opportunities to take part in political culture. Women's clubs soared in popularity in the 1890s to the point that they existed in almost every town for both socialization and reform purposes (Freeman 2000). These clubs focused on social change by creating educational opportunities for girls, starting libraries, electing women to school boards, promoting sanitary reforms, and pushing health legislation (Baker 1984). Further benefits of these clubs for middle- and upper-class women were that:

> They enabled thousands of conventional middle-class women to learn from others, share female values, and work toward common goals. Combining self-help and social mission, they created an avenue to civic affairs . . . and they created a separate space for women in public life. (Woloch 2002, 287)

Despite this separate political culture, some scholars note that women were also involved in mainstream politics. Although women had no power to make decisions in political parties or to vote, feminist scholar Jo Freeman writes that women's activity in the parties increased in the late 1880s: "Women listened to speeches and attended political events with men, were highly regarded as campaign orators, were eagerly employed by the parties to canvas their voters and had their own political clubs and party organizations in some states" (Freeman 2000, 27). During the late 1800s, women were particularly involved in the Prohibition Party, where they served on committees and as convention delegates (Freeman 2000). The mainstream political parties also began explaining how national issues would affect women, as political leaders realized women were not only "exemplars of morality" but also "consumers, household managers, and wage workers" who could potentially persuade their husbands how to vote (Edwards 1997, 61). Women also made gains in their own right by winning local elections, particularly education positions, with the *Woman's Journal* reporting 13 states had women running for public office in 1894 (Freeman 2000; Edwards 1997). As the decade drew to a close, women's participation in electoral politics "soared" in 1896 as they "marched, canvassed, and monitored the polls on Election Day" (Freeman 2000, 36). As the new century approached, women had found a number of ways to become politically involved, thus beginning to blur the lines between men's and women's political cultures.

Yet the first decade of the 1900s was considered "the doldrums" for suffragists (Freeman 2000, 32; see also Anthony 1954, 415). States resisted giving women the right to vote, and Congress did not introduce bills related to the subject between 1896 and 1913 (Freeman 2000). Meanwhile, the debate of whether women were better off "by emphasizing their differences from men or by stressing their similarity" continued (Witt, Matthews, and Paget 1995, 20). However, significant changes and events at the national level between 1900 and 1920 are worth noting as they paved the way for women to finally win the right to vote.

One of the changes that ultimately benefited women was the declining influence of political parties due to election reforms. The introduction of the Australian ballot in the late nineteenth century, voter registration, and the 1913 ratification of the 17th Amendment mandating direct election of senators meant states gained more control over elections (Andersen 1996), thereby reducing the significance of the male political sphere. The 1912 election also saw splintering within the Republican Party as Theodore Roosevelt campaigned as a presidential candidate for the Progressive Party. Political changes such as these resulted in a "growing respect for the independent voter who chose 'the man, not the party,'" (Andersen 1996, 9). Progressive reforms during the time made elections about civic duty instead of party duty (Andersen 1996). In other words, "progressives in effect validated the very disinterestedness [being above politics] that had been associated with women" (Andersen 1996, 33) and therefore gave women more political credibility.

The Progressive era also led to more government involvement in social issues, the domain that played a central role in women's political culture. Anti-suffragists, therefore, became less convincing in their argument that men's and women's political cultures should be separate (Baker 1984):

Suffrage was no longer either a radical demand or a challenge to separate spheres because the concerns of politics and of the home were inextricable. At the same time, it did not threaten the existence of a male political culture because that culture's hold had already attenuated. The domestication of politics was connected, too, with the changed ideas of citizens about what government and politics were for. (Baker 1984, 642)

Along with the Progressive movement, World War I played a critical role in breaking down barriers between men's and women's roles. With men at war and women left to manage the home front and increasingly enter the workforce, suffragists argued that women had "proved their claims to good citizenship" (Baker 1984, 642). With more women working, it became harder to argue that women's role was only in the home (Andersen 1996).

Finally, women's continued involvement in political parties was an important element in their eventual acceptance into mainstream political culture. In cities, party women "did virtually everything necessary to elect candidates that party men did except vote" (Freeman 2000, 63). The Prohibition Party and the Women's National Republican Association were the most popular organizations for women in the late nineteenth century (Gustafson, Miller, and Perry 1999). Both "emphasized women's special obligations as wives and mothers" and "represented alliances of middle-class women and men" (Gustafson, Miller, and Perry 1999, 15). The women's divisions within the Democratic and Republican parties also helped break down barriers between the separate political cultures: "Women had argued for years that whatever affected the home concerned women, and what government did, or could do, affected the home. Progressive men, at least, now agreed" (Freeman 2000, 72).

By the 1910s, women's clubs around the nation had about 800,000 members (Freeman 2000). Still, many women realized their reform efforts at the local level could only go so far and that state and national intervention was necessary to make significant progress (Baker 1984). Anti-suffragists remained problematic with their arguments that God intended for women to be subordinate and that "woman's weak, gentle nature did not fit her for active participation in the world beyond the home—most especially not for the man's world of politics" (Smith 2000, 393). However, with lessons learned from their British counterparts, American suffragists were now ready to engage in more aggressive tactics in what would be the home stretch to national suffrage in 1920 (Smith 2000).

In New York, Rankin began organizing clubs and speaking on the street to garner support; she was soon sent to California to join the suffrage campaign there (Smith 2002). Following that victory, Rankin spent the next few years traveling around the country to campaign for the cause and to lobby state legislatures as a field secretary for the National American Woman Suffrage Association (Smith 2002). Suddenly, Rankin was a "well-established national suffrage leader" (Mead 2004, 156). Newspapers from Washington, D.C., to Florida to Nebraska covered her activity (i.e. "Suffragists Plan Counter Activity" 1913; "May Out Talk the Males" 1913; "Luncheon for Miss Rankin" 1913). The determined efforts of Rankin and her fellow suffragettes resulted in nearly all women in the western United States winning the vote by 1915—including in Montana (Mead 2004).

Rankin's suffrage work in her home state created a critical foundation for her future political campaign. Besides lobbying legislators, Rankin took the suffrage message across the vast state, traveling 6,000 miles via "trains, stages, and borrowed Fords" (Smith 2002, 85). In the span of a month, she covered 1,300 miles and "made 26 speeches, oversaw the election of 20 precinct leaders, and set up county central committees" (Smith 2002, 85). A story in *The Daily Missoulian* noted Rankin was "blazing the suffrage trail in northern Montana" and "stirring press and people" everywhere ("Miss Rankin Gains Good Support in North" 1914, 3). *The Suffrage Daily*

News in Helena wrote of her "unselfish and single devotion" ("Where Tribute is Due" 1914, 2) to persuade Montanans to approve suffrage, which they finally did in 1914.

There are a number of theories as to why Western states were friendlier to suffragists than other states, a topic worthy of further examination since much of Rankin's political campaign coverage came from Western newspapers and since it was a Western state that first voted a woman into national office. Rankin believed that the less rigid class structure in the West played a role in women's progress, as did the popularity of Socialist and Progressive politics (Smith 2002, see also the December 1911 issue of *The Woman's Journal*). Regarding class structure, Western women were generally respected for their hard work helping men on the homesteads and farms, as well as in local businesses (Mead 2004). Pioneer life required assistance from the entire family, and many families were in the same situation of making a fresh start. The societal hierarchy established in the East would have been difficult to maintain in the West, with more people arriving all of the time and towns in a constant state of flux. Mead (2004) expands on the theories for why Westerners were more open to suffrage and points to the "unsettled state of regional politics, the complex nature of Western race relations, broad alliances between suffragists and farmer-labor-progressive reformers, and sophisticated activism by Western women" (1). These arguments deserve further explanation. First, the unsettled regional politics went beyond parties and included the governmental transitions from territories to states in the late nineteenth and early twentieth centuries. What this meant is that suffragists got in on the ground floor, so to speak, and had less-established legislators to work with who were just forming state constitutions (Mead 2004). This made it easier to incorporate women into states' political policies from the beginning. Second, as noted earlier, many Westerners embraced the reform philosophies of the Progressive Party, which welcomed women's participation (Freeman 2000). Progressives believed women voters were necessary in order for political reform to occur (Mead 2004; Freeman 2000). More specifically, they thought women would bring "more democracy and less corruption" to society (Freeman 2000, 47). This "purity" view of women also played into the relationship between suffrage and race. Some Western suffragists argued that women voters would back the interests of white men, thereby (supposedly) decreasing the influence of foreigners in the rural areas and mining towns (Anderson 2002). In other words, women's suffrage was argued as a way to ensure white supremacy (Mead 2004). This argument may seem surprising due to the historical connection between abolition and the women's movement. However, the suffragists' emphasis on how women voters would improve society did include this racist strategy (Anderson 2002). Finally, the 1910s brought the official advent of the concept of feminism, which went beyond suffrage and demanded economic, political, and social freedom for women (Smith 2000). In other words, Woodhull's ideas were gaining more traction, although the movement remained small and was primarily active within the younger generation (Smith 2000; Freeman 2000). Nonetheless, women were increasingly demanding more rights and progress and were getting harder to ignore.

ELECTION OF 1916

With women's suffrage now secure in Montana, Rankin decided to run her own political campaign. After all, she now had the name recognition and network in place after her extensive lobbying efforts across the state. In addition to her prior hard work, she also had luck on her side. The state's population growth meant Montana had earned two congressional seats in 1916, yet redistricting had not yet occurred (Smith 2002). Therefore, candidates were running at-large, an advantage for Rankin who otherwise would have lost to incumbent Democrat (and fellow Missoulian) John Evans. Knowing it would be difficult to beat Evans, Rankin's strategy was to advise Montanans to use their two votes to vote for their local candidate and then vote for her, believing she could then finish second among the field of contenders and still win a seat (Smith 2002). Her brother Wellington, now a wealthy rancher, lawyer, and landholder who had his own political ambitions and connections, backed her campaign, as did many women across the state who would cast their first vote for the woman who helped them secure it (Smith 2002). However, Rankin's campaign wasn't without its problems. For one, not all women supported her ambition. Some—including former National American Woman Suffrage Association President Anna Howard Shaw—thought Rankin should "set her sights a little lower and run for the state legislature" (Smith 2002, 98). Furthermore, current suffrage President Carrie Chapman Catt expressed her displeasure with Rankin's plans: "Catt wrote Jeannette a condescending letter, asking about her program and political ambitions. Catt opposed women sticking their heads up for politicians to chop off until national suffrage was won; whatever one woman did, all would be blamed" (Smith 2002, 98). And while there were men impressed with her national lobbying and media attention, Rankin did not have full support from the Montana Republican Party (Smith 2002). Still, she was not deterred as she never saw herself as a Republican in the first place, despite the fact she ran on its ticket; rather, she focused on running a nonpartisan campaign and believed she could win (Anderson 2002).

Considering both the national and local context of the time, Rankin again had luck on her side in that the United States was still in a period of official neutrality regarding World War I. Whether Montanans would have voted for a woman congressman during wartime seems unlikely, especially considering the furor over Rankin's anti-war vote when she was in office and her unflinching pacifist views. This will be discussed more later in this chapter. However, during her campaign, both the nation and Montana were enjoying booming economies due to war trade and strong commodity prices (Cooper Jr. 2009; Malone and Roeder 1976). Democratic President Woodrow Wilson was heralded for keeping the country out of war and ran for a second term promoting progressive policies, such as health and safety measures and labor reforms (Cooper Jr. 2009). For the time being, Congress also supported neutrality and had in recent years focused on addressing economic and social problems resulting from industrialization. Tariff, banking, and anti-trust policies were among the major items of discussion (Sanders 2004).

Rankin's political priorities included national suffrage, prohibition, child welfare, and maternal and infant mortality (Anderson 2002). In other words, as Freeman (2000) writes, Rankin "ran as a woman" (80). This labeling is perhaps a bit unfair, however, since these were genuine interests of Rankin's and had been for some time. She was also interested in other issues, such as greater transparency in Congress by requiring votes to be public record (Anderson 2002). Still, unlike Woodhull's agenda, Rankin's platform was clearly considered safe as she and other political women "legitimized their public role by claiming to act on behalf of others, not themselves" and "sought to create or reform social institutions to support women's traditional role" (Anderson 2002, 16). So, while she may have been challenging the status quo by seeking a national office, Rankin was doing it within the boundaries of the era's definition of acceptable gender roles, a strategy that Woodhull did not use. Throughout her campaign, Rankin and her supporters traveled the state, spoke on street corners, and organized phone brigades (Smith 2002). On November 7, 1916, Rankin received the second-highest tally of Montanans' votes and made history as the first woman elected to Congress. However, the definitive results were delayed a few days due to the slow process of hand counting votes, leading some to initially report that she lost (Morrison and Morrison 1997; "Miss Rankin Probably Defeated in Democratic Landslide in Montana" 1916; "Democratic Congressmen Elected" 1916). This would not be the first time the press got it wrong in regard to Rankin as "her reticence and desire for privacy unwittingly led to many inaccurate reports of her demeanor, personality, and appearance" (Morrison and Morrison 1997, 137). Examination of this press coverage is now pertinent. First, however, an understanding of the press during the 1910s is important.

A SENSE OF PROFESSIONALISM

By the 1910s, newspapers employed different strategies for reporting than they did in the 1870s. By now, journalists largely controlled the news, not political parties or outside writers (Ryfe 2006). Journalists increasingly came to believe that "the best journalism was the most independent" (Daly 2012, 156) although partisanship remained, particularly through the promotion of candidates for political office (Startt 2004). Other differences are evident in the approach to writing. A 1912 reporting book emphasized the inverted pyramid and starting a story with the most interesting facts, not adhering to the chronological order of events as was used "in the old days" (Hyde 1912, 36). In addition, reports on speeches now centered on the speaker, not the crowds, and the first-person conversational writing style in news stories was no longer a favored practice (Ryfe 2006). In other words, "readers encountered none of the familiarity or intimacy that once abounded in newspapers" (Ryfe 2006, 72). Indeed, the author of a 1911 journalism textbook wrote that "the pronoun 'we' has been banished from the editorial and news columns, and the 'slop' and 'hog wash' known as 'puffs'—that is fulsome compliment and paid-for flattery—has become obsolete" (Ross 1911, 17). The textbook further notes that "the age of personal journalism in its old sense has passed" and warns that a reporter "must refrain from coloring his story with his personal prejudices and opinions" (Ross 1911, 21). The author criticizes the rural newspapers maintaining this old style of journalism, calling them "gossipy neighborhood chronicles" (Ross 1911, 21) rather than modern newspapers. Clearly, journalism had changed in the past 40 years and practitioners during the time sought to differentiate the industry from the style of reporting acceptable in the past.

However, the emphasis on reporters remaining out of the story and instead adhering to "clarity, terseness, objectivity" (Ross 1911, 17) is part of a larger debate about the state of journalism during this time and when objectivity actually became standard journalistic practice. A number of pre-1920s texts mention objectivity, yet there was also still an emphasis on subjectivity and invention (Vos 2011). Therefore, "this early period is characterized more by rhetorical experimentation than rhetorical formalization" (Vos 2011, 445). Indeed, while the 1911 journalism textbook emphasized objectivity (Ross 1911), the 1912 reporting book stated that "many a good piece of news is ruined by a bald, dry recital of facts" and that a "good reporter is always one who can give his yarns a distinctive flavor" (Hyde 1912, viii). It is therefore evident there was "volatility of news conventions in the early 1900s" (Ryfe 2006, 74) due to these differing approaches, thereby making the 1910s a period of journalistic transition just as the 1870s were.

Scholars have also debated the economic reasons for the transition to objectivity as a journalistic standard. As advertising revenue grew and businesses sought to reach as many consumers as possible, journalism became increasingly focused on profits (Kaplan 2002). By 1914, newspaper advertising generated "greater profits in newspaper publishing than had ever been known before" (Mott 1962, 593), setting the industry up for large employment gains in the coming decades (Chambers, Steiner, and Fleming 2004). Journalism flourished in the early twentieth century as readers "devoured" literature, magazines, and newspapers (Jeansonne 2006, 47). Although newspapers faced increasing competition from magazines, they benefited from the expansion of railroads, which expanded their distribution potential (Sloan 2011). Some scholars argue that objectivity served as a marketing effort for newspapers to have "a novel legitimating basis. They needed new compelling reasons to justify their prominence in the public arena" (Kaplan 2002, 190). Yet some scholars dispute this argument, noting that partisanship served as "circulation builders, not circulation losers" (Schudson 2001, 160). Rather, it's believed the era of Progressive reform, the Australian ballot, civil service reform, voter registration, and the direct election of senators played a role in newspapers' shift to objectivity, as well as the rise of science: "Journalists not only sought to affiliate with the prestige of science, efficiency, and Progressive reform, but they sought to disaffiliate from the public relations specialists and propagandists who were suddenly all around them" (Schudson 2001, 162). Kimball (1992) also emphasizes the importance of science during this time, noting that the field became synonymous with "cultural legitimacy" (302). This created an emphasis on specific protocols and professionalization.

The shift to objectivity also offered journalists group solidarity, a means for articulating ideals, a way to exercise control, and creation of a culture (Schudson 2001). Other factors that formalized group solidarity and the creation of a culture were the founding of journalism schools, press clubs, press associations, and ethics codes in the early twentieth century (Barnhurst and Nerone 2009). The push to improve journalistic standards also resulted in the formation of conventions and awards (Daly 2012). By 1917, *The New York Times* had established itself as "the strongest most influential newspaper in the region" (Cose 1989, 125) and was among the early newspapers to adopt the objectivity standard. Other changes during this time included a gradual increase in the number of women journalists, with women comprising 16 percent of journalists by 1920 (Chambers, Steiner, and Fleming 2004). Out on the frontier, the press had a history of supporting civic development, reform, and democratic government (Sloan 2011). All things considered,

Rankin was poised to benefit from a friendlier press environment than Woodhull encountered, which is indeed what happened.

Before discussing the findings regarding Rankin's newspaper coverage, it is worthwhile to note that other scholars have briefly mentioned her relationship with the press. For example, Morrison and Morrison (1997) wrote that Rankin's candidacy "was all but ignored by the state's major newspapers, most of which were owned by the powerful Anaconda Copper Mining Company" (135). Rankin's biographer Norma Smith made similar commentary. However, these claims are odd considering this analysis found 54 articles about Rankin in the *Anaconda Standard* during her campaign months. Furthermore, Smith contradicts herself by referring to Rankin's "bad newspaper coverage" (100) yet also saying that weeklies often published Rankin's public relations material and that there were large papers that treated her fairly. Therefore, this analysis aims to provide a more comprehensive examination of Rankin's campaign coverage by including state and national coverage. First, however, a brief explanation of the data collected is provided.

RANKIN'S NEWSPAPER TRENDS

This analysis involved 256 newspaper articles from 24 states and the District of Columbia between June 1 and November 11, 1916. This allowed for examination of articles throughout Rankin's congressional campaign until four days after Election Day in order to capture post election reaction. Four days were chosen for this post-analysis instead of two days due to the delay in election results.

Before examining the major discursive themes of Rankin's news coverage, a few trends in the news stories are worth mentioning. For one, Rankin's coverage pattern was the opposite of Woodhull's. Woodhull started out strong with a lot of press attention and then saw a decline in coverage until her arrest in November 1872. Rankin was instead a slow burn who gradually gained national attention as the press began to realize she was a viable political player. Rankin's remote location likely played a role in this. Whereas Woodhull was at the center of press attention in New York City, Rankin was far West and away from major Eastern newspapers with influence. Indeed, until November, more than 80 percent of Rankin's coverage in this sample came from newspapers in the West or Midwest. To break that down further, 60 percent of her coverage between June and October was from Montana alone. *The New York Times'* first mention of Rankin doesn't appear until October 13, a day after *The Sun* in New York wrote about her. Therefore, the local, smaller media set the initial agenda for Rankin's coverage as opposed to the larger national media in Woodhull's case. This is a point that will be examined further throughout this book. Another factor to consider in the comparison of Woodhull and Rankin is the fact that Woodhull was running for president, a race of relevance to the entire nation, whereas Rankin was running to represent one state. Therefore, it makes sense that much of the nation's media would not take notice until Rankin became a legitimate contender for making congressional history.

Like Woodhull, Rankin made the front page about one-fourth of the time. The majority of Rankin's front-page play came after Election Day, however, instead of at the beginning of her campaign like Woodhull's. The highest percentage of Rankin's coverage—about one-third—appeared between pages 3 and 6. By now, newspapers had increased in size, with a number of them offering 14 or 16 pages. Newspapers also began incorporating more visuals. A head shot of Rankin accompanied 34 of the articles about her, or about 13 percent. Only two Montana articles included her image. The rest appeared in articles in 17 states and the District of Columbia. Woodhull's image never appeared in her coverage due to journalistic practices of the time. As far as article length, however, Rankin fared worse than Woodhull. More than 85 percent of Rankin's press coverage was merely a brief mention, compared to three-fourths for Woodhull.

Journalists surprisingly controlled 85 percent of Rankin's framing power compared to three-fourths for Woodhull, although—as will be discussed shortly—the discursive tone was considerably different. Rankin and her supporters comprised the rest of her discursive power in the press in articles about her. Yet, of the articles that do include quotes from Rankin, all but one appear *after* Election Day, thereby indicating she did not have direct framing power in the press during her actual campaign. In the mid-1910s, just like the 1870s, journalists were still driving the discursive agenda. One final item of structural interest is that only one article (in Topeka, Kansas) mentioned opponents to Rankin's candidacy. The limited commentary from opposition in both Woodhull's and Rankin's coverage is indicative that objectivity—particularly, the practice of including comments from both sides of an issue in articles—had not yet become mainstream in the journalism community. For Woodhull, this was a disadvantage due to her predominantly negative coverage that would have benefited from more positive commentary. For Rankin, however, journalists chose a much different discursive strategy: one that brimmed with positivity.

The below analysis explores this further as there were five main discursive themes that emerged from examination of the Rankin news stories. The first three are the same as those discovered in the Woodhull analysis: discourse related to her connection to the women's movement of the time; discourse related to her politics; and discourse related to her personal traits. However, two new themes emerged in Rankin's press coverage: discourse related to the historical relevance of the candidacy and discourse related to appearance. These two new themes also align with Murray's (2010) framework regarding women politicians, particularly the gendered news frames concept. By gendered news frames, Murray means the media provide different news coverage for male candidates than female candidates and "frame a candidate in ways which correspond to traditional stereotypes" (8). Subcategories within this concept include appearance and an emphasis on being the "first woman," which is another way of phrasing historical relevance. This is a gendered news frame due to its use as a discursive reminder that women are not considered the norm. With that context provided, this analysis begins with examining discourse related to Rankin's connection to the women's movement.

RANKIN AND THE WOMEN'S MOVEMENT

News coverage about Rankin's connection to the women's movement was significantly different from what Woodhull encountered nearly 45 years earlier. Whereas Woodhull's coverage skewered her as the women's rights candidate and highlighted the friction between her faction and the mainstream movement, Rankin's coverage matter-of-factly accepted her as a suffragist and praised her work on behalf of the cause.

A Prominent Suffragist

More than one-fourth of the stories analyzed in this sample mentioned Rankin's ties to the women's movement. Some simply noted she was a suffragist or, for those opting for more colorful phrasing, "a prominent suffragist of the west" (*Evening Independent*, July 14, 1916, 15; *The Ogden Standard*, July 17, 1916, 4; *Grand Forks Herald*, July 17, 1916, 10; *The Topeka State Journal*, July 19, 1916, 7) or "leading woman suffragist" (*New Castle News*, November 7, 1916, 5; *Logansport Pharos Reporter*, November 7, 1916, 5; *East Liverpool Evening Review*, November 7, 1916, 4). Other articles mentioned her work as a field secretary for the National American Woman Suffrage Association (*The Glasgow Courier*, August 18, 1916, 12; *New York Tribune*, November 10, 1916, 1; *Tulsa Daily World*, August 30, 1916, 5; *New Castle News*, September 14, 1916, 5). Regardless of the exact phrasing, Rankin's career was an accepted fact. There was no discourse judging her choice of profession or her involvement in the overall cause, indicating that suffragists were by and large a normalized aspect of society by the mid-1910s.

This acceptance was certainly important in order for Rankin's campaign to be taken seriously and was missing when Woodhull attempted politics.

Not only was Rankin's suffragist background accepted but the press also saw it as an advantage.

A Source of National Pride

Discourse about Rankin's state and national suffragist ties appeared in a number of news articles to legitimize her qualifications as a political candidate. From a state perspective, an article in *The Daily Ardmoreite* in Oklahoma said Rankin was "the one woman who is credited above all others with having won the ballot for Montana women two years ago" (August 24, 1916, 3). *The Enterprise* in Montana described the "popularity of the woman to whom woman's suffrage in Montana is largely due" (October 12, 1916, 1). The same day, *The Sun* in New York ran an article saying Rankin was "principally responsible for making Montana a suffrage state. For this reason, every woman is said to have taken a vow to vote for her" (October 12, 1916, 4). *The Daily Gate City and Constitution-Democrat* in Iowa also noted Rankin "was a big factor in making Montana a suffrage state" (October 20, 1916, 3). At this point, about 20 percent of U.S. states had granted suffrage. So, while not a new concept, suffrage states were still a minority. Yet newspapers in both suffrage and non-suffrage states viewed Rankin's work as a worthy credential and used this discourse to illustrate her hard work and popularity. Rather than serve as a strategy to derail her credibility, as was used with Woodhull, discourse about Rankin's ties to the movement instead legitimated her.

Similarly, whereas journalists in the 1870s highlighted Woodhull's contentious relationship with women, journalists in the 1910s used an opposite strategy with Rankin. Not only did Montana women love her, but (according to the press) the national suffragists did as well. The *Anaconda Standard* in Montana wrote that "more than one Montana woman has declared that she will never cut her hair or shave until Jeannette Rankin is elected" (October 8, 1916, 4), an interesting feminist commentary and certainly a discursive choice indicative of fervent support and an emotional connection to Rankin. Following Rankin's win, an article appeared in multiple newspapers that said "women voters stood solidly by women candidates in Montana and the election of Mrs. Jeannette Rankin to Congress appears assured" (*Washington Court House Herald* (Ohio), November 8, 1916, 5; *Marysville* (Ohio) *Evening Tribune*, November 8, 1916, 1). Overlooking the fact that Rankin was incorrectly referred to as a Mrs., the "solid" support again contrasts with Woodhull's reported relationship with women and illustrates the emotional investment that women voters had with Rankin. This also illustrates a shift in journalistic culture to support progressivism and advocate on behalf of democracy. Whereas journalists in the 1870s used aggressive discursive tactics against Woodhull, journalists in the 1910s seemed to want to latch onto Rankin's rising star by sharing positive commentary about her.

Perhaps most fascinating is the journalistic discourse about the relationship between Rankin and the national suffragists. As noted earlier, leadership had discouraged Rankin's political ambition, leading to internal friction. While Woodhull's disagreement with leadership was publicized, however, Rankin's situation was apparently kept quiet. There is no indication in her press coverage of a rift. In fact, the opposite is shown. An article in *The Bennington* (Vt.) *Evening Banner* stated that Rankin was "a source of national pride to the National Suffrage Association" and "one of its most valued organizers" (November 9, 1916, 1). A similar article ran in the *Harrisburg Telegraph* in Pennsylvania (November 9, 1916, 9), which also carried an article a few days later noting "so proud are they [the suffragists] that it was their Jeannette who is the first woman elected to Congress" (November 11, 1916, 11). *The Washington Times* also highlighted Rankin's relationship with suffragists by saying those in D.C. were "elated over her coming to Congress," not just because of the perceived victory for suffragists but because it was Rankin herself who won (November 11, 1916, 1).

Some newspapers also included quotes from suffrage leaders to add more viewpoints about the movement's ties to Rankin. Mrs. Walter McNab Miller, first vice president of the National Association for Woman Suffrage, is quoted as saying, "We all love her . . . and nearly every suffragist in the country knows her" (*The Washington Times*, November 11, 1916, 14). Mrs. Mary Dennett, former executive secretary of the national association, is quoted in the *Boston Post* saying Rankin was the one woman "of whom it could be said that all suffragists were her friends" (November 11, 1916, 4). For national suffragists, association with Rankin was a way to build up credibility for their cause as they now wanted to be connected to a winner. In return, she was constructed in the press as an amenable figure loved by all even though she privately had issues with national leadership just like Woodhull publicly did. Clearly, keeping in-house squabbles under wraps is an important factor while campaigning in order to maintain a positive political front. This is also indicative that the press was not aggressive in searching out this information and instead accepted the surface-level discourse. Outside the women's movement, Rankin's political savvy also was evident via the discourse related to her candidacy.

RANKIN AND POLITICS

The articles about Rankin the politician primarily featured her political candidacy in a positive light, although she did face some criticism.

Specifically, the positive discourse emphasized Rankin's celebrity and her political skill.

Jeannette Rankin for Congress

Press coverage supporting Rankin's candidacy frequently used celebrity framing, which involved mentioning her endorsements and her popularity. Several newspapers thought the Missoula Good Government League's endorsement of Rankin was newsworthy, an odd news choice for out-of-state newspapers but indicative of widespread interest in her (*The Ogden Standard*, July 17, 1916, 4; *Grand Forks Herald*, July 17, 1916, 10; *The Topeka State Journal*, July 19, 1916, 7; *Arizona Republican*, July 20, 1916, 4). Locally, the *Cut Bank Pioneer Press* in Montana offered its own endorsement by referring to "Jeannette Rankin for Congress" as words that "carry with them not only something of promise but much of substance" (September 15, 1916, 1). Rankin reportedly had support from women's clubs, good government leagues, and "nearly all big Republican leaders" (*The Topeka State Journal*, November 2, 1916, 3). This included Montana Republican National Committeeman Thomas Marlowe, who made news when he backed Rankin. *The Bismarck Daily Tribune* quoted him as saying Rankin was "certain of election," while the *Daily Inter Lake* in Montana had him saying "I haven't the slightest doubt" of her election (October 4, 1916, 1; October 18, 1916, 2). The biggest reported endorsement came from Theodore Roosevelt, with *The Grand Forks Herald* in North Dakota quoting him as saying, "I very earnestly hope Miss Rankin will be elected" (November 4, 1916, 3). By publicizing that outside groups and major political figures favored Rankin, the press legitimized Rankin to voters. Whether Montanans knew of Roosevelt's reported backing is unknown, but it is possible since Roosevelt and the Rankins shared a mutual friend in Montana Progressive leader Joseph Dixon (Smith 2002). What was clear, however, was Rankin's popularity with Montanans.

The Montana press frequently wrote about the enthusiastic response that Rankin received when she appeared before crowds. Although some news coverage of Woodhull mentioned her favorable audience reaction, her supporters were often immediately criticized in the same news articles. In contrast, Rankin enjoyed a positive popularity with little to no criticism. The *Cut Bank Pioneer Press* in Montana wrote that Rankin was "eagerly awaited by people of all political persuasions" and that "towns and cities all over Montana are clamoring to secure the little lady for speaking engagements" (September 15, 1916, 1). Writing of her upcoming visit to Malta, Montana, *The Glasgow Courier* said a large crowd was expected "as many have expressed a desire to hear her" (October 6, 1916, 5). A month later, the newspaper ran a front-page headline, "Sentiment for Miss Rankin Still Growing," with an article mentioning the "huge crowds" that attended her talks and the "phenomenal" ovations she received (November 3, 1916, 1). This article came out just days before the election and surely boosted her credibility. Anyone still on the fence of whether to vote for Rankin would only have to read these glowing reports to get swept into a bandwagon effect, knowing that so many others reportedly backed her. If nothing else, it had to make at least some people curious as to why she was so popular and prompt them to learn more about her campaign. The *Anaconda Standard* also ran multiple articles about Rankin's popularity and the large crowds at her events (July 12, 1916, 9; August 3, 1916, 3; August 16, 1916, 14). The newspaper told readers of the "wild cheering and applause" and "bursts of applause," with enthusiasm "apparent at all times" (August 3, 1916, 3; August 16, 1916, 3). Similarly, *The Enterprise* wrote that "large audiences and enthusiastic applause have attested the popularity" of Rankin and that she was "supported by men and women and all parties" (October 12, 1916, 1). Although specific voters weren't quoted in these articles, this type of discourse provided multiple viewpoints via the repeated emphasis on crowd approval. Not just crowd approval, but people of different genders and political persuasions. This press construction of Rankin as a celebrity with a loyal following certainly served to legitimize her campaign and illustrated the press was on her side. Perhaps most importantly, the press went beyond the celebrity frame and also highlighted Rankin's skills as a politician. This included coverage about her political qualifications, her platform, and her campaign strategy.

Skilled Politician

Rankin's political qualifications were mentioned in a number of stories, lending further support to her candidacy. *The Glasgow Courier* told readers that Rankin was "thoroughly familiar with governmental machinery, having had legislative experience as the representative of the national suffrage association" (August 18, 1916, 12). The article went on to say that she had appeared before legislatures in New York, New Hampshire, Florida, Delaware, North Dakota, and Montana, and had experience lobbying before Congress. In other words, she was a serious candidate who was qualified for the job, not just a popular celebrity. This is important as this discourse does not use gendered news frames but treats Rankin like a regular candidate. *The Courier* also quoted the *Seattle Times* saying that Rankin was an "excellent speaker" and "skilled politician" (September 22, 1916, 1), a discursive strategy likely aimed at illustrating to Montanans that even outsiders recognized her ability to do the job. Interestingly, there were newspapers that directly said Rankin had the same political qualifications as a man, if not more so. The *Tulsa Daily World* ran an article stating "Miss Rankin knows what she is talking about" and that "when it comes to hand shaking and speech making, no mere man can equal her" (August 30, 1916, 4). Similarly, *The Washington Times* advocated Rankin's qualifications as being equal to a man's by saying: "She has been elected to Congress on precisely the same basis that men are elected in other places and on which, in the future, a good many other women will be sent to Congress: her brains, fitness, public services, and general right to recognition" (November 9, 1916, 6). The newspaper further noted that Rankin was "reputed to be a real student of public affairs over a pretty wide range of phases, [and] an effective speaker." These articles legitimate Rankin as a viable player in the male political world by telling readers that she not only can keep up with them but can outperform them. This discourse notably ran in areas that had not yet granted suffrage, most notably Washington, D.C., the political capital, and could be viewed as a direct challenge to the status quo by legitimating a woman politician. It furthermore illustrates the commitment of the press to promote democracy by indicating that gender should not be an issue.

After the election, a number of newspapers ran articles that mentioned Rankin's college education, another discursive choice likely intended to illustrate her ability (*The Washington Times*, November 11, 1916, 14; *Richmond Times-Dispatch*, November 11, 1916, 1; *New York Tribune*, November 10, 1916, 1; *Boston Post*, November 11, 1916, 1; *New York Times*, November 11, 1916, 2; *Fort Wayne News*, November 11, 1916, 3). The *New York Tribune* offered rare discourse reportedly from Rankin herself discussing her qualifications: "I'm not nervous about going to Congress. I've been working politicians and for political matters so long that I feel I'm a veteran in the game" (November 11, 1916, 1). This framed her as a confident politician— a "veteran," no less—to equalize her among her male counterparts. This contrasts with much of the discourse about her platform, however, which employed a more feminine strategy.

Rankin's Platform

Discourse about Rankin's platform appeared in publications across the country and primarily focused on what are referred to as "women's issues." Before examining this, however, it is interesting to note that—based on the news stories collected for this study—widespread coverage did not mean frequent coverage. In other words, once a newspaper carried an article that included information about her platform, there typically was not further information about it in future editions. One exception was *The Glasgow Courier*, which oddly ran the same article twice in one week. The story stated that

"Miss Rankin stands for national equal suffrage, state and national prohibition, child welfare, and greater publicity in congressional affairs. Her slogan is 'Let the People Know'" (August 18, 1916, 12; August 23, 1916, 12). The *Courier* also ran other articles highlighting Rankin's political priorities, with one only mentioning her dry platform and another stating she "has been speaking on the tariff, the farm loan law, the congressional duties regarding patents and appropriations, and other national questions" (September 22, 1916, 1; November 3, 1916, 1). The latter article is significant since it goes beyond "women's issues" and illustrates that Rankin is knowledgeable about matters discussed by male politicians even though specifics of her commentary weren't provided. This discursive strategy served to legitimize her as capable of entering a "male" position. This was a rare find, however, as the other coverage related to her platform centered on topics that fell under women's issues.

Rankin's stand on prohibition was sometimes the only part of her platform mentioned in news articles, an interesting discursive strategy perhaps aimed at pointing out this was an issue of great importance to women and illustrative that this was an issue of interest to the press (*Evening Star*, September 1, 1916, 3; *New Castle News*, September 14, 1916, 5; The *Glasgow Courier*, September 22, 1916, 1 (citing the *Colorado Spokesman*); *Williston Graphic*, September 28, 1916, 4; *The Sun*, October 12, 1916; 4; *Bismarck Daily Tribune*, November 5, 1916, 14). Other newspapers expanded a bit further and mentioned her interests in suffrage and prohibition (*Bakersfield Californian*, August 31, 1916, 2; *Boston Daily Globe*, September 1, 1916, 1). Therefore, Rankin was primarily framed as a one- or two-dimensional politician, which is similar to the discourse of Woodhull's platform and its heavy emphasis on her free love component. The fact that most of Rankin's coverage entailed brief articles meant there was no space in general for the press to go into much depth.

There were several newspapers across the country that did give Rankin's platform a bit more attention. *The Enterprise* in Montana wrote that the state would "make no mistake in sending so able a representative" who was fitted to consider laws related to women's working hours, education, sanitation, and children (October 12, 1916, 1). Although this was framed positively and was in line with Rankin's own priorities, it also lends itself to "woman politician" discourse rather than simply "politician" discourse, thereby serving as a gendered news frame. In other words, Rankin is discursively constructed as being fit to only address women's issues despite the fact the *Courier* wrote that she spoke on a wide range of issues and had broader interests. Similarly, *The Washington Times* described Rankin as an "ardent advocate of child welfare, prohibition, social insurance and other progressive legislation" (November 11, 1916, 14). Although the article also mentions her interest in greater government transparency, this type of discourse again emphasizes Rankin as a "woman politician" by focusing on women's issues.

A few stories included supposed quotes from Rankin herself talking about her platform. *The New York Tribune* has her saying "social welfare legislation is my chief concern and will be" (November 11, 1916, 1). A rare bylined story that ran in the *Evening Public Ledger* in Pennsylvania—a story surprisingly written by a woman—included a breakout box of Rankin's issues: national woman suffrage, protection of children, state and national prohibition, farm loan law, and equal taxation (November 11, 1916, 6). The story also quotes Rankin as saying: "I am going to Washington to represent the women and children of the West—to work for an eight-hour day for women and for laws providing that women shall be paid the same wages as men for equal amounts of work" (November 11, 1916, 6). This story is interesting since the breakout box includes various national issues, yet the quote emphasizes women and children. Even more noteworthy, the writer, who cites a dispatch from Missoula as the information source, is sure to point out that Rankin was "sewing as she said this today." This was an interesting word choice as it seems to be an effort to make Rankin's political priorities more palatable—or perhaps less threatening—by giving her a housewife-type frame and feminizing her. Surely someone who partakes in a motherly pastime would be respectable. This gendered frame is further emphasized with the writer's repetition that Rankin's platform includes "decent legislation for children and national prohibition," and another quote from Rankin saying "there is not a single woman to take care of the interests of the children" (November 11, 1916, 6). Similar stories appeared in other states (*Fort Wayne News*, November 11, 1916, 3; *The Topeka State Journal*, November 2, 1916, 3; *Des Moines Daily News*, November 11, 1916 1). It's a bit ironic that Woodhull was a mother and Rankin was not, yet Rankin's news coverage had the motherly tone. Still, this clearly was a successful strategy in legitimating Rankin as a candidate and appealing to the moral emotions (and sense of gender norms) of the public. Constructed in the press as having the political skill of a man and the message of a woman, Rankin enjoyed press coverage that clearly aided her candidacy. How reporters covered her campaign strategy also proved beneficial.

Campaign Strategy

Press coverage about Rankin's campaign strategy was overwhelmingly positive and portrayed her as a hard worker and popular speaker—or a "magnetic" speaker as an article in the *Tulsa Daily World* opined (August 30, 1916, 5). *The Glasgow Courier* wrote that Rankin campaigned in every county in the state and "acquainted herself thoroughly with conditions in

Montana" (August 18, 1916, 12). *The Anaconda Standard* called her "one of the busiest campaigners in the state" (August 12, 1916, 9), and *The Sun* in New York said she visited "every town, mountain village and mining camp" in Montana, while also noting her speaking skills (October 12, 1916, 4). One of her stops included standing on a car on Main Street in Deer Lodge, Montana, to give a speech to a large crowd (*Anaconda Standard*, September 3, 1916, 9). Some newspapers referred to her campaign as "strenuous" (*The Washington Times*, October 21, 1916, 8; *Indiana Evening Gazette*, November 11, 1916, 1). To reach out to women, Rankin's campaign planned registration teas in hopes of getting women to come out to socialize and register to vote (*The Glasgow Courier*, September 29, 1916, 1). To hook male voters, Rankin was said to have danced with miners "at the rough and ready social functions in the back woods towns of Montana" (*The Washington Times*, November 11, 1916, 14). Her public relations team reportedly shared Rankin's photo with newspapers and told them she would win (*Evening Star*, November 5, 1916, 14.) On Election Day, her supporters "called every telephone number in the state and asked whoever answered if a vote had been cast for Miss Rankin yet" (*Des Moines Daily News*, November 11, 1916, 1). Clearly, Rankin's suffrage training and her prior efforts to secure voting rights were instrumental to knowing how to score a political victory. More specifically, her role in Montana's suffrage win had already taught her what was effective with Montana voters and what was not. This kind of savviness was missing with Woodhull, who, although a good speaker, focused too much on ideas considered radical at the time rather than trying to appeal to a mass base first. Journalistically, Rankin's campaign strategy was framed as acceptable rather than as a joke, illustrating that the press appreciated her strategy to reach out to as many voters as possible. That being said, Rankin did not have 100 percent support for her candidacy.

Opposition

Although discourse opposing Rankin's candidacy was rare, there was some. An article in *The Topeka State Journal* said her opponents considered her political views "rabid and so radical they are almost socialistic" (November 2, 1916, 3). There is no indication as to who these opponents are or what specific aspects of her platform were considered problematic. A few articles were more specific and mentioned problems Rankin could face from current members of Congress. *The Washington Times* asked readers to "imagine the sensations that would overcome" Alabama Democrat (and white supremacist) James Thomas Heflin if he had to sit next to her in Congress (November 9, 1916, 6). Rankin's potential presence was also said to be "causing some little perturbation among the old war horses of the legislative body" who would have to quit their "violent" language at party caucuses if a woman member were present (*Fort Wayne News*, October 26, 1916, 8). There was also reported to be talks that Congress, "if it wanted to be 'mean,' may refuse to seat a 'congresswoman'" (*The Evening Herald*, October 25, 1916, 4; *Indiana Evening Gazette*, November 11, 1916, 1). It's surprising that there were not more articles raising these kinds of concerns, although, as noted earlier, much of Rankin's press coverage did not come until late in her campaign. In other words, her candidacy or at least her likelihood of winning may not have been well-known enough across the country to generate more criticism. There is also the factor that the national press would have learned about her through reports from the more progressive Montana press, which had already set a positive discursive tone for her. Therefore, the national press possibly opted to simply follow the agenda already set, thereby limiting journalistic negative discourse.

Of more importance to Rankin during her campaign was local news coverage and, although the *Anaconda Standard* ran a number of neutral articles and included positive commentary about her candidacy, there was also critical coverage. A week before Election Day, the newspaper "doubted" her qualifications on national affairs beyond suffrage and said voters were being urged to vote for her merely out of sympathy and to have the first woman congressman (October 31, 1916, 6). A few days later, the newspaper was blunter and specifically told readers not to vote for her since she was not a Democrat like Wilson and wouldn't help his agenda (*The Anaconda Standard*, November 4, 1916, 6). Although sharp in nature, this discourse was nothing like the "Mrs. Satan" kind of discourse that Woodhull received. More specifically, Woodhull's critical news coverage primarily focused on her personal traits, whereas Rankin's focused on her political qualifications and gender. The next chapters of this book will provide insight into how more contemporary women politicians are criticized in the press to see what similarities or differences there are to Woodhull's and Rankin's critical coverage. But overall, from a political standpoint, both Woodhull and Rankin wanted the public to know they would address important national topics that they felt did not get enough attention. Yet Rankin had the smarter political strategy and enjoyed a friendlier journalistic culture, thereby giving her the historic win that they both sought.

RANKIN'S HISTORICAL RELEVANCE

A new theme that emerged in Rankin's press coverage was an emphasis on the historical meaning of her election, a trend that began even before Election

Day results were tallied. Since Rankin received largely favorable coverage throughout her campaign and then ultimately won, journalists were more apt to write about the broader meaning of her candidacy. This historical discourse was absent in Woodhull's coverage, likely due to a combination of the press realizing Grant would win as well as journalists' widespread dislike of her. One could also argue that Woodhull did not meet the minimum age to be president anyway, making any historical reference impossible, but the press did not bring up Woodhull's age or illustrate awareness of it so that does not seem to be a factor. As far as Rankin's historical discourse, a few subthemes were evident: discourse that simply notes she would be a first and discourse that emphasizes the importance of being a first.

First Woman

A number of newspapers ran articles that included one or two basic sentences about Rankin's historical role. For example, *The Butler* (Mo.) *Weekly Times* simply said, "She is the first woman in the state to run for the office" (July 13, 1916, 3). Papers in Oklahoma, Montana, and Washington, D.C., also briefly referenced Rankin as a "first" or "only" prior to her election (*The Daily Ardmoreite*, August 24, 1916, 3; *Cut Bank Pioneer Press*, September 15, 1916, 1; *The Washington Times*, October 21, 1916, 8). After her election, papers around the country carried the news that she won, yet many only ran one or two sentences about this historical moment. The *Rogue River Courier* in Oregon wrote, "One of the big features of the congressional fight is the seeming election of a woman for the first time in the union's history." The paper notes that Rankin appears to have won in Montana and ends its coverage of the matter there (November 9, 1916, 2). Newspapers in Arizona, North Dakota, Iowa, New York, Pennsylvania, Kansas, and Wisconsin also had limited reactions. Some simply said that "an unusual feature" of Election Day was that Rankin appeared to have won (*Bisbee Daily Review*, November 10, 1916, 2; *Arizona Republican*, November 10, 1916, 1; *Mohave County Miner*, November 11, 1916, 1; *The Evening World*, November 10, 1916, 1). Others wrote that "a woman will sit in Congress for the first time in history" or used similar phrasing (*The Daily Gate City and Constitution-Democrat*, November 10, 1916, 2; *Daily Capital Journal*, November 10, 1916, 2). So, although the discourse was brief, the historical reference was still there. One must also keep in mind the practical limitations of journalists covering elections: much news is coming in with only so much space. Plus, this was a time when journalists were still producing a lot of news as briefs rather than stories. However, there were newspapers that believed Rankin's pioneering career deserved more recognition than a declarative sentence as will be explored next.

Progress with a P

Certainly there were newspapers in Montana that trumpeted Rankin's historical run, even if some claims were questionable or simply wrong. *The Glasgow Courier* hyped that "nationwide interest has been aroused" by Rankin's candidacy and that she was appearing "in almost every newspaper in the country" (September 22, 1916, 1). Whether that was true in September seems debatable since the databases searched for news articles for this analysis returned limited results. The newspaper also incorrectly wrote that she was the first woman in the country to run for Congress. Still, clearly an excitement over her history-making potential was there, and this was an emotional strategy to get readers excited as well. In the same article, the *Courier* included snippets of text it collected from other newspapers, quoting the *Seattle Times* as saying Rankin "stands an excellent chance of being the first woman member of Congress" and the *Tallahassee Times* as saying "in the event of her election will be the first congresswoman in the United States" (September 22, 1916, 1). The *Courier* engaged in further cheerleading in November by writing that predictions indicated "Montana will send the first congresswoman to Washington with the biggest majority ever given to any candidate on any ticket in the state" (November 3, 1916, 1). Whether the newspaper really believed this is questionable since Rankin herself knew she would not finish first ahead of incumbent Evans. This was probably more so a discursive strategy to legitimatize her candidacy to readers by indicating that she was a winning cause. *The Enterprise* in Harlem, Montana, also couldn't contain itself over Rankin's history potential by noting in October that it appeared Montana would "have the honor" of electing the first Congresswoman. Furthermore, the paper wrote that, if Montana elected her, the state would "take another step forward in the lime light of progress; and the eyes of the nation will be turned in approval of an act which recognizes ability in its admirable womanhood" (October 12, 1916, 1). In other words, the history wasn't just about Rankin but also about Montana as a whole and its place in the national spotlight. This was an emotional discursive strategy aimed at telling readers that they would all benefit if they chose Rankin, which likely fed into the previously discussed psyche of pioneers to create a progressive civilization. Similarly, the *Daily Inter Lake* in Kalispell, Montana, quoted Republican U.S. Rep. Clarence B. Miller of Minnesota as saying Rankin's election "would be a valuable asset to both the United States and Montana," which would be "an event of more than ordinary importance" and lead to national suffrage (September 27, 1916, 1). Again, this type of coverage is indicating that the election was about more than just Rankin, and the inclusion of multiple viewpoints here and by the *Courier* was intended to legitimize her candidacy and promote its wider significance.

Outside of Montana, other newspapers also pressed the historical importance of sending a woman to Congress. *The Bismarck* (N.D.) *Tribune* wrote that the question of whether voters would do so was "of vital interest to the 4,000,000 women voters in the United States" (October 6, 1916, 5). *The Sun* in New York ran a headline in October already saying "Montana to Elect a Congresswoman" and "surely this was progress with a big P," particularly compared to the "conservative East, which has not even adopted woman suffrage" (October 12, 1916, 4). The *Syracuse Herald* in New York and *Stevens Point Daily Journal* in Wisconsin ran the same article (October 15, 1916, 10; October 22, 1916, 3). This discourse appears to be using Rankin's historical moment (although not yet secured) as an opportunity to challenge the status quo, which is framed as falling behind the times. In other words, the status quo is discursively placed in a position where it would need to play defense rather than maintain an offense in regard to societal norms. This strategy of confronting gender inequality is certainly fascinating and important for the advancement of discourse regarding women. The next discursive themes found in this analysis, however, are decidedly different.

RANKIN'S PERSONAL TRAITS

Upon initial review, news coverage of Rankin's personal traits seemingly had a positive spin. However, closer examination illuminates problematic gendered strategies, including constructions of sexualization and of idealized womanhood.

Look Out Boys!

Interestingly, nearly all of the personal coverage about Rankin came after her election instead of before. *The Glasgow Courier* ran some positive commentary beforehand, quoting *The Sun* as saying "Miss Rankin has a rare personality, a fine intellect, and an unusual perspective" (September 22, 1916, 1). *The Washington Times* called her "an able woman" (October 21, 1916, 8). Otherwise, her personality was primarily described after she became a historic figure, resulting in the press trying to bolster— and romanticize—her image. Her pioneer family roots were highlighted in national media (*The Washington Times*, November 11, 1916, 14; *New York Tribune*, November 10, 1916, 1), a strategy that some regional papers took to the extreme by claiming she hunted bears in the snow for fun (*The Daily Gate City and Constitution-Democrat*, November 11, 1916, 1; *Fort Wayne News*, November 11, 1916, 3). Although this is amusing, the newspapers that chose discourse reminiscent of personal ads are particularly interesting.

In a front-page article headlined "Introducing Jeannette," *The Washington Times* said she was "the Montana dynamo of energy" and further noted that "Jeannette is the best stump speaker in Montana, can dance like a boarding school girl and, believe me, she will lead those Congressmen a merry little two-step when she comes to Washington" (November 11, 1916, 1; see also *The Topeka State Journal*, November 11, 1916, 5). In the same issue of *The Washington Times*, Rankin is described as "young, attractive, quick bright, mighty intelligent looking, and [having] a fine, sharp, well-balanced mind" (November 11, 1916, 14). "A friend" in the article said Rankin's smile "is enough to carry a man off his feet." Although this discourse is meant to legitimize Rankin, the gendered news framing serves to "other" her by drawing attention to her gender. This commentary paired with the metaphor of Rankin dancing with congressmen is prompt for pause, particularly when also considering the *Topeka State Journal* sub-headline: "Best Stump Speaker in Montana and Look Out Boys! She's Good Looking, Classy, Dancer and Isn't Married" (November 11, 1916, 5). A discursive analysis of Rankin's appearance will be discussed momentarily. However, it is noteworthy to immediately consider the discourse of Rankin as a romantic figure. Although it presents her sexuality in a light-hearted way, she is still being presented as a figure *for* men rather than keeping the focus on her work *with* men. Boston newspapers also hinted at Rankin's sexuality by referring to her as "womanly" and "a womanly woman," (*Boston Evening Globe*, November 10, 1916, 7; *Boston Post*, November 11, 1916, 4). Ironically, the latter commentary came from another woman. The *Boston Post* also wrote of how "her femininity, her sweetness, and her direct, but not aggressive, talks won strong suffrage sentiment along those Western trails" (November 11, 1916, 4). Surely this imagery of a "sweet" woman out in the rough-and-tumble Western trails created a romanticized view of Rankin. It's ironic that Woodhull faced media criticism for being oversexed, while the single Rankin was discursively served up on a platter by the press. The slight loosening of sexual norms associated with the first wave of feminism is likely a factor as to why. One could argue that the above commentary is innocent enough and the close reading is an exaggeration, yet this seems to be the beginning of discursive sexualization still faced by women in Congress today (Rhodan 2014).

Additional gendered news framing included the construction of Rankin as an ideal housewife. A number of newspapers focused on her cooking and sewing skills, with headlines and sub-headlines like "Congresswoman No. 1 Good Cook and Seamstress," "Can Dance, Speak and Sew," "First Congresswoman Said to be Splendid Cook," "Able to Sew and Cook," and "First Congresswoman Trims Her Own Hats, Makes Her Clothes, and Can Cook, Too" (*The Topeka State Journal*, November 11, 1916, 5;

The Washington Times, November 11, 1916, 14; *The Daily Gate City and Constitution-Democrat,* November 11, 1916, 1; *Indiana Evening Gazette,* November 11, 1916, 1; *Newark Advocate,* November 11, 1916, 5; *Indianapolis Star,* November 11, 1916, 3; *Hammond Lake County Times,* November 11, 1916, 1). A few newspapers ran an article pointing out that Rankin "refused to forsake the old household arts, cooking, and needlework" (*Fort Wayne News,* November 11, 1916, 3; *Evening Public Ledger,* November 11, 1916, 6; *Des Moines Daily News,* November 11, 1916, 1). Again, it is worthwhile to repeat that these gendered stories primarily came out *after* the election, not before. Now that the challenge to male-dominated national politics was reality, some in the press (perhaps unconsciously) seemed to feel a need to back-pedal. This feminization of Rankin was likely a discursive strategy to downplay her masculine ambition to have a career in politics and ensure the public that she still knew her proper gender role and would not become too manly. In other words, she was not challenging gender roles to the point of being alarming to the status quo, like Woodhull did. The next theme, the focus on Rankin's appearance, also served this strategy.

ATTRACTIVE IN APPEARANCE

Discourse regarding Rankin's appearance was another new theme that emerged in the analysis of her press coverage and is an extension of the gendered news framing mentioned above. Although Woodhull's appearance received some attention (i.e. *New York Herald,* May 11, 1872, 10; *The Orangeburg* (S.C.) *News,* May 18, 1872, 1), it was not a noticeable trend like it clearly was with Rankin. However, it was not Rankin's clothes that received attention; it was primarily her hair. An entire brief in *The Daily Gate City and Constitution-Democrat* in Iowa focused solely on Rankin's hair color. The article noted that her hair was likely light brown or auburn and "looks red only to her opponents" (November 6, 1916, 4). On its own, this article seems strange. However, it's clearly part of a wider press discourse. An earlier story in *The New York Times* also obsessed over her hair color: "If she is elected to Congress, she will improve that body aesthetically, for she is said to be 'tall with a wealth of red hair.' Even when good, Congress is not beautiful and needs adornment. Nothing is more beautiful than red hair" (October 13, 1916, 10). The reporter was not yet done and also added that "Congress needs Representative Rankin, needs her badly. She cannot, single-headed, make the House beautiful, but a little red hair will go a long way toward it" (October 13, 1916, 10). Bizarre as this may be, it prompts a point of serious concern: The reporter is legitimizing the notion that women should be seen and not heard. In other words, this story is saying that Rankin will simply be something nice to look at in Congress and completely ignores that she could also make an educated contribution. She is reduced to "adornment" despite her nationally recognized career as a successful suffragist/lobbyist. *The New York Times* continued to make note of her hair in its other coverage of her as well. One article mentioned her "wealth of red hair" (November 5, 1916, 2), while another called her a "tall and red-headed Republican" (November 9, 1916, 1). After Rankin won the election, the paper wrote that "Miss Rankin, who has great oratorical power and a striking presence with the advantage of good looks and brilliant red hair, is likely to make a figure at Washington" (November 10, 1916, 5). Although it helps that the reporter mentioned her political skill, the emphasis on her appearance arguably diminishes that since the discursive strategy places "the advantage" on her appearance, not her skills. There is no explanation as to why good looks and red hair were advantageous for serving in Congress. Yet *The New York Times* wasn't the only newspaper to think so. *The Sun* and the *Syracuse Herald* in New York both ran articles about Rankin that said "tall and with a wealth of red hair, she is one of the most striking figures ever seen on the hustings," or campaign trail (October 12, 1916, 4; October 15, 1916, 10). Rankin's news coverage appears to set a precedent that a woman's looks are important for a political career, a concept likely further enforced by the fact that she won. Although the press gave notable attention to Rankin's platform, the above discourse serves to simplify her candidacy by placing so much emphasis on her appearance, particularly *The New York Times*. Rankin's local media placed little emphasis on her appearance, yet outside and national media did, again illustrating the differing gender norms (and journalistic cultures) between the frontier and the East.

Interestingly, other articles found red hair to be disadvantageous and attempted to "cover" for Rankin's hair color. A Rankin supporter is quoted in a *Harrisburg* (Pa.) *Telegraph* article saying Rankin "won't do anything rash even if she has red hair" (November 11, 1916, 11). *The Washington Times* also felt the need to defend Rankin's hair, writing she has "red hair of the sort that nowadays is called titian and is accounted a mark of beauty rather than a disfigurement as in the rude days of our childhoods it was supposed to be" (November 9, 1916, 6). Regardless of whether her hair was described as light brown, auburn, or red, a point of apparent disagreement in the press, Rankin's hair color was also mentioned in newspapers in Missouri, Indiana, and Wisconsin, (i.e. *Holt County Sentinel,* November 10, 1916, 1; *Indiana Evening Gazette,* November 11, 1916, 1; *Fort Wayne News,* October 26, 1916, 8; *Logansport Times,* October 20, 1916, 4; *Stevens Point Daily Journal,* October 22, 1916, 3). For the record, her biographer described her hair as having "a glint of red" (Smith 2002, 41). To spend even this much space describing hair discourse seems excessive, yet it was clearly a significant factor in Rankin's news coverage, a finding that should raise red flags (pun mostly intended) for journalists.

Beyond her hair, other aspects of Rankin's appearance were also discussed. A number of newspapers ran articles describing her as "small" and "slight" (i.e. *Holt County Sentinel,* November 10, 1916, 1; *Indiana Evening Gazette,* November 11, 1916, 1; *Richmond Times-Dispatch,* November 11, 1916, 1; *Oklahoma City Times,* November 11, 1916, 1). Others noted her "picturesque" (*Fort Wayne News,* October 26, 1916, 8; *The New York Times,* November 5, 1916, 2) or "attractive" appearance (*The Glasgow Courier,* September 22, 1916, 1; *Tulsa Daily World,* August 30, 1916, 5). Some publications were more colorful with their descriptions, such as "tall, straight as a mountain pine" (*The Daily Gate City and Constitution-Democrat,* October 20, 1916, 3) and "quiet, comely, gray-eyed young woman" (*Boston Evening Globe,* November 10, 1916, 7). The *Fort Wayne* (Ind.) *News* opted for "intelligent looking" (November 11, 1916, 3), which is perhaps the best discourse that Rankin received about her appearance. Although this coverage overall had positive or neutral tones, the gate had clearly opened to make appearance discourse a significant aspect of a woman politician's news coverage. How this plays out in future campaigns and its broader significance will be discussed further in coming chapters.

DISCUSSION

After Rankin won the election, *The Washington Times* declared she would "appear in the school histories of the future" (November 9, 1916, 6). One hundred years later, Rankin is largely forgotten, although her past provides illumination of the future. The next two chapters will examine how discourse regarding Rankin set a precedent for how future women politicians were covered by the press. First, however, a final recap of Rankin's discourse is necessary, including how it compared to Woodhull's.

Rankin's connection to the suffragists and the women's movement was an important factor to her success, just as it initially was for Woodhull, and how this played out discursively was even more important. Woodhull's public break with the mainstream movement furthered journalistic discourse of her as an extremist out of touch with societal mores. Rankin was smarter and kept her disagreements with national leaders under wraps, so the public was unaware that she did not have their support. In addition, the press during Rankin's era was not as aggressive as it was during Woodhull's, thereby leaving this information out of the newspaper pages. As a result, this perceived unity, combined with her work on behalf of Montana women, gave Rankin a legitimated edge since she was discursively constructed in the press as an amenable figure much beloved by fellow women. With a seemingly united front, there was less room for criticism and for drama for the press to latch onto. However, it is also important to remember the lack of consternation by the press overall over Rankin's career as a suffragist, and that Montana men had agreed the year prior to grant suffrage in the state, indicating a majority support for women's formal involvement in politics. This is again a reminder that Rankin had advantages in temporal, socio political, and physical locations that Woodhull did not. In other words, Rankin was not just the smarter politician but also clearly benefited from the context of her times. During this era, at least some journalists wanted to see progressive change and the word choices in their stories indicated as much. By promoting Rankin and women's progress as a symbol of pride, newspapers undoubtedly helped reinforce these attitudes within readers as well, as evidenced by Rankin's support at the polls. Although one may argue over how much power the press has to influence public opinion, it is certainly noteworthy that journalism and public opinion aligned in Woodhull's and Rankin's respective cases. Rankin received positive coverage and won her race; Woodhull received mostly negative coverage and had limited public support. Clearly, the journalism of both eras reflected public opinion, if not had some role in influencing it. This again supports the argument of Richardson (2007) that society influences writers of texts, which also influence society.

From a political standpoint, Rankin had the political skill of a man, the message of a woman, and the political savvy and networking to tie it all together. Although she was challenging the male-dominated world of politics, her platform's primary focus on women and children was in line with the longtime "women's sphere" philosophy and with progressives' beliefs that women were needed for reform. She also focused on running a nonpartisan campaign in order to broaden her appeal. Had Woodhull tailored her message to be more palatable to the mainstream, she likely would have held onto her initial popularity and fared better in the short term. But this also raises the question: Which is the better strategy? Does slow and steady win the race, or is an explosive challenge needed to spur faster change for the future? Certainly national suffrage leaders during Rankin's time favored the former even though their pace was slower than what Montana voters were ready to do. Rankin knew better and took the plunge. Unlike Woodhull, her short-term political strategy proved victorious. However, it is also notable to point out that, unlike Woodhull who challenged gender roles, Rankin "ran as a woman," or at least that's what her discursive construction in the press was. Although her political victory was beneficial for future women (and men) to see that it was possible, the long-term consequences of this strategy still reverberate today and are expected to be evident in the next two case studies. By "running as a woman" to appease the short term, Rankin's press discourse set a long-term precedent for future women—and men—that this is how a woman can win.

In addition to the "running as a woman" discourse, the gendered news frames regarding Rankin's personal traits and appearance set a worrisome precedent, even though they were used to create positive discursive constructions at the time. On the one hand, the appearance discourse makes sense when taking into account the context of the time. Journalism was increasingly interested in visuals, as is evident by the fact that Rankin's picture ran about three dozen times compared to the zero times a Woodhull photo ran. Therefore, it stands to reason that this interest in visuals would lead to discourse of visuals as well—in other words, description of what Rankin looked like, particularly if a photo wasn't available. In an era before color photos, television, and social media pages, newspapers needed to use words to provide visual information. The fact that Rankin was a historic figure who lived half a country away from Washington, D.C., would spark curiosity as to who this woman was and what she was like. Therefore, the discourse in and of itself at that time is understandable due to the technological limitations of the time. Similarly, discourse of Rankin's "housewife-" type activities would make sense in that time since women were fairly limited to what they could do and this was in line with gender norms of the time. On the other hand, the fact that media today focus so heavily on the appearance of women politicians and how they compare to an old-fashioned housewife standard is indicative that the precedent set in 1916 with Rankin was not left in the time from which it came. In other words, journalists may not have evolved in their discursive strategies concerning women politicians in the past 100 years. If so, this should certainly be cause for reconsideration of current practice and whether it is indeed useful in current contexts. Before reaching definitive conclusions, however, journalistic discourse of two more women politicians will be explored in the upcoming chapters.

Before moving on from the Woodhull/Rankin comparisons, however, a few more points of interest are useful. As previously noted, Rankin had a lot of luck on her side as far as the political and journalistic cultures of her time. Woodhull was running against a beloved Civil War hero during an unstable time as the nation grappled with Reconstruction and unification. She also lived in the cutthroat partisan journalism world of New York City with a press that set the national agenda. Rankin benefited from a unique twist of fate in Montana politics, which allowed her to run at-large in a state where she had just finished campaigning for suffrage. The nation had not yet entered World War I and was enjoying a period of prosperity, including an increasing number of states granting women the right to vote. Journalism overall was shifting to become more professional, and her early campaign coverage came from Western states more amenable to women's involvement in politics. By the time the national media caught up, Rankin had already been constructed in the regional press as a winner and a celebrity at that. This variable of local vs. national media agenda setting will be considered further in the next two chapters.

Another interesting difference in Rankin's discourse compared to Woodhull's is the historical buy-in from the press and members of the public. Excitement of a first woman in Congress was evident in the mid-1910s to the point that the *Anaconda Standard* warned about merely voting for Rankin to have a historic first (October 31, 1916, 6). In contrast, the 1870s press gave no regard whatsoever to the potential of a first woman president. This emphasizes the importance of a favorable relationship with the press in order to get positive coverage. Woodhull attempted to do this through her own newspaper, but still lacked the mainstream media's valuable support.

Ironically, what was missing from Rankin's historical-themed coverage was Woodhull herself or, to put it more broadly, historical context of women in politics. Neither news coverage of Rankin's campaign nor coverage in the immediate days following her election mentions Woodhull or the other women who had previously vied for national office—in other words, the women whose trailblazing helped give Rankin and her fellow suffragists the opportunities they had. Woodhull, who by then had spent the past 40 years living in England, had already largely faded in American memory. *The Evening Times Republican* in Iowa ran an article in 1917 that chided newspapers for forgetting about Woodhull and claiming Belva Lockwood was the only woman presidential candidate in U.S. history (June 5, 1917, 11). Another missed opportunity was whether Woodhull had a reaction to Rankin's election since she was still alive at the time. Her biographers do not mention it (Underhill 1995; Gabriel 1998), nor do news articles in the Chronicling America or Historical News York Times databases. Yet without women like Woodhull shaking the status quo to prompt change for the future, historical contexts and victories like Rankin's wouldn't be possible. This study, therefore, is aiming to remedy this gap.

The next chapter will focus on the 1960s and press coverage of the first woman to receive a nomination for president at a major political party's convention. First, however, a brief epilogue of Rankin's story is provided.

By the time Rankin was seated in Congress in 1917, the national landscape had changed. As a result, her brief political career began with her casting

a controversial vote against entry into World War I. Although 49 men also
voted no, the press had a field day with Rankin. The *Rogue River Courier*
in Oregon blared a front-page headline declaring "Woman M.C. Votes
Against the War" (April 6, 1917, 1). An article in *The Daily Gate City and
Constitution-Democrat* in Iowa said that Rankin was tearful as she cast
her vote, pointing out "her evident grief and the signs of mental struggle"
(April 6, 1917, 1). Other newspapers also made a point to use her war vote
to illustrate Rankin's purported weakness. *The Ogden Standard* in Utah
and *Rock Island Argus* in Illinois were among the papers to carry an article
describing Rankin as "trembling, obviously badly frightened, and with a sob
in her voice" as she cast her vote (April 6, 1917, 3; April 6, 1917, 1). Through
this coverage, the press was clearly indicating that a woman was emotional
and not strong enough for the job. This is likely the precedent for the longtime stereotype that women in politics can't handle military and defense
affairs. What is especially problematic is that the coverage wasn't true.
Besides Rankin herself saying she didn't cry, *The Congressional Record* and
Democratic Rep. John Raker of California also denied it (Smith 2002), but
the damage was done. Rankin spent the rest of her term promoting suffrage
and her other priorities, but her war vote and her efforts to help a Butte miner
strike had alienated the Anaconda Copper Mining Company, a powerful
force in Montana (Smith 2002). Rather than face stiff competition in a House
re election, Rankin chose to run for the Senate but still lost. Her career in
politics appeared to be over.

Rankin spent much of the remainder of her life living in Georgia with
financial support from her brother and her father's inheritance (Morrison
and Morrison 1997). She continued to promote pacifist views and to lobby
for labor reform and for children. In 1940, she made a brief return to formal
politics when Montana re elected her to Congress. Now she was one of nine
women in the U.S. House (*Women in the U.S. Congress 2015* 2015), indicating gradual progress for women in politics. Ironically, however, Rankin
ended up facing another congressional vote over whether the United States
should enter a world war. This time, she was the only member to vote no,
again sparking controversy (Morrison and Morrison 1997). Her political career was again limited to one term as she realized she would not be
re elected, and she returned to Georgia. During the Vietnam War, Rankin
again rose to national prominence when, at 88, she led a peace march dubbed
the Jeannette Rankin Peace Brigade. During the 1968 event, "5,000 women
convened in Washington, D.C., to protest what they saw as the disgraceful
human and capital waste of the Vietnam War" (Morrison and Morrison 1997,
155). Three generations later, Rankin's pacifist beliefs were now popular, a
woman ahead of her time just like Woodhull.

When Rankin died on May 18, 1973, at 92, *The New York Times* focused on her anti-war stance and described her as "a lifelong pacifist and one of the country's earliest women's suffragists" (McFadden 1973). A decade later, the state of Montana donated a bronze statue of Rankin to the National Statuary Hall Collection in Washington, D.C. Today, Rankin stands tall in the U.S. Capitol Visitor Center as a permanent reminder of her historical significance.

Figure 4.1   In 1964, Maine Republican Senator Margaret Chase Smith became the First Woman to be Placed in Nomination for the Presidency at a Major Party's Political Convention. *Source*: Photo courtesy of Margaret Chase Smith Library.

Chapter 4

Media Negligence of
Margaret Chase Smith

In a 1986 interview, Margaret Chase Smith was adamant that she was not a woman politician, not a woman senator, and not a feminist (Sherman 2000). Smith, who spent 32 years in Congress on behalf of Maine, was the first woman to win election to both chambers, to win election to the Senate in her own right, and to be nominated for the presidency at a major party's convention. Yet despite her groundbreaking achievements on behalf of women, Smith was so vocal about separating herself from feminism that it was mentioned in her obituary (Severo 1995). Although Woodhull and Rankin had complicated relationships with the women's movement, Smith offers a new level of complexity in the quest to understand the relationship of women, media, and politics throughout history.

This chapter focuses on news coverage of Smith's 1964 presidential campaign from her announcement in January 1964 through her loss at the Republican national convention that July. Her presidential campaign rather than her first Senate campaign is being analyzed for a number of reasons. Not only was the presidency a more ambitious goal, but the journalistic, feminist, and political contexts of the early 1960s combined to create an unusual time in history—a time not conducive to a woman breaking a new political barrier. Therefore, Smith's experience had the potential to be similar to Woodhull's, thus providing a valuable point of comparison, while also allowing for contrast against Rankin since both had political success in securing a seat in Congress. Smith's presidential campaign is also of interest due to its absence in literature about the 1964 election. Pulitzer Prize-winning author Theodore White only mentions Smith's name once in his 400-page *The Making of the President 1964* (White 1965). Other books about Barry Goldwater, the eventual Republican nominee, fail to mention Smith at all even though she was vying for the same nomination (i.e. Volle 2010; Iverson

1997; McDowell 1964). Is this a case of a male, hegemonic version of history or was Smith's campaign so insignificant that it was not worth mentioning? Certainly Smith ran a campaign considerably different from the aggressive approaches used by Rankin and Woodhull. Still, Smith's press coverage provides important insight into the progression of women and media, and the forthcoming comparison of her coverage to Rankin's and Woodhull's illustrate both continuing trends and new discursive approaches toward women in politics. Before discussing this, however, a further understanding of Smith and how she became a political woman pioneer is pertinent to explore. The colorful story began when an older man asked a 16-year-old girl to give him the time of day.

FROM POLITICAL WIDOW TO PIONEER

Born in Skowhegan, Maine, on December 14, 1897, Margaret Chase Smith grew up in a rural town as the oldest of six children born to George and Carrie Chase. Her father worked as a local barber, and her mother worked various jobs at times to help support the family, illustrating to her daughter the importance of being self-sufficient (Wallace 1995). As a teenager, Smith worked for the local telephone company as a part-time operator, a position that meant she was well-connected to the town's residents and well-versed in the local happenings. More important, however, was the smooth-talking older man who called her at the switchboard every night to ask for the time. Clyde Smith, a prominent local politician and businessman, was recently divorced (Wallace 1995). Even though he was 21 years older, Clyde took an interest in her and became the critical factor in her career, both in the short and long term. When she was 17, he offered her a part-time job recording tax assessments, which helped her learn about budgeting, taxes, and governmental procedures (Wallace 1995). After high school, she dabbled in careers in teaching, customer service, and newspaper work, moving from job to job due to better pay as opposed to any particular passion (Graham Jr. 1964; Sherman 2000). It was marriage to Clyde that ultimately set up Margaret Chase Smith for her future in national politics.

Sixteen years after their first switchboard conversation, the couple married in 1930. At the time of their marriage, she was 32 and he was 53. She would later say their marriage was also a political arrangement as Clyde, well-known around town for his womanizing, was interested in running for governor and needed a wife (Sherman 2000). By this time, she had served as local and state president of the Business and Professional Women's Club and had recently accepted a post on the Republican State Committee (Wallace 1995; Graham Jr. 1964). Therefore, she was a "politically astute, well-spoken young woman with a positive state reputation of her own" (Sherman 2000, 27). Throughout the 1930s, Smith traveled with her husband and helped manage his political campaigns, learning from him the ins and outs of running for office (Wallace 1995). Although his dream to serve as governor never materialized, Clyde Smith won his first election to Congress in 1936. In a twist of fate, his victory paved the way for his wife's future career.

Shortly after her husband's election, Margaret Chase Smith won her first political victory, even if it was a personal one. She expected to be rewarded for her role in Clyde's win and asked for a paid position on his staff. Her husband reluctantly gave in after she rallied voters back home to petition on her behalf (Wallace 1995), indicating she had her own level of political savvy and support. Smith's new job provided her with experience managing a congressional office, attending committee meetings, handling mail, and observing research, speech writing, and voting (Wallace 1995; Sherman 2000). She noticed that young, female assistants handled much of the congressional work, yet at the time there were only eight women serving in Congress (Wallace 1995; *Women in the U.S. Congress 2015* 2015). It wouldn't be long before Smith was one of those women. Less than two years after their arrival in Washington, D.C., Clyde suffered a heart attack, prompting his wife to take on more of his congressional responsibilities in hopes of preserving his strength (Wallace 1995; Sherman 2000). His health continued to fail, however, and, shortly before his death in April 1940, his doctor advised him to name his preferred political successor (Wallace 1995). Within hours of endorsing his wife of 10 years, Clyde Smith was dead.

Margaret Chase Smith had to act fast, with the special election for Clyde's unexpired term planned for June and the general election set in September (Chamberlin 1973). Within a week of her husband's death, she released a statement to the press announcing her candidacy. The release said, in part, that "this decision has been reached at this time because of the desire of my husband that I should undertake to the best of my abilities, if the people approve, to carry on the work in which he was so much interested throughout his life" ("Mrs. Clyde Smith Enters Primary to Succeed Husband in House," *Daily Kennebec Journal*, 1940, 1). Smith noted her experience helping her husband in Congress and her support of his agenda, while also saying that women should have a role in determining government policy. Her biggest public relations boost came from the sympathetic press, however, who wrote of her "carrying out her husband's death-bed wish" (Wallace 1995, 47). Smith also benefited because political widows historically were more successful in securing support if they had previously played a role in their husband's career (Swain 1997; Gertzog 1995). The majority of women who served in Congress in the first decades after suffrage received the job due to their husband's death, a nod to coverture wherein the widow inherited her husband's authority (Witt, Matthews, and Paget 1995). During her campaign, Smith "ran as a widow," as newspaper photos often showed her doing housework while stories featured her talking about her husband and his unfinished agenda (Wallace 1995, 47). Yet a biographer noted that Smith personally "was in pursuit of no cause and motivated by no principle, aside from what she had pursued since childhood, a better job" (Wallace 1995, 55). This same kind of attitude would be apparent in the press coverage of her presidential campaign nearly 25 years later.

In the meantime, the year 1940 marked the 20th anniversary of woman's suffrage, and Smith was one of 30 women running for Congress, along with Jeannette Rankin (Wallace 1995). Smith won and spent the next eight years in the U.S. House, benefiting from a Republican-dominated Maine and a plum assignment on the Naval Affairs Committee during World War II (Wallace 1995). Despite this political experience, her decision to run for the Senate in 1948 was controversial. Although other women had served in the Senate, they had either initially been appointed or won a brief interim election, making Smith the first woman to secure a seat via a regular election (Graham Jr. 1964). Smith herself discussed the challenges she faced in this race in a later story titled "No Place for a Woman?" that ran in *Ladies' Home Journal*:

> When I ran for United States Senator in 1948, one of the arguments most emphasized against me by the opposition was that I am a woman. The most repeated phrase of the opposition was 'the Senate is no place for a woman.' The voters of Maine answered that phrase by giving me a victory in which I polled more votes than my three men opponents put together. That phrase made the women of Maine mad. (Smith 1952, 50)

One of Smith's first biographers wrote that women voted "in unprecedented numbers" in Maine that year (Graham Jr. 1964, 57). Yet despite this support, Smith was not known for her support of women, beyond legislation related to women and the military, and she insisted throughout her career that she was not a feminist (Wallace 1995; Graham Jr. 1964). Aware that prior woman senators were treated as a joke, Smith was determined to be taken seriously (Wallace 1995). She believed that no politician "could afford to align herself with one-half of her constituency when the powerful half was threatened by that allegiance" (Sherman 2000, 56). Her top assistant and companion Bill Lewis Jr. publicized Smith as "female but not a feminist" (Wallace 1995, 79). One author explained Smith's approach this way:

> Her chief protection came from a personal style that exuded traditional femininity and left critics little room to claim, apart from her candidacy itself,

that she was a threat to the existing sexual and social order . . . even as she simultaneously created a self that thrived outside of the culturally prescribed role for women. (Schmidt 2005, 378)

Smith's "simultaneous affirmation and denial of gender" (Sherman 2000, 4) throughout her career resulted in mixed messages, which will be examined in her presidential campaign coverage later in this chapter. First, however, it is worthwhile to back up and explore the women's movement in the years between Rankin's groundbreaking congressional victory and Smith's own pioneering campaign since this context helps explain Smith's gender dilemma.

AFTER SUFFRAGE

After the national changes to elections and the victory of women's suffrage in 1920, both men's and women's political cultures had arguably transformed into one. However, this is not to say that men and women were on equal footing or that the challenges for women in politics were over. Just as there were disagreements among women over suffrage, there were also varying approaches to political involvement. In the early 1900s, there were three main types of female political activists: the feminists, the reformers, and the party women (Freeman 2000). All had an interest in suffrage, but their goals widely varied. The feminists focused on suffrage, while the reformers had a broader women's rights agenda. Meanwhile, the party women worked for inclusion in mainstream politics and the good of the party, not for a specific women's agenda (Freeman 2000). Once women received the right to vote, the common thread that linked these three perspectives vanished, and disagreements widened "on the roles and nature of women and on how to achieve those goals they shared" (Freeman 2000, 123). Gradually, the party women gained prominence while feminist and reform support declined until the 1960s (Freeman 2000).

In party politics, women slowly gained ground in political offices after Rankin's election. Between 1916 and 1932, 14 women were elected to Congress (Freeman 2000). At the state level, Nellie Tayloe Ross, a Democrat in Wyoming, became the first woman elected governor in 1924 following her husband's death. By 1931, nearly 150 women served in state legislatures. However, the decline of the first wave of feminism was evident, and the 1930s have largely been considered "a bleak period for women" due to the lack of a strong feminist movement (Ware 1981, 2). This view is short-sighted since a number of women contributed to New Deal programs—which "offered greatly expanded roles for women in public life"

(Ware 1981, 1)—and Frances Perkins became the first woman to serve in a president's cabinet. Yet challenges for women in politics remained, such as the expectations "to remain womanly, to avoid displaying political ambition, and to be interested primarily in a narrow range of women's issues" (Andersen 1996, 17). For example, despite Perkins' prominent role, Labor Department New Deal policies "left little room for a notion of women's rights that did not depend on their family roles" (Deutsch 2000, 465). Similarly, education, children's issues, and other topics related to family and caregiving were still viewed as the women's sphere (Freeman 2000). As noted earlier, women who did win major political office in the early half of the twentieth century were often seat fillers following their husband's deaths (Witt, Matthews, and Paget 1995; Freeman 2000). Yet a number of these early political women took pride in what they were doing, as they knew they were "pushing the limits of what was considered expected or acceptable" (Andersen 1996, 132) and were providing more opportunity for future women.

The National Women's Party also set out to push the limits of acceptability with its advocacy of the Equal Rights Amendment. Initially proposed in 1923 to amend the Constitution to provide equal rights for women, the controversial amendment lingered in national politics for 60 years before its ultimate defeat. Following the home-front work of women during World War II, advocates believed they had momentum for the amendment's passage. However, they failed to get support from Eleanor Roosevelt and the political mainstream (Freeman 2000). Roosevelt did advocate for women to have positions in her husband's administration, however, and this growing visibility for women in politics benefited Smith, among others.

During the 1950s, a number of women viewed party work as an opportunity to contribute in their free time while still maintaining their primary roles as housewives (Freeman 2000). Indeed, their work for the parties has been referred to as "the housework of government" since they often did the "day-to-day work that received little glory but was critical to sustaining and building the party" (Rymph 2006, 133). This included conducting surveys, compiling voter lists, organizing candidate talks, registering voters, driving voters to polls, and generally doing grassroots volunteer work (Rymph 2006). Women who did seek political office were more likely to serve in local or state politics since this allowed them to maintain their home lives more easily than a national position would (Rymph 2006). Often, women's politics were referred to as "as a women's moral crusade" since "moral, spiritual and family matters traditionally have been among the few political arenas in which men grant women authority" (Rymph 2006, 126, 127). These values received a significant shakeup in the late 1960s during the second wave of feminism since the social movement brought feminists and reformers together to pursue similar goals. Yet when Smith ran for president in the early 1960s, the political, feminist, and journalistic contexts of the time were not on her side.

ELECTION OF 1964

Smith's rise to national prominence was gradual. Although her committee work during World War II brought her some national press coverage, arguably the biggest moment in her career came in 1950 when she addressed one of the most serious issues in the nation at the time: McCarthyism. In the early days of the Cold War, the fear of Communism spread rapidly throughout the country fueled in large part by Wisconsin Senator Joseph McCarthy's claims that there were Communists within the government. After seeing no evidence of these claims, Smith gave a speech in the Senate known as the Declaration of Conscience in which she criticized the "selfish political exploitation of fear, bigotry, ignorance, and intolerance" and said "Democrats and Republicans alike have unwittingly but undeniably played directly into the Communist design of confuse, divide, and conquer" (Wallace 1995, 106). Her speech made headlines across the country, both positive and negative, thereby increasing her national presence (i.e. Associated Press 1950c, 1950b, 1950a). Two years later, Smith was considered a potential candidate for the Republican vice presidential nomination, although how much support she would have received is unclear. A United Press story noted that "not many of Mrs. Smith's sister Republicans gave her much chance of getting the nomination, not in 1952 at least" (Meiner 1952, 6). However, the article also said Smith was "perhaps the most successful U.S. woman politician of any year." Smith ultimately was not nominated since supporters withdrew her name after facing party pressure (Sherman 2000), but by the early 1960s, rumors arose of Smith's aspirations for the presidency. President John F. Kennedy, who faced criticism from Smith for his handling of the Cold War, was widely quoted as saying Smith would be a "formidable opponent" (Wallace 1995, 156). Kennedy undoubtedly did not regard Smith as a serious presidential threat, but he would not live to face off against his former Senate colleague. On November 22, 1963, the assassination of Kennedy drastically changed the 1964 presidential race. Smith, however, still moved forward and declared her intention to run during a speech at the Women's National Press Club on January 27, 1964. Her timing, however, like Woodhull's, came at a point in history when she had no chance of winning.

Not only did Kennedy's assassination change the political landscape of the 1960s, but the gender and journalistic contexts also worked against Smith. To understand the early 1960s, one must go back to the prior decade first. During the 1950s, Americans grasped hold of the American Dream and the promise of advancing their social and economic status (Greene 2010). After the long years of depression and war, many wanted stability at home and a traditional family life (Greene 2010). Societal views regarding this were so strong that challenges to the status quo and traditional gender norms were met with sharp criticism, to the point that "women not content with domestic life were variously labeled neurotic and not well-adjusted or communist and un-American" (Weiner 2005, 371). The mass media contributed to this culture by focusing advertising on women's role as housewives (Greene 2010), thereby indicating this was the proper role for women. Yet a number of women had experienced life outside the home during World War II, or at least were now aware there were more options, and felt like they needed more in life than being a wife and mother (Greene 2010). This inner conflict and the mass media culture contributing to it became the focus of Betty Friedan's *The Feminine Mystique* released in 1963, a year prior to Smith's presidential campaign. The publication of *The Feminine Mystique* served as a rejuvenating moment in the history of U.S. women and feminism (Chafe 1972). In an effort to illuminate the isolation of American housewives, Friedan wrote

> a powerful critique of women's roles in contemporary American society . . . [and] attacked a host of institutions, including women's magazines, women's colleges, and advertisers, for promoting images of women deliriously happy with—and limited to—the domestic life of a housewife. (Fermaglich and Fine 2013, xi)

Friedan's book about the unhappiness of many American women due to rigid gender role expectations was not a magic bullet in and of itself to launching the second wave. Although the book generated a powerful response following its release (Fermaglich and Fine 2013), the real strength of the second wave of feminism did not rise until later in the decade (Giardina 2010; Krolokke and Sorensen 2006). By then, an increasing number of young middle-class adults in the 1960s attended college, where they learned to be "skeptical and critical of the social standards and practices that prevailed in the middle class" (Chafe 2000, 531). Furthermore, much like the abolition movement motivated women to become politically active in the 1800s, the Civil Rights Movement in the mid-1900s paved the way for further advances in women's equality and the second wave of feminism. However, in 1963 and 1964, the focus was still more on race than gender. Therefore, Smith was running for president at a point in history when society was clinging to traditional gender roles rather than advocating for their advancement, a context contrary to what Rankin encountered. In other words, Smith did not have strong enough feminist winds behind her to help push her forward.

From a political perspective, women occupied just 5 percent of seats in state legislatures and 14 congressional seats at the time of Smith's campaign (Hartmann 1989; *Women in the U.S. Congress 2015* 2015). However, the legacy of Kennedy was the biggest hurdle to overcome. In the months after Kennedy's murder, Lyndon Johnson had worked to maintain the martyred president's legacy by asking Kennedy men to stay on staff, promoting Kennedy policies, and mentioning Kennedy often (Caro 2012). Johnson's succession was going so well that by early 1964, "it was becoming simply a fait accompli, an accepted fact of American political life" (Caro 2012, 598). A nation rocked to its core by Kennedy's death was clearly going to elect his heir apparent to continue his work, leaving Smith in a position similar to Victoria Woodhull, who was up against Civil War hero Ulysses S. Grant. In other words, these women entered a contest that they had no chance of winning. In addition to incumbency, the sympathy vote, and "an atmosphere permeated with a desire for continuity" (Kearns 1976, 206), Lyndon Johnson had a long political record of his own to run on. Born in Texas in 1908, Johnson won a seat in Congress in 1937 and served on the Naval Affairs Committee with Smith when she joined in 1940. Coincidentally, both Johnson and Smith won election to the Senate in 1948, thus continuing their similar career paths. Johnson became minority leader in 1953 before securing the majority leadership and becoming known as the "master of the Senate" for his savvy in persuasion, power, and politics (Caro 2002; Kearns 1976). Although they were from different political parties, Smith and Johnson liked each other, and she considered him a good leader (Wallace 1995). In 1960, Johnson sought the Democratic presidential nomination and instead ended up elected as Kennedy's vice president. Within his first several months of inheriting the presidency, Johnson had outlined his plan for a Great Society, declared his War on Poverty, and pushed through the Civil Rights Act (Kearns 1976). A victory at the polls in November was all but in the bag.

The man who would ultimately beat Smith and other contenders for the Republican nomination and face Johnson in the 1964 general election was Barry Goldwater, an Arizona senator known as Mr. Conservative (McDowell 1964). Born in 1909 in Arizona Territory, Goldwater was the anti-Johnson candidate, with an emphasis on limited government, states' rights, and capitalism. Smith would say in her news coverage that she was a moderate option to Goldwater, whose *Conscience of a Conservative* book was viewed as "the first serious attempt to challenge the New Deal and the welfare state along with the civil rights movement by a politician" (Volle 2010, 9). Like Smith, Goldwater expected to challenge Kennedy, not Johnson, in 1964 (Iverson 1997). Unwilling to let down his supporters and the conservative cause, however, Goldwater pushed forward and lost to Johnson in a landslide in November (Iverson 1997).

With the state of feminism and political culture in the early 1960s reviewed, it is now pertinent to further explore the state of the press. Although now operating under a paradigm of objectivity, the journalistic culture of the era proved just as unfriendly to Smith's political ambition as the other historical factors of the time.

THE PROBLEM OF OBJECTIVITY

By the 1960s, the practice of objectivity resulted in journalism much different from the decades prior. However, a number of scholars note this did not mean better journalism. Although contemporary journalists were taught in textbooks to practice objectivity (Miller 1962), this often meant simply passing along information without critiquing its credibility, a practice particularly evident in the media's compliance with spreading McCarthy's claims (Daly 2012). Newspapers were said to be "naively trusting of government," and stories often lacked attribution, "simply passing along an unquestioned, quasi-official sense of things" (Stepp 1999, para. 40). In other words, reporters "reproduced a vision of social reality which refused to examine the basic structures of power and privilege" (Schudson 1978, 160). One journalism historian put it this way: "Journalism was like a horse wearing blinders, making its regular rounds oblivious to all sorts of activity just outside its field of vision" (Daly 2012, 339), including its stereotypical coverage of blacks and women. Coverage of Congress in the 1950s and the early 1960s was "overcooperative" (Matthews 1960, 207; see also Fink and Schudson 2014), and the press overall was "generally respectful of the political establishment" (Zelizer 2007, 230).

The 1960s were a time of high readership, however, with nearly 81 percent of adults reading newspapers in the mid-1960s (Larsen 2001). At the time "virtually everything qualified as news," including birthday or bridge parties, minor speeches, and other personal and social items (Stepp 1999, para. 54). Unlike Woodhull who campaigned at a time when there was a sharp partisan press, Smith wasn't likely to receive news coverage that was blatantly negative due to the embrace of objectivity in journalistic culture. However, like Woodhull, Smith also wasn't running for election at a time when the press would favor a radical change to the status quo and, as a result, would make its discursive choices accordingly. In other words, selection of sources, story framing, and select word choices would be indicative of journalistic attitudes as opposed to straightforward inclusion of opinion. For the press of the 1950s and early 1960s, the status quo of writing for and about women typically meant women's pages and sections "firmly focused on woman as wife/homemaker/caretaker" (Beasley and Gibbons 2003, 147). During this decade, the leadership of the press was generally controlled by middle-aged white men, almost all of whom were "part of a broad conservative-centrist consensus" (Daly 2012, 320). The journalism workforce overall was largely undereducated and underpaid (Larsen 2001), and it was difficult for women to receive jobs and serious assignments (Chambers, Steiner, and Fleming 2004; Bradley 2005). By the end of the 1960s, women comprised about 20 percent of daily newspaper journalists (Bulkeley 2002).

Smith's firm denials that she was a feminist illustrated a clear understanding of the underlying current against the women's movement at the time. A study of press coverage later in the decade found the mainstream media portrayed feminists as "dysfunctional and pathological figures" (Hesford 2013, 73). Most mainstream journalists were "bewildered or downright hostile" to second wave feminism (Daly 2012, 348), for "journalism was relatively slow to change" despite the cultural transformation throughout the decade (Chambers, Steiner, and Fleming 2004, 47). This context, therefore, suggests that coverage of Smith's presidential campaign, while not as hostile as Woodhull's, would not be as favorable as Rankin's. Although Smith made a point of separating herself from feminism, she was still embarking on a mission that challenged traditional gender roles at a time when this was widely unacceptable and the press had little interest in challenging the political structure.

It is also important to note that Smith personally had a contentious relationship with members of the press. So much so that reporters formed an Order of the Wilted Rose, a reference to the rose Smith wore daily, with membership conferred after being harshly criticized by Smith if she believed they had wronged her (Wallace 1995). Smith was said to have "abysmal relations" with both the local press in Maine and the national press in Washington (Wallace 1995, 171). How much this was a factor in her presidential campaign coverage will be speculated on shortly. Before analyzing this coverage, one more point about the journalistic culture of the 1960s is worthwhile to consider. From a structural standpoint, press coverage in the 1960s focused more on providing fewer but longer stories with a greater emphasis on photos, graphics, and design (Barnhurst and Mutz 1997), thereby moving away from the strategy of the past to place numerous briefs on a page. The influence of television played into the newspaper industry's move toward more visuals and greater story depth to stay competitive (Barnhurst and Mutz 1997). As a result of stories increasing in length, the inverted pyramid structure of placing the most important information first became standard (Miller 1962). Therefore, reporters were exercising judgment about how newsworthy each piece of information was when determining how high or low to put it in the story. This provides insight into a reporter's line of thinking on a particular subject and what elements were considered worthy of playing up. Consideration of story structure will be among the contextual elements taken into account in the following analysis of Smith's presidential campaign coverage.

SMITH'S NEWSPAPER TRENDS

This analysis involved 533 news articles from 38 states that ran between January 27 and July 18, 1964. This allowed for examination of articles throughout Smith's presidential campaign until two days after the Republican National Convention to capture reaction to her failed bid.

While reviewing Smith's press coverage, it became glaringly clear that the Associated Press and United Press wrote the majority of the articles, indicating a significant shift in journalistic culture from the first two cases analyzed in this study. This finding allows for a continuation of the discussion from the prior chapter about the role of local vs. national media in relation to campaign coverage. Although it was evident in both Woodhull's and Rankin's coverage that newspapers were sharing stories among themselves, there was diversity in coverage and more of a conversation, so to speak, about their campaigns. To put it another way, there was clearly local control over content but also an awareness of other journalistic discourse on the matter. With Smith, the discursive power of the political press was clearly being corralled into the hands of a few by the 1960s, thereby giving national media organizations sizeable control of the agenda and framing of national politics. While one could argue that local news organizations still make the decision of whether or not to run this content, they also have little choice if they want to provide readers with national news since the wire service is more cost effective and efficient. This trend clearly increases the importance of analyzing the content generated from these national news outlets due to the widespread use of their coverage. The cases selected for this study and the comparisons among them, therefore, allow for examination of this shift from local to national discursive control.

Before examining the themes that emerged from Smith's coverage, however, a few other data trends are worthwhile to note. The majority of articles that mentioned Smith only briefly referred to her, such as simply noting that she was a candidate or listing her in primary results. Of the sample analyzed, Smith made the front page nearly 30 percent of the time, slightly improving on Woodhull's and Rankin's rates of about 25 percent. The largest percentage of Smith's front-page play came in April when she performed better than expected in the Illinois primary. Since Smith's campaign announcement came so late in January, it's difficult to compare her coverage to Woodhull's based on month alone. However, an analysis of two weeks of coverage after each woman's announcement found that Woodhull received nearly twice as much front-page placement as Smith. Whether this is due to the novelty of Woodhull being the first woman to run for president, to the journalistic conventions of the time that allowed for more articles to run on the front page, or to some other reason is unclear. Still, it is an interesting difference.

As far as comparison to Rankin, Smith had fairly steady press coverage in the first few months of her campaign but then press interest declined, as opposed to the gradual increase in Rankin's coverage throughout her campaign. This suggests the press is more likely to cover a candidate if she is perceived to be a winner. Although this makes sense, it also raises the question of whether the press is indeed fulfilling its democratic mission by having these varied standards. This is relevant in relation to an earlier point: Even though journalists of the era embraced objectivity, their discursive choices would still be indicative of attitudes of the time. Although Smith's news coverage could be considered overwhelmingly neutral, particularly when contrasted against Woodhull's negative coverage and Rankin's positive coverage, the fact that discourse about Smith was largely missing is just as important to consider and raises questions about how objective the coverage actually was. The type of coverage she received, combined with the fact that she was not expected to win, perhaps explains why photos of her were so rarely used in news stories. Only 25 articles in the sample included a visual of Smith, amounting to the inclusion of a visual less than 5 percent of the time, compared to Rankin's 13 percent. (As a reminder, Woodhull's photo never ran, but this was also a time in journalism history when photos were not common practice.) Half of Smith's visuals ran within the first two weeks of her announcement, and one-fourth of her visuals ran in New York newspapers. Surprisingly, only two photos of Smith were included in the news articles analyzed from July, the month of the Republican convention. It's interesting to note that half of Rankin's visuals ran following her election. Was Rankin's overall greater visual exposure due to the fact she was a relative political newcomer or because she was a winner or both? The next chapter of this study may help provide clarity on this, but it is interesting to note now that Smith and Rankin had varying media experiences.

As far as coverage length, Smith fared the same as Rankin with 85 percent of her press coverage entailing a brief mention in comparison to three-fourths for Woodhull. The journalistic convention of the 1960s to write longer stories clearly did not improve a woman politician's odds of receiving more space within an article. Journalists controlled three-fourths of Smith's framing power, which again was an analysis of which sources were discussing her in news articles. This rate was the same as Woodhull's but lower than the 85 percent for Rankin. The remaining discursive power was divided among Smith, those who opposed her candidacy, and those who favored it. Use of opponent and supporter sources was fairly even in Smith's case, as would be expected in an era focused on objective coverage. What is particularly interesting, however, is that, of the nearly six months of campaign coverage analyzed, half of Smith's own discursive power came within the first three weeks of her campaign. In other words, journalists started out including commentary from Smith in articles, but then rarely did so in the final five months. The same trend is evident in Woodhull's campaign coverage, if articles about her arrest are excluded. This would indicate that journalists are curious enough to initially cover a pioneer woman politician and grant her discursive power, but they then lose interest shortly thereafter. This perhaps only applies to politicians considered unlikely to win, since this was not the trend with Rankin. Regardless, it is interesting to note that journalists maintained a super majority of the discursive power among all three women.

With this overview now complete, it is time to discuss the four main discursive themes that emerged from examination of the Smith news stories. Two of the themes were also found in Woodhull's and Rankin's coverage: discourse related to her politics and discourse related to her personal traits. Since Smith did not have a connection to the women's movement like Woodhull and Rankin did, this theme was not present in her campaign coverage. However, the politics theme includes discourse related to women's reactions to Smith. Smith's last two themes were in line with Rankin's: discourse related to the historical relevance of the candidacy and to her appearance. Specifically, much of the news coverage of Smith's appearance was related to her age, which is another one of the factors in Murray's (2010) framework. Murray refers to age as one of the "double binds" that women candidates face. Double binds are a combination of ingrained gender stereotypes and gendered news frames, which create "lose-lose scenarios" for women (Murray 2010, 16; see also Jamieson 1995; Lawrence and Rose 2010). This will be described in further detail within that theme in this chapter. First, this media analysis examines discourse related to Smith the politician.

SMITH AND POLITICS

The articles about Smith the politician included positive and negative public reaction to her candidacy as well as commentary about her campaign related to her platform and to her level of effort in the race.

More Power to Her

Following Smith's entry into the presidential race, a number of journalists sought commentary from public officials and the general public to gauge reaction to her candidacy. Therefore, the discursive strategy of equalizing, or including multiple viewpoints, was much more common in Smith's news coverage than in Woodhull's or Rankin's, another sign of the transformation in journalistic culture and the efforts to be objective. Interestingly, many of the comments from public officials regarding Smith's candidacy were positive. A United Press story that ran immediately after Smith's announcement featured Vermont Republican Senator George Aiken calling her candidacy "very refreshing," while Republican National Chairman William E. Miller said he was "delighted" (*Provo Daily Herald*, January 28, 1964, 12; *Santa Fe New Mexican*, January 28, 1964, 2; *Huron Daily Plainsman*, January 28, 1964, 1; *Statesville Record and Landmark*, January 28, 1964, 1). Aiken was also quoted in the *Des Moines Register* as saying Smith's campaign was "a serious challenge to other Republican contenders" as he praised her "devotion to her country and her duty, her understanding of the problems of ordinary people, and her many years of legislative accomplishment" (*Des Moines Register*, January 28, 1964, 5). Clearly, Aiken is trying to legitimize Smith's candidacy with his discussion of her patriotism, empathy, and career record, along with his emphasis that she was serious. Elly Peterson, assistant chairman of the Republican National Committee, also offered support by highlighting Smith's "superb background" and noting Smith "has advanced the cause of women" (*Cedar Rapids Gazette*, July 12, 1964, 7C). Journalists for the AP and UP also lent discursive legitimization to Smith by including in their stories Kennedy's prior description of Smith as a "formidable" candidate (i.e. *Des Moines Register*, January 28, 1964, 5; *New Castle News*, January 27, 1964, 1). Whether or not Kennedy was serious when he made the comment is irrelevant since the journalists in 1964 framed the discourse as favorable to Smith. Certainly praise from the martyred former president was a boost for Smith's cause, and a bit of an emotional tactic on the part of the press.

In another story, former national Republican Chairman Thurston Morton of Kentucky was quoted using more colorful language when discussing Smith's candidacy and said "if she proves in the primaries she can bring us the suffragettes and the old maids, she's in" (*Greenfield Recorder Gazette*, April 11, 1964, 3). In other words, Smith would be acceptable if she could benefit the party by attracting a new contingent of Republican supporters. However, this discourse is problematic as it presumes that a woman candidate would only be able to attract fellow women, thereby presuming the existence of a women's bloc and reaffirming separate spheres. Smith's fellow Republican opponents also lent support to her candidacy in interesting ways. Goldwater believed Smith would "get more votes than some people think," according to Associated Press and *New York Times* reports (i.e. *North Adams Transcript*, January 29, 1964, 8; *Berkshire Eagle*, January 30, 1964, 30; *The New York Times*, January 29, 1964, 16). This word choice is noteworthy because, even though Goldwater's words lend credence to Smith, they also vocalize a public belief that she wouldn't get many votes. In other words, his discourse is both legitimizing her and delegitimizing her by calling attention to the underlying assumption that she will lose. Nelson Rockefeller gave a more polished reaction, as he thought "the entry of additional candidates, including Margaret Chase Smith of Maine, into the primaries was healthful for the party" (*The New York Times*, January 29, 1964, 17). He later was quoted as saying Smith's entrance into the race was "a tribute to her and to the quality of opportunity of all in this country" (*Lowell Sun*, June 28, 1964, 76). Although this discourse can be considered politically safe, there is also a hint of belittlement as Smith is treated as an "other" who is benefiting from the nation's graciousness. Pennsylvania Governor William Scranton kept his reaction simpler by saying, "I know of no reason why a woman could not become president" (*Lowell Sun*, June 28, 1964, 76). Like the others, Scranton's discourse was not exactly a glowing endorsement of Smith's candidacy but offered some legitimization nonetheless. Although some of the public officials' comments only lent surface-level support to Smith, the fact that she received any discursive legitimization from the political sector is noteworthy. This is certainly an improvement upon discourse surrounding Woodhull's candidacy and an indication that a few more cracks were being made in the glass ceiling. This strategy is also illustrative of the journalism culture at the time as far as journalists seeking out opinions from sources rather than blatantly writing their own opinions into news articles.

Beyond public officials, Smith also generated some support from the general public and was said to have "brought down the house" when she declared her candidacy (*Altoona Mirror*, January 30, 1964, 21). In addition, the press reported on the "encouraging" mail that she received from all 50 states, including letters from women asking how they could help (*Burlington Daily Times News*, March 12, 1964, 8C). This emphasis on crowd reaction was also used with Woodhull and Rankin. Expanding on this strategy, the *Independent Press Telegram* in California was one of a number of newspapers that employed a "man on the street" approach of asking members of the public about Smith's candidacy or the idea of a woman president in general. This is interesting as it again means the journalists are giving up some discursive control and allowing others to have discursive power in the political process, an improvement upon Rankin's coverage, as noted earlier. Several of the *Telegram's* sources supported the idea of a woman president. Local employment agency director Clair Carmody thought "a woman would be very good in the presidency. By nature, she is good at detail and works well under pressure" (February 2, 1964, W4). However, Carmody also believed a woman "has to be twice as good as a man to gain equal position," an insightful commentary on the difficulty for women of the time to earn legitimacy in the public sphere. Similarly, in the same story, local school board president Elizabeth Hudson thought "a woman putting her hat in the ring is either very silly or very courageous. But more power to her. Someone had to start it." This quote is interesting for a few reasons. Hudson rightly notes the challenge of pushing gender boundaries, a discourse that was largely absent in the rest of Smith's news coverage and that should have received more attention. In addition, Hudson's comment that "someone had to start it" is interesting, as it is indicative of her ignorance of Woodhull, who actually "started it" nearly a century earlier. This lack of knowledge, from a school board president no less, suggests that discourse about women's political history was largely absent during this time. This is problematic because it leaves subsequent political women to have to "start it" over each time they challenge a barrier (see also Murray 2010; Falk 2010; Jamieson 1995), making the battle that much more challenging and the public frustratingly ill-informed. This is a key reason why this study is attempting to bring to light this history and its discursive trends, for without knowledge of history, the lessons of the past cannot inform the future.

Two other sources in the same *Telegram* story are also important to examine for their broader implications. Dr. Michael Singer, referred to as a leading psychiatrist, was interviewed, likely to respond to claims that women were too emotional to be president. Singer told the press, "I would say, unequivocally, that women are emotionally equipped for the job" (*Independent Press Telegram*, February 2, 1964, W4). Singer's inclusion in this story is particularly striking since it was the only expert commentary found in the news stories examined. In other words, the press did not seem to go to much effort to interview sources or include discourse that would debunk stereotypes about women. Also of note is local Chamber of Commerce vice president Harry Krusz, who was quoted as saying that a woman president was an "intriguing idea" and that "some of the greatest things in the world have been accomplished by women—as queens, religious leaders, and scientists." Yet, beyond Krusz's comment, this type of discourse was also glaringly missing from press coverage about Smith during her campaign in 1964. The newspaper articles examined did not even mention that women throughout the past 50 years had served alongside men in Congress, a political territory that previously excluded women but had overcome that barrier. Including this type of discourse is important for perspective as a woman president should not be viewed as such an oddity when considered within the broader context of women in leadership throughout history. Yet the continual treatment of women in politics as "other" serves to delegitimize the idea that women could serve as president. The missing context, analysis, and depth in reporting on Smith's candidacy is indicative of the journalism of the time, and the general absence of the above points surely played a role in the continuation of negative attitudes toward the idea of a woman president. The specific negativity that Smith encountered in 1964 is explored next.

A Man's Job

Smith's candidacy generated an outpouring of negativity that was all too familiar to Woodhull nearly a century earlier. However, whereas much of the criticism of Woodhull focused on her personal life and platform, much of the criticism of Smith focused on her gender. Now, to clarify, certainly the criticism of Woodhull's personal life and platform were due to her challenges of gender norms and, therefore, were gender related. With Smith, however, Smith herself was often irrelevant. In other words, the attacks were generally aimed at the idea of a woman president as opposed to being aimed at Smith personally. Evidence of this is abundant in an article in *The Salina* (Kan.) *Journal*, which was among the newspapers to ask its readers what they thought of Smith's candidacy. In a story headlined "Candidate Smith Gets Little Support From Her Own Sex," Mrs. Lowell Lefoureau is quoted as saying "no matter what her qualifications or party affiliation, I wouldn't vote for her" (January 31, 1964, 5). In the same article, Mrs. Robert Myers said she wouldn't vote for Smith "because I don't have enough confidence in her. Women are too emotional." Both Lefoureau and Myers are simplifying the issue and disregarding Smith herself. Lefoureau freely admits gender is the problem and Smith is irrelevant, while Myers gives no evidence as to how Smith specifically is emotional and criticizes women in general more so than Smith herself. This same "emotional" argument appeared in the *Lebanon* (Pa.) *Daily News* when high school seniors were asked to "give their views today on a woman's chances of attaining the nation's highest office" (February 7, 1964, 11). Daniel McKinley, 17, thought "women are too emotional for such a position," while Janice Mathias, 17, said "women generally let their emotions guide their decisions." Mrs. Myrtle Coburn, a receptionist in Massachusetts, had similar views: "Oh, goodness, a woman's makeup is such that she can't accept criticism. She's too sensitive—and I mean any woman is" (*Fitchburg Sentinel*, January 29, 1964, 25). This "emotional" discourse is noteworthy for a few reasons. For one, neither age nor gender appeared to hinder the use of this emotional argument. Both men and women, and high school students and married women, found this argument rational and acceptable. Second, by repeating a stereotypical discursive construction of women, these sources are perpetuating the stereotype without any basis in fact and further cementing it into discursive practice. Third, the sources offer no specifics as to how their argument relates to Smith personally, thereby lumping her by default into a gendered discourse that negates her candidacy on no basis of who she actually is. Beyond the fact that the above sources are delegitmizing Smith simply because of her gender, it is also important to notice that the journalists evidently did not prompt the sources to explain their comments further. This is again indicative of a journalistic culture that lacked in inclusion of context. By simply running emotional commentary, these journalists are not getting at the bigger issue of gender norms and stereotypes.

Salina Journal readers also delegitimized Smith by declaring that the presidency was "a man's job." R.E. Shipe said, "I don't feel it's a woman's place to be president of the United States. She's a big lady in political ways, but it's too much of a job even for her" (January 31, 1964, 5). Mrs. Rollin E. Cobb stated, "I definitely am not in favor of her because I feel we aren't ready to have a woman in the White House. Being president is a man's job." Voters in Kansas weren't the only ones who felt this way. In Massachusetts, high school student Charles Hummel said, "There is too much prestige involved in this post for a woman to handle" (*Lebanon Daily News*, February 7, 1964, 11). In California, Bill Boyd, a local public relations man, told the *Independent Press Telegram* that "women make wonderful wives . . . but I think top leadership roles belong to men. I think we should keep it that way" (February 2, 1964, W4). In Pennsylvania, 17-year-old Barbara Brubaker also thought "this office should be filled by a man," noting that women's first responsibility is "to their home and family" (*Lebanon Daily News*, February 7, 1964, 11). Similarly, *The New York Times* wrote that Smith was "undeterred by the idea that a woman's place is in the home" (January 28, 1964, 17), thereby underscoring popular sentiment that women belonged in the private sphere with the public sphere left to men.

Celebrities offered commentary along these same lines. An Associated Press story headlined "Smith Divides Women" quoted Sandra Dee as saying, "I wouldn't respect a woman's opinion on world affairs as much as I would a man's. It's the man's right to make the major decisions" (*Pasadena Independent*, January 29, 1964, 9). Actress Lucille Ball also reportedly thought a woman president was "a bad idea" since "the boss should be a man" (*Lowell Sun*, June 28, 1964, 76). Considering Ball was the first woman to run a major television studio, this commentary is ironic at best if she indeed said it. Regardless, readers in Lowell, Massachusetts, were told she did, thereby serving as a celebrity un-endorsement and negating Smith's cause. Again, sources are opposing a woman for president more so than opposing Smith herself, with no concrete explanation as to why Smith personally was problematic and journalists not pushing for or including additional context from sources or themselves. As a result, the news coverage became a defense of the current state of gender norms, a state attacked the prior year in *The Feminine Mystique* and challenged again with Smith's candidacy. This emphasis on a "man's job" casts a gender role on an occupation and is a discursive strategy clearly aimed at maintaining a gender barrier and separate spheres between men and women. This discourse is essentially serving as a defensive shield irrelevant of who tries to break it or their qualifications. This is indicative that, until the defense of traditional gender norms is lowered or there is more of an open conversation about these norms, women have little chance of securing the presidency.

In addition to emotional and "man's job" arguments, a number of voters across the country said the nation simply wasn't ready for a woman president. Genevieve Blatt, the first woman elected to a state office in Pennsylvania, said Smith likely would have been considered for the presidency "long before this" if she were a man (*Somerset Daily American*, January 30, 1964, 2). However, Blatt felt "it would take a qualified candidate and a receptive electorate to send a woman to the White House," and "she questioned whether the voters were receptive enough at present." Readers of the *Independent Press Telegram* in California tended to agree. Housewife Mrs. Robert Heinsohn said she wouldn't vote for a woman and further noted "this is one thing women aren't ready for yet. Our country either" (February 2, 1964, W4). Although Mrs. John Goerwitz, a past president of the League of Women Voters, thought a woman should run for the presidency, she did not think a woman could win "in our stormy sea of politics" (*Independent Press Telegram*, February 2, 1964, W4). Fashion designer Ceil Chapman doubted Smith's chances, saying "the day will come when we will have a woman president but it has not arrived" (*Fitchburg Sentinel*, January 29, 1964, 5). Similarly, high school seniors viewed a woman president as a concept for the future. Cheryl Stumpft believed a woman would be president "someday," while Karen Shellenhamer thought a woman "will eventually be elected president." So did William Spancake, although "I don't expect to see it in my lifetime" (*Lebanon Daily News*, February 7, 1964, 11). The repeated discourse that the nation wasn't ready for a woman president further cemented the idea, thereby legitimizing the rationality of the argument even though no specifics are provided as to why Smith personally was unqualified. By pushing a woman presidency to the future, the public was essentially saying it was not comfortable having a discussion about gender norms in the present and that the future could deal with it. By not pushing sources to further discuss their views, the press was also kicking the can down the road.

Smith herself attempted to counter this gendered discursive strategy against women by saying:

I see no special qualifications or disqualifications for women for I think they are people just as much as men are. I think they are no more and no less capable than men. Whether a man or a woman, the candidate should be judged on his or her ability and record rather than on his or her sex. (*Lowell Sun*, June 28, 1964, 76)

Other women also lent Smith support regarding this same point. Mrs. Walter E. Cosgriff, reported to be the only woman general manager in professional baseball at the time, said, "I don't think the sex of a candidate would matter once she got elected. It would be a matter of ability. I would have to be convinced she had the ability" (*Fitchburg Sentinel*, January 29, 1964, 25). Actress Bette Davis, who had met Smith before, told the press, "I find her totally impressive as a woman in politics. I feel this is as great a step forward as Mr. Kennedy being nominated as a Catholic" (*Pasadena Independent*, January 29, 1964, 9). However, the Associated Press article quoting Davis was headlined "Smith Divides Women," and the journalist wrote in the story that Smith's candidacy "brought expressions of mild or strong disapproval from many of her sex." In other words, the framework of the journalist's story discursively negated attempts to legitimize Smith, thereby reducing the impact of the positive comments from Davis. Overall, Smith's press coverage entailed a discursive agenda against a woman president that was too strong and, without enough supporters to counterattack, supportive discourse on the issue fell flat.

The closest that news coverage came to attacking Smith personally involved word choices that downplayed her chances of winning. One report said Republican politicians did not think Smith would receive enough votes in New Hampshire to continue in the presidential nomination process (*Madison Wisconsin State Journal*, March 8, 1964, 6B). Other stories referred to her as "a woman without a chance" or used similarly worded language (*Ada Evening News*, April 16, 1964, 10; *The News*, June 8, 1964, 19; *Freeport Journal Standard*, July 15, 1964, 1). Yet these comments are still more so aligned with Smith's gender than with any personal attacks on her character or platform, as was the case with Woodhull. Why was there a change in discursive tactics from Woodhull to Smith? There are a few possible explanations. The differences in the partisan and objective press likely played a role, as the partisan press was about bringing the fire while the objective press is about bringing a sanitized version of the news. However, Smith herself was probably the biggest reason why she did not generate personal attacks. Although she was running for president and challenging a gender norm, her long career of refusing she was a feminist made her less threatening than Woodhull, who wanted to turn gender norms upside down. In addition, the lack of substance to Smith's campaign provided less ammunition and less reason for opponents to attack her than was the case with Woodhull, thereby making the position Smith sought the problem as opposed to her message. For unlike Woodhull and Rankin, Smith did not aggressively pursue her campaign.

Severe Limitations

As noted previously, the most common theme in all of Smith's presidential campaign coverage was a barely there mention of her candidacy. For example, the *Oneonta Star* mentioned Smith was a Republican candidate in an article about the Oregon primary (February 29, 1964, 1), while *The New York Times* ran an AP brief simply noting Smith was on the Oregon ballot (March 6, 1964, 40). Similarly, the only mention of Smith in an AP story headlined "Goldwater Heads for New Hampshire Today" was that she, too, was on the ballot (*Centralia Evening Sentinel*, March 2, 1964, 2). Other common coverage of Smith was simply noting her vote total in articles about primary results (i.e. *Danville Bee*, March 14, 1964, 9). This coverage cannot simply be blamed as a blatant disregard of her candidacy by the press, however. It didn't help that Smith did little to support her own cause, beginning with the announcement of her candidacy.

Before a gathering of several hundred supporters at the Women's National Press Club, Smith said the arguments against her candidacy were "far more impelling" than those for it (*The New York Times*, January 28, 1964, 1). She then announced that is why she decided to run. There is no doubt that Smith used this discourse to be dramatic and build suspense with her supporters. However, it's interesting to note that the discursive tone she adopted from the beginning was indicative of how press discourse regarding her campaign would play out. Instead of being *for* something and on the offensive, Smith's discourse indicated that she was running merely to prove she could be a candidate. Smith also did not legitimate her own candidacy when she said that her campaign "would be a lean one, with little or no money and no paid workers" and that she "would not purchase political time on radio or television or advertisements in newspapers" (*The New York Times*, January 28, 1964, 1). Furthermore, Smith said she would not have a campaign headquarters and would only campaign when the Senate was not in session. She then acknowledged the odds against her were heavy (*The New York Times*, January 28, 1964, 1; (i.e. *Arkansas City Daily Traveler*, January 27, 1964, 1; *Rocky Mount Evening Telegram*, January 27, 1964, 1; *Salina Journal*, January 27, 1964, 2). In other words, Smith is telling the public from the beginning that she plans to put little to no effort into her campaign and that she also doesn't think she can win, not exactly the discursive strategy of someone determined to win an office. Not coincidentally, the key discursive themes that soon emerged in her campaign press coverage were the minimal effort she put into her campaign and her lack of a clear platform.

Low-Keyed Campaigning

Not only did Smith begin her campaign by saying she would put in minimal effort, but she continued this discourse throughout her run. As a result, the press grabbed hold of this and repeated it, resulting in a number of articles alluding to the fact that Smith was not a serious candidate.

Following Smith's announcement, the next major step in her campaign was the New Hampshire primary. Although Smith received positive framing for campaigning bright and early when it was 28 degrees below zero, the Associated Press also noted she was the last among the Republican candidates to start campaigning (*Biddeford Journal*, February 10, 1964, 1). Smith's limited time in New Hampshire became an issue as to how legitimate her campaign was. Smith herself acknowledged that "I've not done a regular campaign," yet said she was "happily surprised by the warmth of the reception and the interest I have met in my candidacy so far in New Hampshire" (*The New York Times*, February 13, 1964, 18). However, this reception did not change her campaign or discursive strategies, as she noted that she would go to Illinois to campaign "when I get a chance" (*The New York Times*, February 13, 1964, 18). This response implies that the Illinois primary was not a priority for her, even though she is running for the nation's highest office. By saying this, Smith is again delegitimizing herself, a discursive strategy she couldn't afford when so many others were already doing that for her. Yet she continued this strategy, and the press continued using it.

This was particularly evident in Smith's hesitation of whether to campaign more or to return to Washington, D.C., to maintain her record of 1,600 consecutive roll call votes. After completing a six-day, 1,000-mile campaign in New Hampshire, Smith was said to be considering additional campaigning: "It would take a lot to break my [roll call] record, but I'm on the verge" (*The New York Times*, February 16, 1964, 48). The Associated Press ran similar commentary about how Smith "said she is tempted to break her long string of Senate roll call votes in order to push her campaign harder" (i.e. *Joplin Globe*, February 15, 1964, 2). United Press reported that after "winding up a week of low-keyed campaigning in the New England state, [Smith] said she might return before the election if there was no pressing business in the Senate" (i.e. *Billings Gazette*, February 17, 1964, 9; *Western Kansas Press*, February 18, 1964, 2). By indicating that the Senate and roll call voting were her priorities, Smith (and the press) again is telling voters that her campaign was not as important to her. This was reinforced when Smith did not return, as *The New York Times* reported in March that Smith "remained in Washington to protect her unbroken skein of roll calls" and noted that it had been several weeks since her visit to New Hampshire (March 8, 1964, 1). This furthered the opportunity for the press to continue hammering the message that Smith was not taking her candidacy seriously, a discourse that would only chip away at her candidacy's legitimacy. The Associated Press wrote that Smith "might have done better in New Hampshire if she had not returned to Washington to protect her never-absent Senate roll call record" (i.e. *San Antonio Light*, March 9, 1964, 3; *Reno Evening Gazette*, March 9, 1964 1; *Burlington Daily Times*, News March 9, 1964, 1).

The New York Times noted that Smith "took the primary so lightly that she reported no campaign expenses. She did not have any" (March 9, 1964, 1). Another reporter pointed to Smith's "low pressure" campaign in New Hampshire without bands or sound trucks, noting that she instead "drove quietly about by private car, like a favorite aunt calling on relatives" (*Elyria Chronicle Telegram*, February 17, 1964, 2). With this type of discourse, any hope for Smith's campaign was clearly dashed within the first few weeks of her candidacy. If Smith was not aggressively pursuing her own campaign, journalists had no reason to, either, and used this ammunition to point out the faults of her campaign.

Discourse in regard to Smith's campaign did not improve during the Illinois primary, both in regard to journalistic discourse and her own. Smith again reiterated that she was "conducting a political experiment" and had "no time to campaign, no money, and no organization" (*Petersburg Progress Index*, March 22, 1964, 3). While Goldwater spoke at a rally of 10,000 people, Smith "quickly made the rounds at colleges and small gatherings" (*Salisbury Times*, April 15, 1964, 1). *The New York Times* wrote that "her visits to private homes and other small gatherings gave observers the impression she was being received more like a favorite aunt from the state of Maine than a politician" (April 19, 1964, 81). This media construction of her as a "favorite aunt" implied the limited scope of her campaign and thus further minimized her as a candidate and indicated to the public that she was not a serious option. However, what is interesting to note from this media discourse is that, when Smith did campaign, the press did cover her. In other words, the press of the time was clearly event-centered, meaning it was more likely to provide coverage if there was a specific event happening. Because Smith rarely campaigned, the press found little reason to go out of its way to write about her candidacy. This is certainly a significant reason why so many articles throughout her campaign barely mentioned her. Smith did not campaign in Oregon. As a result, her press coverage during this period merely noted that she wasn't campaigning there, that her name was on the ballot, or that she was a Republican candidate (i.e. *Appleton Post Crescent*, May 14, 1964, 2; *Lock Haven Express*, May 14, 1964, 20; *Baytown Sun*, May 14, 1964, 1), whereas she received more substantial coverage when she did campaign in New Hampshire and Illinois.

Although Smith occasionally insisted she was a serious candidate or "a bona fide candidate" (*Greenfield Recorder Gazette*, April 11, 1964, 3; *The New York Times*, July 7, 1964, 24), the majority of news coverage regarding her candidacy indicated otherwise. Clearly, Smith took a different approach to campaigning than Rankin, and this was one factor as to why Rankin had success and Smith didn't. The women also greatly differed in their platforms.

Why She's in the Race

Although Rankin's campaign coverage made clear that her platform included national suffrage, prohibition, child welfare, and maternal and infant mortality, Smith's campaign coverage provided little insight into what she stood for politically. A number of articles indicated she was running simply to challenge the gender barrier to the presidency. While pointing to the public's belief that the presidency was no place for a woman, Smith said she wanted to "destroy any political bigotry against women on this score just as the late John F. Kennedy had broken the political barrier on religion (*Des Moines Register*, January 28, 1964, 5). Similarly, Smith was reportedly tired of being told "this is a man's world and that it should be kept that way" (*Amarillo Daily News*, January 28, 1964, 2) and was running to "repudiate the argument" that women shouldn't run for president (*Altoona Mirror*, January 30, 1964, 21). In other words, Smith is saying that she wanted to run and win merely because she was a woman, a discursive strategy that would do little to legitimize her candidacy in the climate of the early 1960s. This discursive choice is also interesting coming from a woman who insisted she wasn't a feminist or a woman candidate, although it's important to note that Smith was not promoting women's issues like Woodhull and Rankin did. She was not seeking the office to promote women's legislation but instead to break the barrier of access to the office. Still, this discourse provides additional clarity as to why so much of Smith's campaign coverage was gender-focused: At least early in her campaign, Smith herself was also making it about gender rather than her personally and why she was qualified for the position.

Smith's apparent lack of a concrete platform didn't go unnoticed and became one point of criticism from the press. When writing about Smith's candidacy, Associated Press news analyst James Marlow wrote "she herself is extremely vague on why she's even trying" (*Arkansas City Daily Traveler*, February 5, 1964, 12; *Lowell Sun*, February 5, 1964, 35) and later noted that "she never got around to explaining why she's in the race at all except to say she wants to beat the other candidates" (*Joplin News Herald*, February 13, 1964, 5; *Alton Evening Telegraph*, February 13, 1964, 9; *Kingsport Times*, February 13, 1964, 8; *Sandusky Register*, February 13, 1964, 18). Smith would describe herself throughout the race as a moderate providing a choice between the "liberal" Nelson Rockefeller and more conservative Barry Goldwater (*Salina Journal*, January 27, 1964, 2; *Biddeford Journal*, February 25, 1964, 8; *Salisbury Times*, April 15, 1964, 1). She also mentioned that she was running on her congressional record and had "never dodged an issue or walked out of a vote on any controversial matter" (*Des Moines Register*, February 11, 1964, 10; also see *The New York Times*, February 12, 1964, 21). Yet this provided little legitimacy for why Smith should be president.

Buried within the mountain of articles with little of substance about Smith's campaign were slivers of what Smith stood for as a candidate. Smith brought up foreign policy issues, particularly in relation to the Cold War, but either she provided few details on her views or the press opted not to include them. For example, the Associated Press reported Laos, Cuba, Panama, Vietnam, and "all the rest of the trouble spots in the world" were issues of her campaign, yet her proposals for handling them weren't included (*Biddeford Journal*, February 10, 1964, 8). During a speech at Northeastern's graduation ceremony, Smith called for a government with more "courageous leadership" and "precision of purpose" to battle Communism and said the nation had "a tragic lack of clear-cut national objectives and national strategy" (*The New York Times*, June 15, 1964, 32). However, the article was only three sentences long total, thereby giving no clues as to whether Smith provided examples of objectives or strategies. Either way, the press did not go to the effort to find out or include them, thereby continuing the discursive strategy to simplify Smith's platform and further illustrating the lack of interest in context within journalism during this time.

Some articles offered more specifics about Smith's views, with Smith noting that she opposed recognition of China and its admission to the United Nations and that she would tell Soviet leader Nikita Khrushchev to tear down the Berlin Wall (*Des Moines Register*, February 11, 1964, 10). She pledged to be "as strong as any man" when dealing with the Soviet Union and said being a woman "would not weaken her stand with Khrushchev" (*Berkshire Eagle*, February 11, 1964, 3). Smith also criticized Kennedy's handling of the Bay of Pigs invasion of Cuba, saying she would have provided air cover or never attempted the mission at all (*Berkshire Eagle*, February 11, 1964, 3; *The New York Times*, February 11, 1964, 1; *Des Moines Register*, February 11, 1964, 10). There were hints of her attitude regarding social issues, with Smith saying she wished the party platform had "a stronger civil rights plank" (*San Antonio Express and News*, July 18, 1964, 6). In regard to women, Smith thought the Equal Rights Amendment would be "the most effective and efficient way to make our women first-class citizens" (*Salisbury Times*, April 11, 1964, 14). Yet, she went on to say that

too many women who militantly advocate the Equal Rights Amendment are not willing to give up their special feminine privileges and thus actually do not support equal rights in the fullest sense of the word. They want to have their cake and eat it, too. (*Salisbury Times*, April 11, 1964, 14)

Glimpses like these into Smith's beliefs were too far and in between, as well as too short and lacking in context, however, to get a clear grasp on what a Smith presidency would have been like. Certainly Smith shares in the responsibility for this due to her minimal campaign. However, the press also is to blame for giving little effort to providing coverage about what her presidency would actually entail. This was a case where missing discourse served to delegitimize Smith's campaign as much as what was covered. Interestingly, there was also a lack of news coverage surrounding Smith's personal life.

SMITH'S PERSONAL TRAITS

What is most interesting about Smith's personal coverage is what was left out of news articles rather than what was included. Whereas the romantic lives of Woodhull and Rankin were of interest to journalists of their times, the 1964 political press was silent about Smith's living arrangement with aide Bill Lewis and their evident closeness. In a rare exception, a newspaper in Oklahoma, the home state of Lewis, ran a story noting that "whenever you see Mrs. Smith, you usually see Lewis" (*Ada Evening News*, February 9, 1964, 12). However, the article focused on his political importance to her rather than exposing a romantic connection. There also was no interest in examining Smith's marriage to Clyde. So why was Woodhull persecuted in the press over her marriage, living arrangements, and views of free love, while Smith received a free pass? The answer lies in large part with the journalistic culture of the time to not question the actions of government officials. Just as Kennedy's love affairs were kept out of the newspapers, other public officials benefited from this politician/press understanding to keep private lives private. Although Smith had been a widow for 24 years and Lewis was single, their cohabitation surely would have prompted voter gossip and criticism had it been mentioned in the press. This kind of privacy for a presidential candidate is unlikely to occur again, making Smith a unique case.

The other interesting discursive strategy used in Smith's personal traits coverage was a dynamic of referring to her as both tough and womanly at the same time. This is another one of the double binds that Murray (2010) includes in her framework. Essentially, this means that "male" leadership qualities are deemed necessary to be viewed as competent, yet women must also maintain femininity to conform to gender norms, resulting in political women struggling to be the "correct" amount of masculine and feminine. In Smith's press coverage, an AP story discussed her history of taking on "powerful opponents," such as McCarthy, thereby indicating she had the toughness of a man. Yet the story went on to say that Smith was "known to lecture service secretaries, generals, and admirals like the school teacher she once was" (*Des Moines Register*, January 28, 1964, 5). The juxtaposition from military personnel—a man's profession—to her past as a teacher—a woman's profession—is one example of this double-bind dynamic and is an interesting one since Smith worked as a teacher for less than a year before she quit (Wallace 1995). In other words, the comparison was a stretch. Yet the discursive choice was still made to provoke an imagery of a stern schoolmarm, womanly and manly at the same time. Another story told of Smith's impressive resume on the Naval Affairs, Armed Services, and Space committees, pointing out that she was the first woman to sail on a destroyer during wartime and that "very few people have conferred with as many leaders of nations throughout the world as she has" (*Altoona Mirror*, January 30, 1964, 21). Yet the journalist also noted that Smith "can make cool, delicious blueberry muffins" and that "muffins made from her recipe were served and enjoyed at the press luncheon." By emphasizing homemaking skills, the press belittles the professional qualifications of a woman as a politician and confines her to her gender. This type of discourse illustrates that media were not yet cognizant of the problems with gender bias and gendered news frames at this historical juncture, the eve of the second feminist movement. The discursive strategy employed in the above stories seems to indicate a fear of challenging gender norms and an uncertainty of how, and whether, to lend legitimacy to Smith's candidacy. The journalists seemed to feel a need to balance out the "manly" aspects of Smith by including feminine discourse, a strategy that Smith apparently was participating in as well with her muffin making.

Whether the journalist writing the story was a man or a woman did not seem to make a difference when it came to using this strategy. A story written by Jerry Klein reported that Smith was "an acknowledged defense expert, having toured overseas defense posts, but also is a great lover of flowers" (*Ogden Standard Examiner*, July 12, 1964, 55). Following the same pattern, Judith Stahl touched on Smith's record number of roll calls votes, but then also discussed her simple dresses, "attention-getting high heels," and "slender 118-pound figure" that didn't require dieting (*Burlington Daily Times News*, March 12, 1964, 8C). A headline in *The New York Times* also constructed this male/female balance: "A Chic Lady Who Fights: Margaret Chase Smith" (January 28, 1964, 17). This discursive struggle of how to handle a woman challenging gender norms is apparent. Whereas the press had no question that Woodhull and Rankin were running as women, so to speak, how to handle Smith was entirely different, resulting in a confused discourse with both legitimizing and delegitimizing components. Both the press and the candidate appear unsure of how to discursively construct a woman candidate, a telling sign of the discursive trouble to come in the future.

FIRST WOMAN EVER

Although the press offered little substantive discourse regarding Smith's platform and campaign, newspapers freely offered discourse about the historical relevancy of her candidacy. On the cusp of Smith's announcement, the United Press told readers of her "bid to become the nation's first woman president" (*New Castle News*, January 27, 1964, 1), while the Associated Press wrote "she would be the first woman ever to run on the national ticket of a major political party" (*High Point Enterprise*, January 27, 1964, 2). Another United Press story called Smith the "first female aspirant for the presidency from a major party and the first woman candidate since Belva Lockwood" in 1884 (*Provo Daily Herald*, January 28, 1964, 12; *Santa Fe New Mexican*, January 28, 1964, 2; *Huron Daily Plainsman*, January 28, 1964, 1), one of the few references to women's political history. Similarly, an AP story leading up to the Republican nomination mentioned both Lockwood and Woodhull, "two women in minor parties who tried to make it on their own, almost a century ago" while noting that Smith would make history that day: "For the first time in the history of any major party, the name of a woman will be placed in nomination today for president" (*Freeport Journal Standard*, July 15, 1964, 1). Beyond a few instances such as these, however, Smith's historical achievement was treated as an isolated event, with no context of prior women who made her climb possible, thereby simplifying what her run meant in the broader scope of history and making her a novelty. Some stories referenced Smith's prior historical achievements as the first woman elected to the Senate without being appointed first (*Des Moines Register*, January 28, 1964, 5) and the "only woman ever to have been elected to three full terms in the U.S. Senate and only woman to serve both houses of Congress" (*Altoona Mirror*, January 30, 1964, 21). But primarily, historical references were limited to Smith's presidential bid, with more colorful language chosen as the Republican convention approached. The Associated Press called Smith the "first woman to try to make a contest with male colleagues in an important primary" in its coverage of the New Hampshire primary (*Hutchinson News*, March 11, 1964, 1). A local reporter called Smith "history's first fully accredited woman candidate for president" (*Logan Herald Journal*, June 25, 1964, 2). In a way, this helps legitimize her since she is deemed "fully accredited," yet it still suggests that her candidacy is a novelty.

The most amusing and telling commentary came from a vendor selling Smith's campaign materials at the nation convention: "I've never had a hotter item than them Smith buttons. If I wasn't so dumb, I would have ordered thousands of them" (*North Adams Transcript*, July 17, 1964, 4; *Portsmouth Herald*, July 18, 1964, 6). It is interesting that so many people appreciated the historical moment of Smith's candidacy that they wanted to buy buttons, yet they did not give her actual candidacy the same regard nor did the press. Journalism loves "firsts" because of the emphasized news value of novelty, hence why this theme developed. Yet, as was stated in Rankin's chapter, "first woman" discourse is a gendered news frame, if further context is not provided, which serves as a discursive reminder that women in politics are not the norm and therefore are less credible. Although a historical theme emerged in both Rankin's and Smith's campaign coverage, Rankin clearly benefited from a more legitimizing discourse and, not coincidentally, Rankin won her election. As was discussed in the prior chapter (see pages 67–68), Rankin's history-making campaign prompted pre election discourse about "an event of more than ordinary importance," "progress with a big P," and "another step forward." In other words, there was an emotional discursive strategy to get readers to buy into Rankin's campaign that was absent in the objectivity-focused, plain language used to describe Smith. This wasn't the only discursive theme with differing results between Smith and Rankin.

SMITH'S APPEARANCE

Like journalists of Rankin's era, the press of the 1960s placed an emphasis on Smith's appearance. However, the journalistic approaches toward the two women noticeably differed. Whereas Rankin's news coverage focused on her hair and attractiveness, news coverage related to Smith's appearance focused on clothing and her age.

Bonnet in the Ring

References to throwing a bonnet in the ring were impossible to miss while perusing news articles after Smith's campaign announcement. The *Independent Press Telegram* ran the headline "Ballots and Bonnets: Should the Next President Be a Woman?" and noted Smith had "thrown her bonnet in the presidential ring" (February 2, 1964, W4). The *Des Moines Register* ran a prominent headline at the top of its front page declaring "Mrs. Smith's Bonnet in Ring" (January 28, 1964, 1). Other newspapers chose "tossed" or similar phrasing in their word play on bonnet (i.e. *Arkansas City Daily Traveler*, January 27, 1964, 1; *Rocky Mount Evening Telegram*, January 27, 1964, 1). Although this study did not focus on analyzing news photography, it was eventually determined that the bonnet phrasing was related to an image of Smith actually throwing a bonnet through a ring and a cutline saying she was illustrating "an old cliché by tossing her bonnet into a ring in her Washington office" (*Daily Journal*, January 28, 1964, 1). The image did not appear with many of the stories using the bonnet phrasing, however, thereby leaving most readers with the impression that newspapers were simply using a gendered play on words. It is noteworthy that Smith brought this gendered discourse upon herself, a fact that previously mentioned psychiatrist Dr. Michael J. Singer bemoaned: "I was sorry to read Mrs. Smith's comment, however, that she had tossed her bonnet in the ring. Why not a hat, like Rockefeller?" (*Independent Press Telegram*, February 2, 1964, W4). Indeed, this was an unusual move for a woman who insisted that she was not a woman senator or a woman candidate throughout her career, which indicates Smith herself wasn't sure how to navigate these new political waters and gender expectations.

Beyond the bonnet, references to a handbag also appeared in Smith's press coverage, with the United Press writing that Smith "stuffed 14 Republican convention votes into her handbag today and set out to remove the 'for men only' sign at the White House" (i.e. *Provo Daily Herald*, January 28, 1964, 12; *Tyrone Daily Herald*, January 28, 1964, 1). Critiquing the use of handbag and bonnet word choices by journalists may seem trivial. However, the gendered word choices are part of a discursive strategy to "other" Smith and call attention to her gender. Certainly newspapers were not discussing Goldwater stuffing votes into his wallet. Therefore, it is not just the word choices that are problematic but the uneven use of gendered discourse depending upon whether the candidate is a man or a woman. By calling attention to her gender, the press is pointing out that Smith is different, which chips away at her legitimacy.

Interestingly, there was not as much focus as expected on what Smith wore, but the fact that she rarely campaigned and that most of the articles about her were simply listing her as a candidate or mentioning her primary results are certainly contributing reasons as to why not. Still, there was some news coverage of her clothing. *The New York Times* described her "black suit and brown alligator heels. Her only accessories were two strands of pearls and a yellow rose pinned to her lapel" (January 28, 1964, 1). Reporter Judith Stahl wrote that Smith wore simple dresses, red roses, and "attention-getting high heels" (*Burlington Daily Times*, News, March 12, 1964, 8C). In the same story, she referred to Smith as a "high-heeled campaigner for the presidency." Smith's three-quarter length coat of beaver skins and the fact she wore no hat also attracted attention while she campaigned in New Hampshire (*The New York Times*, February 11, 1964, 1; *Des Moines Register*, February 11, 1964, 10; *Phoenix Arizona Republic*, February 11, 1964, 11).

As far as Smith's predecessors, the press gave only slight attention to Woodhull's clothing and none of the articles in this analysis discussed Rankin's. This was perhaps due to her remote location since newspapers struggled to even determine Rankin's hair color, let alone her clothing.

Regardless, during the 1960s, there was an increased focus on a female candidate's fashion choices, another discursive strategy that emphasized her gender. Smith also faced another type of news coverage that Woodhull and Rankin didn't: an emphasis on her age.

White-Haired Widow

Whereas Rankin's hair and features were constructed in the press as positive and beautiful, Smith's press coverage served to remind readers that she was old. As mentioned earlier in this chapter, age is one of the double binds mentioned in Murray's (2010) framework. Women who are younger are considered inexperienced and are expected to be at home with their children, while women who are older are considered "past their prime" (18), resulting in a very limited window of potential age acceptability for women in politics. In Smith's case, the press often emphasized her older age. A United Press story described Smith as "the white-haired lady from Maine" (*New Castle News*, January 27, 1964, 1), while the Associated Press referred to her as a "gray-haired 66-year-old veteran of 15 years in the Senate" (*Salina Journal*, January 27, 1964, 2; *High Point Enterprise*, January 27, 1964, 2). The following day, the United Press mentioned Smith's age and called her a "white-haired widow" (*Provo Daily Herald*, January 28, 1964, 2; *Santa Fe New Mexican*, January 28, 1964 , 2; *Huron Daily Plainsman*, January 28, 1964, 1; *Statesville Record and Landmark*, January 28, 1964, 1). This wording makes it sound like Smith was a frail, elderly woman rather than the active woman she was. The fact that Smith had been a widow for nearly 25 years—this was not a new occurrence—makes the word choice even more peculiar. The discursive strategy was clearly used to elicit a particular image of Smith, one that seemingly served to delegitimize her as a serious candidate by emphasizing her age.

To drive the point in further, a news analyst for the Associated Press wrote that Smith was the "oldest of the candidates at 66" (*Arkansas City Daily Traveler*, February 5, 1964, 12). This goes back to the earlier point that seemingly objective press coverage isn't necessarily so. Was it true that Smith was 66? Was it an observable fact that she had white/gray hair? Was it true she was older than Barry Goldwater, Nelson Rockefeller, and Richard Nixon? Yes. However, the negative implications of these facts were easily understood. Smith herself did not appreciate the press focus on her age and fired back in what would be a rare decision by the press throughout her campaign to include direct discourse from her. An Associated Press story noted Smith "took firm issue today with any idea that her age, 66, should be a barrier to her quest for the Republican presidential nomination" (*Monroe News Star*, February 6, 1964, 1). *The New York Times* ran the headline

"Mrs. Smith Says Her Age Is No Bar to Presidency" and carried an AP story with Smith saying "almost every news story" began by mentioning her age (February 7, 1964, 14). This statement is important to consider. Because journalists were now primarily using the inverted pyramid style of writing, the high placement of Smith's age is indicative that journalists thought it was important information for readers to know. What makes this problematic is that Smith went on to say that "I haven't seen the age played up in the case of men candidates" (February 7, 1964, 14). This is a very telling indication of gender bias in journalistic discursive choices and is illustrative of women in politics attempting to fight back at perceived sexism. Another wire service story had Smith saying her age was "referred to almost daily" and pointing out that Dwight Eisenhower was seven years older than her and "many of the national leaders were much older" (*Des Moines Register*, February 11, 1964 10). Again, Smith is attempting to draw attention to the double standard that older men can seek leadership roles without receiving attention as to their age while she couldn't. (As a note of reference, Eisenhower was 62 when he first assumed the presidency and 70 when he left office compared to Smith's age of 66 at the time of her presidential run.) A similar story ran in *The New York Times* a few days later. Ironically, the story still referenced Smith as "silver-haired" even though Smith is arguing in that very article about the ageism against her (February 11, 1964, 1), thereby indicating at least some journalists paid little heed to Smith's complaint. When NBC "Today" show reporter Martin Agronsky pointed to the belief that women were the weaker sex and asked Smith if she could stand all-night crisis conferences as president, Smith replied that women lived seven years longer than men (*The New York Times*, February 7, 1964, 14). This did not end discussion of her age, however.

A few journalists chose to defend Smith's age, but not many. Writer Judith Stahl wrote that "despite her 66 years, observers agree that she brings to her work the energy of a Beatle fan and the steely discipline of a JV determined to make varsity" (*Burlington Daily Times News*, March 12, 1964, 8C). Beyond the colorful comparisons, what is interesting to note is that discourse of Smith's age was still ongoing in March. Furthermore, in addition to repeating ageist discourse by also referring to Smith as "silver-haired," Stahl was again reminding readers that Smith's age was perceived to be an issue even though her intent was clearly to be helpful.

The discursive theme of age provides an interesting insight into journalistic practice of this era and the development of a new discursive device for delegitimizing a woman politician. Woodhull was not even old enough to serve as president in 1872, yet the press made no note of her age. Similarly, the news articles about Rankin did not call attention to her age even though, at 36, she could have been considered young for Congress. Yet the focus on Smith's age was clearly an evolution of the emphasis on physical characteristics that emerged during Rankin's campaign coverage and suggests the growing importance of appearance discourse in relation to women in politics. Smith's complaints were not treated seriously in the 1960s and how this plays out in the 2000s will be examined in the next chapter.

DISCUSSION

Among the letters of support from around the country that Smith received was one from a 10-year-old girl who "expressed her gratitude to Mrs. Smith for paving the way for her to grow up to be president" (*Burlington Daily Times News*, March 12, 1964, 8C). Fifty years later, that little girl is still waiting for a woman president. Unlike Rankin who benefited from a historical time conducive to breaking a gender barrier, Smith launched a campaign at a point in history similar to what Woodhull encountered: a nation committed to re electing the current president and to firmly defending traditional gender norms. From a journalistic standpoint, Smith personally did not encounter discourse as piercing as Woodhull did, yet the press of the 1960s had its own discursive efforts to delegitimize her campaign via lack of context and in-depth reporting. Still, an examination of Smith's news coverage indicates some progress was made in the path to a woman president even though some additional setbacks were added.

Smith surprisingly received support in the press from male politicians during her campaign, a benefit that Woodhull never had. Although some of the politicians' commentary indicated only surface-level support and her opponents surely did not see her as a legitimate threat, the fact that mainstream politicians went on the record to lend a word to her candidacy was a significant improvement from the tarring and feathering that Woodhull encountered. Newspaper articles also included some positive discourse on Smith's behalf from members of the general public, whereas Woodhull's supporters were primarily feminists or other populations derided by the press. However, the emotional reflex to defend traditional gender norms had significant strength in the early 1960s just as it did in the 1870s. As a result, Smith did not stand a chance of winning a presidential nomination even if the makeup of candidates during the 1964 presidential race had differed.

Whereas Woodhull encountered attacks on her platform and her personal life, the negative discourse surrounding Smith's presidential ambition centered more so on the fact that a woman in general was unacceptable to be president than on opposition to Smith herself. In a way, this discourse was useful in that it addressed the real issue—*any* woman was problematic—rather than taking out this matter on Smith personally. Yet the surface-level discussions of this hot-button topic did little to nothing to advance the issue. Sources frequently stated that the presidency was a man's job, that women were too emotional, and that the nation was not ready for a woman president without giving any indication as to why Smith in particular was problematic beyond her gender. In other words, discourse reinforcing that gender in and of itself was a rational argument for repressing women appeared all too often in Smith's campaign coverage. Journalists legitimated these discursive strategies by rarely challenging stereotypical claims or providing more context or depth. The press also rarely referenced prior women's political history or women in leadership positions, which would have put Smith's campaign in a broader context that would have made it appear less foreign. Woodhull was only briefly mentioned a few times in the sample of Smith's coverage, and there was no discussion of the challenges that women in U.S. history had faced to make advancements. Like the journalists' sources who believed a woman president was a concept for the future, journalists of the early 1960s did not seem to want to embark on a conversation about gender norms, leaving that can of worms for the future to handle.

Yet the press of 1964 had no choice but to discursively construct a woman presidential candidate and clearly struggled with how to handle a woman seeking a "man's" job. This resulted in journalists using discourse that described Smith as both tough and qualified but also feminine, in a bizarre effort to balance her out. This was certainly better than most of Woodhull's coverage, which often constructed her as a villain or troublemaker. Yet it illustrated a double bind for women in politics to need to appear competent but to also properly perform their gender. The discursive construction of Smith also included the emergence of the double bind of age, as well as an increased emphasis on appearance, all of which certainly would have implications for future women politicians as well.

Smith's previously mentioned "abysmal relations" with the press seemed to factor little into her coverage, however, as her campaign itself was the biggest discursive focus of the press, as opposed to her personal traits. Smith herself did little to help her own cause by rarely campaigning and not establishing a clear platform from the beginning beyond running simply because people thought she shouldn't. Although Woodhull had a platform, her campaign has similarities to Smith's, in that both women lacked an understanding or willingness to do what was necessary to run a campaign of their particular scope. Rankin, on the other hand, had a clear understanding of her audience and a clear strategy for her platform and campaign. Perhaps most importantly, she entered a race she thought she could win, unlike Smith and Woodhull. Smith was clearly aware that she had little odds of securing the Republican nomination and no chance of defeating Lyndon Johnson, as evidenced by her own press commentary. Because she did not aggressively pursue her own race, she gave little reason for others to do so. As a result, the event-centered press either gave her minimal coverage or often used discourse that indicated she was not a serious candidate. Although the press noted the historical implications of Smith's candidacy, the discourse lacked the emotional pride that accompanied Rankin's campaign, indicating a lack of buy-in to Smith.

Smith said she was influenced to run by the argument that other women had paved the way for her political career "and that I should give back in return that which was given to me" (*Cedar Rapids Gazette*, February 3, 1964, 15). Although Smith's candidacy did indicate some discursive improvement on the part of the press when compared to Woodhull's, Smith ultimately did little to help the women who would come after her. Indeed, one of Smith's biographers noted that Smith's "firsts were more for herself than for inspiring other women" (Wallace 1995, 163). Smith's management of her campaign and her own discourse about it did little to advance the argument that a woman should be considered a serious presidential contender and resulted in press coverage that further legitimized the status quo. Although she put cracks in the glass ceiling by being the first woman nominated for president at a major party's convention, Smith, like Woodhull, also ended up creating future discursive trouble for subsequent women in politics, as is discussed in the remaining chapters of this book.

The next chapter focuses on the 2000s and press coverage of the first Republican woman vice presidential candidate. First, however, a brief epilogue of Smith's story is provided:

Smith secured 27 votes for the Republican presidential nomination, but was ultimately crushed by the 883 votes for Goldwater. She resumed her work in the U.S. Senate, where she would remain until 1972 when she was defeated at the polls after 32 years in Congress. Then 74, Smith faced questions during her final campaign about her age and her ability to keep up with her duties. Furthermore, Smith's conservativism and detachment from Maine prompted criticism that she was out of touch with constituents (Wallace 1995; Sherman 2000). Her longtime stance against feminism also caught up with her at a time when the second wave was flourishing, and she failed to secure support from women's groups (Wallace 1995). Smith later complained that feminists "had not recognized her accomplishments nor realized the limits of her power" during her career and said they did not understand she would not have been politically successful if she had embraced a feminist approach (Sherman 2000, 217).

During her retirement, Smith continued to live with her companion and former congressional aide Bill Lewis. She put her energy into lecturing at colleges, serving on boards, and renovating her Skowhegan home into a library that would highlight her career (Wallace 1995). She lived to see

Geraldine Ferraro in 1984 become the first woman to win a vice presidential nomination, an honor that alluded Smith 30 years earlier. In 1989, Smith received the Presidential Medal of Freedom, earning praise from President George. H. W. Bush for her "historic and courageous speech" denouncing McCarthyism in 1950 (Associated Press 1989). Smith died May 29, 1995, at age 97. The Margaret Chase Smith Library continues to operate in Skowhegan, Maine, today.

Figure 5.1   The Official Governor Portrait of Former Alaska Gov. Sarah Palin. In 2008, Palin became the first Republican woman vice presidential candidate. *Source*: Photo courtesy of Alaska State Library, Palin-Sarah-1. New permission form would be required for a paperback format.

Chapter 5

Media Celebritization of Sarah Palin

In her autobiography, Sarah Palin recalled the day when she and John McCain made history. "John believed in change, the power of independent and committed individuals, the power of women. He thought it was time to shake things up," she wrote (Palin 2009, 223). Shake things up indeed. McCain stunned the political world on August 29, 2008, when he announced the Alaska governor was his choice for a vice presidential running mate. Relatively unknown to the general public at the time, Palin soon became a household name as her admission into national politics rejuvenated the Republican Party and entered her into history as the first female Republican vice presidential candidate. However, questions quickly arose as to whether Palin was qualified for the job, and she became a popular target for tabloids and late night TV shows like "Saturday Night Live." Reminiscent of the days of Victoria Woodhull, Palin and her family soon found criticism of their personal lives splashed across the media.

This chapter's focus on Palin is an opportunity to come full circle in order to understand how press coverage of female politicians has and has not changed since Woodhull's groundbreaking run for national office in 1872. Like Woodhull, Palin's political views were considered extreme to some and her family's private affairs drew intense scrutiny. Like Rankin, Palin was an avid campaigner and serious contender whose personal appearance drew more attention than her platform at times. Like Smith, Palin's candidacy did not mean the securing of the (mythical) women's vote, but her ambition received praise for advancing women in national politics. Clearly, attitudes and discursive strategies used in regard to women in politics have improved somewhat in the past 140 years, as evidenced by the fact that Palin and Democratic presidential contender Hillary Clinton made it as far as they did in 2008. Yet, as this chapter will illustrate, discursive remnants of the past continue to infiltrate press coverage today, resulting in gendered discourse best left in the late nineteenth and early twentieth centuries.

This analysis focuses on newspaper coverage of Palin's vice presidential campaign from the announcement of her selection in August 2008 through her loss at the polls that November. This chapter includes discussion of the key discursive themes that emerged from Palin's news coverage as well as compares and contrasts these findings to how Woodhull, Rankin, and Smith were covered by the press. As was the case with the other women, it is first necessary to provide an overview of Palin's life and the political, feminist, and journalistic cultures of the time in order to better understand her media experience. This chapter begins at the same place where it began for Palin: Alaska.

THE ALASKA POLITICIAN

Sarah Heath Palin was born February 11, 1964, in Sandpoint, Idaho, but the future governor of Alaska did not remain in the Lower 48 for long. Within months of her birth, her parents moved the family to Alaska to pursue a new job opportunity for her father (Palin 2009). Growing up in Alaska had a tremendous influence on Palin, the third youngest in a family of four children. As a child, she developed a love of hunting and the great outdoors as well as formed her religious faith and competitive spirit, all of which were factors in her later political career (Palin 2009; Benet 2009). In high school, Palin played basketball and was a member of the state championship team her senior year, a fact the press would bring up during her vice presidential campaign along with her nickname "Sarah Barracuda" (Benet 2009). Palin would later say that basketball taught her how to set goals, be disciplined, and work as a team in order to be successful (Benet 2009).

Palin grew up during the height of the second wave of feminism, but later said she had mixed feelings about the movement. "I didn't subscribe to all the radical mantras of that early feminist era, but reasoned arguments for equal opportunity definitely resonated with me," she wrote in her autobiography (Palin 2009, 29). After high school, Palin attended college and one of her activities—beauty pageants—would later be emphasized in her vice presidential campaign coverage. After graduating from the University of Idaho in 1987 with a degree in broadcast journalism, Palin returned to Alaska to work as a sports broadcaster on television (Benet 2009; Palin 2009). Although Woodhull had her own newspaper and Smith had experience working for the newspaper industry, Palin is the only politician in this study who had formal journalism training, notably in a field that emphasizes public speaking and appearance. Her journalism career was short, however.

She married her high school boyfriend, Todd Palin, on August 29, 1988, which was 20 years to the day before she was announced as a vice presidential candidate. Like many professional women of her generation, the birth of their first two children (of the eventual five) soon after their marriage prompted Palin to leave her television career behind to spend more time with her children. But Palin, who "believed that she'd had a religious calling to serve in politics since she was a teenager" (Benet 2009, 68), soon found herself a new career: local politician.

Palin's rise in politics began in 1992 when she was elected to the Wasilla City Council. Four years later, she won the seat for mayor after promoting fiscal responsibility and criticizing the city's "good old boys" network (Benet 2009, 74), the same kind of messaging she would later use in her national political career. At this early stage, Palin was already taking on challenging political races by opposing the incumbent mayor (a fellow Republican) and positioning herself as the candidate with fresh energy and ideas (Benet 2009; Palin 2009). Even though the mayoral position was nonpartisan, Palin received the backing of the state Republican Party as well as the National Rifle Association at a time when conservative candidates were popular nationwide (Benet 2009). After a heated race, Palin's early days as mayor sparked additional controversy, including when she asked all of the city's department heads to resign and reapply for their jobs (Benet 2009). Still, Palin was reelected mayor and, throughout her tenure, she focused on lowering property taxes, improving city infrastructure, and finding ways to cut the city budget (Palin 2009).

In 2002, Palin sought the Republican nomination for Alaska's lieutenant governor. Although she lost the primary, she had gained statewide exposure. In 2005, she filed for governor, setting up a direct challenge to fellow Republican Frank Murkowski and, as Palin put it, "taking on the entrenched interests and the political machine" (Palin 2009, 116). She won the office in 2006, becoming Alaska's youngest and first female governor at age 42. A *New York Times* story published days before the election declared "Novice Stands Her Ground on Veterans' Turf in Alaska" (Yardley 2006, 25). This foreshadowed the discourse that would become prominent during her vice presidential campaign, as did a news article a few days later that noted an opponent called her "inexperienced" ("The 2006 Elections: Alaska" 2006, P13).

During her first year in office, Palin's popularity as governor and her push for a gas pipeline resulted in national media exposure, and another big break came in April 2008 when she gave a keynote speech at the Republican Governors Association meeting in Texas (Benet 2009). Palin was in the early stages of labor with her youngest son, Trig, but did not want to miss the opportunity and continued with her speech before quickly returning to Alaska to give birth (Palin 2009). Her son, who was born with Down syndrome, would attract his own share of media attention in the months ahead. The Palins also discovered that their teenage daughter Bristol was going to have a baby of her own. In addition, the Alaska legislature began an investigation in summer 2008 regarding Palin's firing of the state's public safety commissioner amid accusations that she did so because he would not fire her ex-brother-in-law, a state trooper. Palin denied she abused her power as governor, but the event quickly became "a publicity nightmare" (Benet 2009, 194). The media attention was soon to become even stronger.

In August 2008, Palin found herself on a plane headed for Arizona to be vetted and ultimately selected as McCain's running mate. Within hours of the public announcement, media stories abounded with both praise and criticism, with a heavy emphasis on Palin's lack of experience and questions as to how well McCain's staff vetted her (Benet 2009). Why would McCain choose a relatively unknown governor with two years of executive experience and with personal issues sure to set off the national press? An examination of the political culture of the time provides clues as to why.

ELECTION OF 2008

By 2008, the United States was entering its fifth year of war in Iraq, and George W. Bush's administration faced increasing criticism and sagging poll numbers from a war weary country (Lansford 2012). The 2006 midterm election brought sweeping victories for Democrats, including the rise of Nancy Pelosi as the first woman speaker of the House. In the waning months of the 2008 campaign, the downward spiral of the economy became a critical issue in the country as the housing bubble burst and unemployment rates spiked (Brands 2010; *The 2000s in America* 2013a). The growing crisis in the banking and financial industry resulted in a $700 billion government bailout just weeks before Election Day (Lansford 2012; Brands 2010). A recession was clearly taking hold as stock prices eroded, consumers stopped spending, and layoffs escalated (Lansford 2012). In 2008, mass layoffs hit a seven-year high, according to CNN (Smith 2009). Not surprisingly, foreign policy, the economy, and a clamor for new leadership were critical factors for the public heading into the 2008 election (*The 2000s in America* 2013b).

A few other political factors are also worth noting. The 2008 election marked the first time in more than 50 years that neither an incumbent president nor vice president was seeking the nation's top office (Balz and Johnson 2009). Therefore, the path to the White House was essentially cleared for a newcomer, hence why such a diverse field of candidates emerged. On this same note of diversity, the United States' population was shifting and minorities now comprised one-third of the nation's citizens

(Balz and Johnson 2009). Women held 16 percent of the seats in Congress, still not representative of half of the nation's population, but significantly improved from 2.6 percent in 1964 when Smith ran for president (*Women in the U.S. Congress 2015* 2015). Between 1917 and 1972, women never occupied more than 5 percent of Congress (Chamberlin 1973; *Women in the U.S. Congress 2015* 2015). However, the second wave of feminism had advanced women's rights and opportunities, which were now benefiting women during the third wave in the late twentieth and early twenty-first centuries. Democrat Walter Mondale's selection of Geraldine Ferraro as his vice presidential running mate in 1984 was a historical achievement that ultimately paved the way for Palin and other prominent women politicians. By the mid-1980s, women who ran for office began to make some gains as the "pattern of running in impossible races had reversed itself" (Witt, Matthews, and Paget 1995, 103). Women began to have the mentality that they could win, not merely be "sacrificial lambs" (Witt, Matthews, and Paget 1995, 103).

This was particularly the case in 1992 after another critical moment in women's political history: Anita Hill's 1991 sexual harassment testimony against Supreme Court nominee Clarence Thomas. Hill became "a symbol of women's status in American life and, in particular, their exclusion from the halls of power" (Witt, Matthews, and Paget 1995, 1). Hill inadvertently sparked "more women than ever" to run for political office as well as launched "the most unprecedented mobilization of women voters" in the 1992 election (Witt, Matthews, and Paget 1995, 4, 2). As a result, 24 new women won seats in the House, with more women winning seats in that one election than they typically would in a decade (Weatherford 2012, 166). Just as the Hill hearings buoyed women in politics, they also served a prominent role in the launch of the third wave of feminism in the early 1990s. Third wave feminists have promoted greater inclusiveness for people of varying races/ethnicities, classes, and sexual orientations and have criticized the second wave of feminism for racism, classism, and heterosexism (Bronstein 2005). One of the most recognizable aspects of the third wave is the emphasis on "girl power," or the empowerment of girl culture (Lorber 2012). Still, despite these advances, women in politics continued to struggle with sexist attitudes of whether they could handle "men's issues" like finance and war, while also needing to illustrate that they were running for office with permission from their husbands (Witt, Matthews, and Paget 1995).

With all of the above influences taken into consideration, the social and political landscape of the United States was increasingly becoming more accepting of diversity by 2008, even though problems remained. Cognizant of the support for presidential candidate Hillary Clinton and the buzz over the potential first black president, Barack Obama, Republican candidate John McCain decided to create a diverse and historic ticket of his own with the selection of Palin as his running mate. To better understand the 2008 election, a further review of the major political players is useful.

Born in 1936, McCain spent his early adult years continuing his family's legacy of enrolling in the Navy and famously spent five and a half years as a prisoner of war in Vietnam (Alexander 2008). After a brief stint in the U.S. House representing Arizona, McCain embarked on his current Senate career in 1986 by capturing the seat of the retiring Barry Goldwater (Alexander 2008). McCain became well-known for his expertise on defense and national security matters, as well as for his criticism of pork barrel spending (Balz and Johnson 2009). He positioned himself as a "maverick," or a challenger of the establishment (Balz and Johnson 2009, 35), a persona that Palin had developed as well. In 2000, McCain entered the presidential race, but lost the Republican nomination to George W. Bush. McCain again entered the presidential arena for the 2008 election, this time winning his party's nomination. Yet internal struggles within his campaign staff and worrisome fund-raising numbers beleaguered his campaign as did polling results indicating women preferred Obama (Balz and Johnson 2009). McCain had met with Palin earlier in the year at a National Governors Association meeting (Palin 2009) and saw her as an opportunity to boost his campaign. McCain believed "he needed someone dramatic to transform the presidential race" (Balz and Johnson 2009, 226). With the addition of Palin, McCain had his own historic ticket with the promise of a woman as vice president. However, the campaign of his rival and a shift in political winds would prove to be too much to overcome.

Like Palin, Obama seemed an unusual candidate for the 2008 presidential election due to his background and limited national political experience. Born in 1961 to a Kenyan father and an American mother, Obama spent his childhood in Hawaii and Indonesia. He attended Columbia University and Harvard Law School and made his home in Chicago, where he worked as a community organizer, taught constitutional law, served as a civil rights attorney, and was elected to the state senate (Balz and Johnson 2009). He set his sights on a U.S. Senate seat in 2004. That same year, he gave an "electrifying" keynote speech at the Democratic national convention that cemented his future as a rising political star (Kantor 2012, 22; Balz and Johnson 2009). He entered the 2008 presidential race despite the fact New York senator and former first lady Hillary Clinton was the clear front-runner for the Democratic nomination (Brands 2010). Yet Obama's campaign message of hope and change for the future wooed voters as did his positioning as the anti-George Bush candidate who would improve the economy, end the war in Iraq, and repair the nation's reputation abroad (Lansford 2012). The promise of the nation's first black president also appealed to voters, as did Obama's savvy campaign strategy that took advantage of new media. By 2008, the media landscape had become a whole new world for both candidates and journalists and was strikingly different from what Margaret Chase Smith and her rivals encountered in the early 1960s.

THE RISE OF NEW MEDIA

To understand the state of the media in the 2000s, it is useful to back up and explore the changes for the industry that took place in the 1960s. By the middle of the decade, the alternative press grew as "the climate for youth-oriented, antiestablishment newspapers had quickly become fertile" (McMillian 2011, 31). These new alternative journalists challenged the status quo and its defenders with "unprecedented levels of scrutiny and ridicule" (McMillian 2011, 31). This rise of critical culture "deeply affected [mainstream] journalism" (Schudson 1978, 179). Reporting became more probing as journalists "grew less deferential to politicians" (Fink and Schudson 2014, 4). The 1964 New York Times vs. Sullivan Supreme Court case that offered greater protection for media against libel lawsuits was also a pivotal moment in this decade, thereby allowing journalists to become more critical of public figures. By the end of the decade,

> fact-centered and detached reporting seemed too limited an approach for exposing larger political dilemmas like McCarthyism or White House lies about Vietnam and Watergate. It led to calls to "blend" the hard-news paradigm with analytic and interpretative elements. (Esser and Umbricht 2014)

This approach to journalism occurred during the rise in prominence of major industry players, such as Katherine Graham, Arthur Ochs Sulzberger, and Al Neuharth. The resulting development of corporate culture under this leadership "affected the content of the papers at least as strongly as it did their organizations" (Cose 1989, 15), a trend that would become increasingly evident by the 2000s. As newspaper companies bought up properties, the industry became increasingly dominated by concentrated corporate ownership that put pressure on newspapers to earn money (Hachten 2005). Complaints arose of newsrooms operating with too few reporters in order to keep costs down and increase profits (Weaver et al. 2007). At the same time, changes in technology created financial strain. Readers and advertisers found other opportunities on the Internet, leading to the publication of books such as *The Vanishing Newspaper: Saving Journalism in the Information Age* (Meyer 2004). To attract readers, newspapers began putting more emphasis on entertainment news, including gossip, scandals, and celebrities (Hachten 2005). Yet readership and news credibility polls continued to decline, with some journalists blaming this emphasis on soft news for these problems (Sloan 2011). However, a number of journalism fabrication and plagiarism scandals, and a decline in reader interest in hard news, continued to beleaguer the industry, as did the rise of 24-7 cable news and increased pressure to turn out content as quickly as possible (Marshall 2011; Barnhurst and Nerone 2009; Weaver et al. 2007). As newspapers transitioned to multimedia reporting, books advised reporters that this new style of reporting meant "being flexible enough to provide news and information to anyone and everyone, anytime and all the time, anywhere and often everywhere" (Kolodzy 2006, vii). The news industry was described as being "in a state of flux" or "disarray" due to "technological, social, and economic changes" (Kolodzy 2006, 3), similar phrasing as that used to describe newspapers in the 1870s. Also similar to prior journalism history was continued gender imbalance in newsrooms, as women comprised one-third of journalists in the early 2000s (Weaver et al. 2007).

Following the political corruption and backlash against the government in the 1960s and 1970s, a more cynical press had developed by the 2000s (Hachten 2005). Presidential election coverage grew increasingly critical and began to focus more "on the 'game' of politics rather than the policies proposed by candidates" (Fink and Schudson 2014, 6; Patterson 1994). Along the same lines, journalism began to focus more on analysis and contextualization of politics, which meant a heavy emphasis on interviewing experts, using quotations, and weighing pros and cons (Esser and Umbricht 2014). Reporters faced criticism for being biased both in favor of and against the government, particularly following September. 11, 2001, leading at least some in the public—and some journalists themselves—to believe that the media had abandoned objectivity (Sloan 2011).

The state of the relationship between media and politics during the 2008 presidential campaign, specifically, is perhaps best summarized in an article written by former *New York Times* reporters David Carr and Brian Stelter: "Not since 1960, when John F. Kennedy won in part because of the increasingly popular medium of television, has changing technology had such an impact on the political campaigns and the organizations covering them" (Carr and Stelter 2008, B1). The growth of YouTube and Facebook as new media tools, the rise of new media outlets like *The Huffington Post*, and an increased focus on Internet presence by mainstream media outlets (and political candidates) brought monumental change to information sharing in the mid- to late 2000s. No longer were mainstream media bound to the platforms of the morning newspaper and evening broadcasts (Carr and Stelter 2008). Advances in technology led to the creation of a constant news cycle for all media, not just the cable channels, and resulted in additional competition. As a result of this diversified and ever-present media state, the 2008 presidential election became "a kind of hybrid in which the dividing line between online and off, broadcast and cable, pop culture and civic culture, has been all but obliterated" (Carr and Stelter 2008, B1). The increased competition to break news created a mindset that "pits each against all" (Daly 2012, 458), an environment compounded by the downturn in the mainstream media industry in 2008. By late summer, headlines announcing hundreds of newspaper job cuts became all too common (Sonderman 2012), resulting in the industry struggling to find ways to maintain revenue. This begins to shed light on why the Palin family was splashed across the press the way it was, although there were other reasons for this discursive practice as well. Political analyst Larry Sabato has pointed to Watergate as a turning point when the media began to place heavier scrutiny on the character of political candidates, although some say the shift began in the late 1960s (Sabato 2000; Fink and Schudson 2014). Regardless, by the latter half of the twentieth century, journalists believed that their job was to serve as the "screening committee" for political candidates in order to "[filter] out the weaker or more unlikely contenders" and to let the public know about flaws that could affect the candidates' public service (Sabato 2000, 42). The personal lives of political candidates, including their character traits, generated increasing press scrutiny (Barber 2009; Sabato 2000). Journalists believed this type of coverage was what the public wanted and expected (Sabato 2000).

Going beyond political coverage in particular, the structure of newspaper stories overall had also shifted by the early twenty-first century. Stories were now longer with a greater emphasis on context and analysis, which meant frequently using quotes from official and expert sources (Fink and Schudson 2014; Barnhurst and Mutz 1997). Newspapers began to focus more on "second day stories," rather than one-day events, as this strategy "keeps the story alive and maintains its value in the marketplace, by telling the story better, with greater depth, explanation, and background" (Barnhurst and Mutz 1997, 45). Although differentiating themselves from television is often cited as the reason why newspapers pursued this strategy, other factors must also be considered. Barnhurst and Mutz (1997) suggest that a change in the newspaper industry itself played a role. No longer was it common for cities to have more than one newspaper in town. Even though the competition was now gone, the remaining newspaper wanted to tout itself as providing "complete, authoritative coverage" (47), which meant writing longer and more in-depth stories. In addition, the greater education level of journalists in the early twenty-first century may have prompted more interest in providing analytical and interpretive news stories (Barnhurst and Mutz 1997). Finally, some journalists have said that the complexity of today's global society has made it necessary to provide more explanation to readers (Barnhurst and Mutz 1997). No matter the specific reason for longer media stories, the trend was clearly evident in the 2008 presidential election, which saw some news-papers writing 1,800- to 5,000-word stories about Palin, McCain, Obama, and Democratic vice presidential candidate Joe Biden (The Project for Excellence in Journalism 2009).

With a better understanding of the context of the times, it is now pertinent to analyze Palin's press coverage to generate a more detailed understanding of the discursive strategies that journalists used during her campaign.

PALIN'S NEWSPAPER TRENDS

This analysis involved 228 news articles from 20 states and Washington, D.C., that ran between August 29 and November 6, 2008. This allowed for examination of articles from the day when the selection of Palin as a vice presidential candidate was announced through two days after Election Day to capture reaction to her failed bid.

The fact that this chapter involves analysis of the fewest number of articles from the fewest number of states, when compared to the other cases in this book, is a point worth clarifying. The number of states listed above is misleading because all but a handful of the Palin stories were from wire services. In other words, an Associated Press story that ran in a New Mexico newspaper counted as one result and one state, even though the reality is that daily newspapers across the country use Associated Press material and it's quite likely that one story appeared in assorted newspapers in all 50 states. Therefore, the scope of the Palin data actually is comparative or even larger than the other cases in this book even though the initial statistics seem to indi-cate otherwise. This is an instance where the reality of the real world needs to be taken into consideration along with the statistics. Furthermore, nearly 45 percent of the articles about Palin were stories as opposed to briefs. This compares to 15 percent for Smith and Rankin and 25 percent for Woodhull. Therefore, there was as much data—if not more—in the Palin analysis since journalists wrote longer articles about her than they typically did for the other women. Therefore, the Palin data overall was as comprehensive of a sample as the other women's, if not more so, once the numbers are understood.

The fact that wire services wrote all but a handful of the Palin articles in the data sample is indicative of a journalism culture that has increasingly trans-formed in the past 140 years. As previously noted, Woodhull's and Rankin's coverage exemplified local control and was much more diverse as far as who wrote content. In contrast, Smith's coverage and even more so Palin's illustrate that discourse of national politics has fallen under the control of a few national media organizations in the past 50 years. This shift has placed great discursive power into the hands of a few. The fact that the press favored writing longer stories in 2008 is also important to consider. Was Palin better served than her predecessors because she was more apt to receive lengthier coverage? Was she better served by having nearly all of her press coverage originate from national media organizations that are viewed by the industry as the best and most objective? These points will be explored further throughout this chapter and into the next.

First, however, a few other trends related to the Palin news articles are worthwhile to note. Of the sample analyzed, Palin made the front page 15 percent of the time compared to about 30 percent for Smith and 25 percent for Woodhull and Rankin. This decline is surprising, but one must also consider the context of newspapers during this time. In 2008, editors only selected a handful of stories for the front page as opposed to past practice where as many short articles as possible were placed on the front page of the newspaper. Therefore, there was a much stricter standard for front-page placement in 2008. Daily newspapers were also larger and involved multiple sections, as opposed to the eight-page papers common during Woodhull's time. Therefore, it's difficult to make comparisons concerning front-page placement. However, it is noteworthy that the majority of Palin's front-page coverage occurred within the first two weeks of her joining the Republican ticket, indicating a trend similar to Woodhull's coverage. Palin's articles were in the A section of newspapers, the section considered the most important for news, 75 percent of the time.

Remarkably different from press coverage of prior women politicians, 25 percent of the articles about Palin included a visual of her, compared to 13 percent for Rankin, less than 5 percent for Smith, and zero for Woodhull. Like Rankin, Palin was a newcomer to the national political scene, which likely increased interest in using visuals of her. During this period in journalism history, newspapers overall were more interested in visuals and design, a stark contrast to Woodhull's and even Rankin's days when pages were loaded with text.

What is perhaps the biggest difference in Palin's coverage compared to the other cases, however, is the change in discursive power, or who discussed her candidacy within news articles. Whereas journalists controlled 75 percent of Smith's and Woodhull's framing power, and 85 percent of Rankin's, they accounted for less than 40 percent of Palin's. In other words, journalists were employing an equalizing discursive strategy more often by frequently providing multiple viewpoints, that is, incorporating more sources in their stories. This significant change is illustrative of the journalism culture of the era to not only strive for objectivity but to also heavily rely on experts, officials, and outside sources to help shape their stories. Palin and her supporters comprised 40 percent of her discursive power in articles that mentioned her, while those who opposed her candidacy comprised about 16 percent.

The remaining sources were neutral/did not take a stand for or against Palin. Although it may seem like Palin had an advantage compared to her predecessors, this was not necessarily the case. When discourse from Palin and her supporters is broken down further, Palin herself had relatively the same amount of discursive power as Woodhull and Smith, with direct commentary from Palin included in about 11 percent of the data. The fact that the McCain campaign largely restricted Palin from interacting with the press certainly played a role in this, but it is still interesting to note that, in the course of 140 years, women politicians still largely have little discursive control over their own campaigns.

Statistics aside, Palin's news coverage as a whole could be considered neutral just as Smith's initially appeared to be, particularly when contrasted against Woodhull's negative coverage and Rankin's positive coverage. There were articles that were clearly negative toward Palin, but they were balanced out by those that were positive toward her. The vast majority of articles strived to be neutral, which isn't surprising considering nearly all of the Palin articles came from wire services. However, as was the case with Smith, particular word choices in Palin's news articles raise questions about how objective the discourse actually was.

Six main discursive themes emerged from examination of the Palin news data. As was the case with the three prior women, two of the themes are discourse related to her politics and discourse related to her personal life/traits. Like Woodhull and Rankin, another theme was discourse related to Palin's relationship with the women's movement. Like Rankin and Smith, the Palin data also generated themes related to the historical relevance of the candidacy and to her physical appearance. A new theme to emerge in Palin's news coverage was direct discourse about the sexist nature of her media coverage. This review begins with an examination of Palin the politician.

PALIN AND POLITICS

The discourse about Palin the politician primarily focused on public reaction to her candidacy and on her platform. These trends were also evident in the prior cases examined in this book, although the type of discourse varied.

Unlike Rankin and Smith, there was no emphasis on Palin's campaign effort or strategy. The other women were at the top of their political tickets whereas Palin was the No. 2 behind McCain, so that helps explain the difference. Also unlike Smith, Palin did not have decades of experience in Washington, D.C., a fact that generated a fair amount of news coverage in Palin's case. Interestingly, Smith's wealth of experience should have been a benefit to her campaign but was instead largely ignored by the press and public of the 1960s, suggesting there have been differing discursive tactics used regarding women candidates' level of experience.

There were political similarities between Palin and the other women. Like Smith, Palin's media availability for self-promotion was limited. However, in Palin's case, this was more so due to her handling by the McCain campaign and her joining the campaign just 10 weeks prior to Election Day, as opposed to Smith who chose to put in minimal effort. As was the case with Rankin, reaction to Palin's candidacy included news coverage emphasizing her celebrity, although Rankin generated more respect as a politician. Perhaps most interestingly, Palin's news coverage had similarities to the negative scrutiny that Woodhull encountered nearly 140 years prior. The negative reaction to Palin's candidacy is explored first.

A Polarizing Figure

By far the most prominent negative discourse in Palin's news coverage was the public and press questioning whether she had adequate experience to be vice president. One of the first stories after McCain's selection of Palin as a running mate noted that she was a "40-something candidate with two years in major office and no significant foreign policy experience" (Baker, *The New York Times*, August 30, 2008, A1). The story further said that Palin "spent just two years as governor of a state with a quarter of the population of Brooklyn" and reiterated that she did not have "deep experience." Another story in the same issue of *The New York Times* further emphasized that Palin was not qualified for the job, pointing out her lack of foreign policy experience, her only two years of experience as governor, and her lack of travel outside of the country (Cooper, A1). An Associated Press story said that Palin "has more experience catching fish than dealing with foreign policy or national affairs" (Quinn, *Hutchinson News*, August 30, 2008, A1). The fact that the nation was at war during this time is the reason for the frequent references to foreign affairs. This discourse is also in line with the journalism context of the era in which journalists considered it their job to vet candidates and serve as watchdogs on behalf of the public. Yet this press discourse also served to discursively delegitimize Palin's candidacy from the beginning, which contradicts journalistic goals of promoting democracy and adhering to objectivity. The question then becomes: How do journalists balance these roles? Certainly thinking more about their word choices would help. Snide commentary about Palin having more experience catching fish was not necessary when readers simply could have been told that, as a governor, her role did not involve foreign policy. Providing more historical context also would help. Mentioning that other governors in U.S. history have been on presidential tickets or writing about the prior qualifications of vice presidents would have put Palin's candidacy into a broader context. It is not like Palin was the first governor to enter a presidential campaign or the first candidate who did not have foreign policy experience. Yet the constant discourse about her inexperience made it seem like she was indeed an outlier.

Journalists weren't the only ones questioning Palin's resume. A Republican lobbyist said the right wing would be happy with the selection of Palin, but he also called her "a gamble" (Baker, *The New York Times*, August 30, 2008, A1). Opponents to her candidacy posed the question as to whether Palin needed "the qualifications to immediately step into the role of commander in chief" and called her selection a "desperate, cynical, or dangerous choice, given Ms. Palin's lack of any experience in national security" (Cooper, *The New York Times*, August 30, 2008, A1). In this same story, an Alabama Republican questioned McCain's choice, saying, "We're in a global war, we're in a global economy, so it's less than honest if someone says that this woman is qualified to lead America right now." Obama's campaign staff also emphasized Palin's lack of foreign policy experience and reminded the public she would be "a heartbeat away from the presidency" (Associated Press, *Alton Telegraph*, August 30, 2008, A1). Democratic Wisconsin Governor Jim Doyle used the same discourse, noting Palin would be a "heartbeat away from being commander in chief" and calling McCain's choice of her a "panic pick" (Wehrman, *Madison Wisconsin State Journal*, August 30, 2008, A10). The same wire story quoted Alaska conservative talk radio host Rick Rydell saying it would be "very scary to have someone with such a lack of knowledge and experience . . . one heartbeat away from the presidency."

This repeated "heartbeat" discourse is clearly an emotional discursive strategy intended to instill fear into voters, particularly when combined with mentions of McCain's age. Historically, the vice president of the United States has had a minimal role, with few exceptions, in the running of government. In addition, only 20 percent of the time since the founding of the country has the vice president ascended to the presidency either due to death or resignation. Yet the above discourse is frequently implying that Palin would have a monumental role that she was ill-prepared to handle and that her odds of becoming president were imminent.

The emphasis on Palin's lack of political experience did not fade after the initial announcement of her joining the Republican ticket. In September, news articles told readers that Palin "got her first passport last year," thereby suggesting she had limited world experience, and questioned whether she would "display enough command of the issues to convince voters that she is qualified to move into the Naval Observatory" (Bumiller, *The New York Times*, September 18, 2008, A24; "The Mayor," *The New York Times*, September 29, 2008, A17). Another story said she received "a crash course in running for vice president," which suggests to readers she doesn't even know how to secure the job let alone maintain it (Espo, *Daily Sitka Sentinel*, September 16, 2008, A1). Palin's infamous interviews with CBS anchor Katie Couric also generated a number of news stories. One noted that Palin "struggled through her questions about her foreign policy credentials during an interview with CBS News," while another said the interviews "have raised questions about her grasp of the issues" (Nagourney, *The New York Times*, September 26, 2008, A1; Seelye, *The New York Times*, October 2, 2008, A26). One journalist wrote that Palin was "starting to seem very, very vulnerable" while noting her "stumbling interview" with Couric (Associated Press, *Amarillo Globe News* September 30, 2008, B4). The press also reported that the McCain campaign "tightly limits Ms. Palin's availability to the traveling press corps" and "limits her exposure to the news media," thereby suggesting the campaign itself did not think she was experienced enough (Bosman, *The New York Times*, October 19, 2008, 25; "McCain, Palin," *Syracuse Post Standard*, September 11, 2008, A9).

Not surprisingly, after weeks of discourse among the press and public officials on the matter, voters also began to recycle and reproduce the discourse that questioned Palin's experience. A substitute teacher and homemaker interviewed by the *Lawrence Journal World* in Kansas said she liked Palin, but was "a little worried that she doesn't have a ton of experience" (Riley, *Lawrence Journal World*, September 12, 2008, A5). An information technology consultant interviewed in the same story said he was "leery" that the McCain campaign was limiting Palin's media access and seemingly keeping her "on a script." Interviews with Long Island, New York, residents led one reporter to determine that Palin "stood out as a polarizing figure. A few voters proclaimed themselves fans, while more characterized her as an unprepared running mate" (Lambert, *The New York Times*, October 26, 2008, LI1). Specifically, an 80-year-old retired nurse said she would have voted for McCain if Palin wasn't on the ticket: "It's not because she's a woman, but she's certainly not ready" (LI6). A real estate agent told the same reporter, "If something happened to McCain, Palin is not ready. I'd like to have a woman, but not Palin" (LI6). In early October 2008, the Associated Press reported poll results that found "just 25 percent of likely voters believe Palin has the right experience to be president" (Associated Press, *Daily Herald Suburban Chicago*, October 2, 2008, 13).

This poll is interesting considering Palin was running for vice president, not president. Yet so much of the discourse surrounding Palin's candidacy focused on whether she was qualified to be president even though there were low chances of that happening. These poll results are indicative of the power of the discourse of the press, which is why it is so important to study press coverage and strive to improve its discourse. In Palin's case, journalistic discourse certainly seems to have played a significant role in delegitimizing her as a candidate. Voters who repeated the press discourse that Palin was unqualified further cemented the delegitimization of her candidacy.

In a rare story that included Palin defending herself, she said that she was ready to be president if necessary. When ABC News anchor Charlie Gibson pressed her on her foreign policy credentials, Palin said she had never met a head of state, adding, "If you go back in history and if you ask that question of many vice presidents, they may have the same answer that I just gave you" (Associated Press, *Indiana Gazette*, September 12, 2008, A13). Now, one could go back to the Alabama Republican's comment that the United States was now in a global war and a global economy and, therefore, past vice presidential resumes were irrelevant. However, one also has to question how many vice presidents were qualified to address the major issues of their particular era and how many of them were prepared to assume the presidency. Again, this is why historical context is so important in order to put the times into perspective. Yet historical reference was virtually absent throughout Palin's press coverage, with the exception of a few brief mentions of Dan Quayle, "a barely known senator from Indiana," who was selected as the running mate on George H. W. Bush's winning ticket 20 years earlier (i.e. Cooper, *The New York Times*, August 30, 2008, A1).

Just days before the election, the press still made note of Palin's inexperience, using discourse such as "Obama is a relative newcomer to national politics, Gov. Sarah Palin even more so" (Healy, *The New York Times*, November 2, 2008, AR1). The level of scrutiny that Palin faced regarding her readiness to serve in national office was not something that the other pioneer women politicians featured in this study had to endure. Rankin's news coverage touted her ability to serve, with discourse noting she was "reputed to be a real student of public affairs over a pretty wide range of phases, [and] an effective speaker" (*The Washington Times*, November 9, 1916, 6). Smith, who served in Congress as long as Lyndon Johnson did and belonged to prominent committees, also did not face scrutiny over her resume. In Woodhull's case, the press was too busy criticizing her platform and her personal character and had no intention of seriously weighing her as a candidate.

None of the articles in the Palin sample discussed the challenges that women face to gain the credentials that would make them "president worthy," so to speak. These stories possibility existed in other press coverage, yet were not present in this sample. Instead, in an era of infotainment, the press devoted space to highlighting a simpler form of discourse: the rise of Palin's celebrity.

Rising Star on the Right

The discourse about Palin the politician wasn't all negative. The press also wrote about her popularity with crowds and how her selection as a vice presidential running mate boosted the Republican Party, thereby adding a different kind of emotional discursive strategy to her coverage. This strategy of benign discourse often emphasizes the popularity of a female politician rather than the substance of her campaign. Immediately after her selection, *The New York Times* noted that she was a "rising star on the right" and that she "electrified" the Republican National Convention (Baker, August 30, 2008, A1; Bumiller, September 4, 2008, A1). She was credited with "the resulting jolt of energy among Republican voters" and was said to have "dominated the [political] stage" the week after joining the race (Nagourney, *The New York Times*, September 12, 2008, A1; Zeleny, *The New York Times*, September 10, 2008, A20). The Associated Press reported that Palin "rocked the GOP convention with a star-turning performance" (Johnson, *Bedford Gazette*, September 4, 2008, 5). Within a week of her addition to the Republican ticket, the press noted Palin was greeted at an outdoor rally in Michigan "like an international celebrity as rock music blared and the crowd chanted" her name (Bumiller, *The New York Times*, September 6, 2008, A13). This repeated discursive emphasis on celebrity is indicative of the celebrity culture that dominated the 2000s. Yet it was also a strategy that served to legitimize Palin to some extent by building up credibility that she was personally popular, even if detractors did not necessarily think she was professionally qualified.

Local journalists used this same celebritization strategy in their stories. In Alabama, the *Athens News Courier* quoted a local Republican official who said there was a rush for campaign signs after Palin joined the presidential ticket (Cole, September 9, 2008, A4), thereby indicating her popularity. In Pennsylvania, the *Tribune-Democrat* reported that Palin would "get a rock star's welcome" as "at least 6,000 people" were expected to attend her speech (Faher, October 10, 2008, A1). In New Mexico, a *Roswell Daily Record* headline said "Palin's Visit Fires Up GOP," while the story noted her visit "rallied a crowd of more than 10,000 supporters" (Toney, October 21, 2008, A1, A6). It's interesting to note that, when there were local press stories, they were generally positive about Palin, which is in line with what Rankin encountered as well. However, unlike Rankin's case, the national press set the dominant discursive tone for Palin's campaign rather than the local press. This begs the question of whether the local press is too lenient or the national press is too tough. The answer is perhaps both. This is not to say the national press did not cover Palin's popularity. Besides the above examples, *The New York Times* also wrote about a group of Palin fans at a political rally who were chanting her name ("The '08 Campaign," November 4, 2008, A1). In addition, a teaser in the newspaper described Palin as a "hometown heroine" to Alaskans, while one of her former Alaskan opponents was quoted as saying "she wouldn't have articulated one coherent policy and people would be fawning all over her" ("On nytimes.com," *The New York Times*, September 5, 2008, A4; Yardley, *The New York Times*, August 30, 2008, A1). Yet certainly the national press articles in the sample were far more critical of Palin than the few local press articles were. In a way, this makes sense since the national media cover these candidates day after day, whereas a campaign stop is a special event for individual towns and their local press. The discrepancy is still noteworthy, however, and suggests that national politicians would be wise to make more time for the local press.

It is also interesting to note that the press, politicians, and public were "celebritizing" Palin at the same time they were questioning her credentials, as was described in more detail above. When considered together, the contrasting discursive strategies used with Palin seemingly suggest that it was fine for her to be a cheerleader and a face for the cause, yet she should not be considered a serious political player in the game. This certainly differed from Rankin's celebrity status, which considered her to be a legitimate politician as well as a celebrity. Then again, one must consider the difference in what it meant to be a celebrity between 1916 and 2008. By 2008, reality television and YouTube meant anyone had the potential to become a celebrity, particularly if they were viewed as unusual/unique, and their personality or back story was the draw, not any kind of particular stance or message. Indeed, a "Saturday Night Live" sketch that mimicked Palin drew more than 5 million hits on YouTube and NBC's website, and the press noted that Palin "has become a favorite character, for lack of a better term, for SNL" (Stelter, *The New York Times*, September 17, 2008, E2; Stelter, *The New York Times*, October 11, 2008, A13). The Drudge Report referred to the "Sarah Show," a discourse that again made Palin into more of a character than a woman seriously vying for the second-biggest job in the nation (Stelter, *The New York Times*, October 4, 2008, A15). This goes back to the commentary by David Carr and Brian Stelter about the blurred lines between pop culture and civic culture during this time. Even the politicians themselves were caught between these blurred lines, as Palin further fed into her celebrity status by appearing on "Saturday Night Live" as herself. She not only appeared in an opening sketch wearing the same clothing that comedian Tina Fey wore when mimicking her, but also joined another sketch: "She joined in a rap routine that made fun of Senator John McCain's smile, and she cheerfully waved her arms in the air when the chant ordered 'all the mavericks in the house' to raise their hands" (Bosman, *The New York Times*, October 19, 2008, 25). Clearly Palin wanted to appear good-natured about her celebrity status as well as garner additional publicity for the campaign. Yet activities such as this, combined with the prior questions of her suitability for office, further legitimized the discourse that she was more of a celebrity than a serious politician. This is not to suggest that Palin is the reason the Republicans lost the election.

As previously discussed, the context of 2008 played the decisive hand in Obama's victory. Yet it is interesting to consider the following:

After McCain and Palin lost the election, an Associated Press writer referred to Palin as among the "prospective White House hopefuls" and "GOP rising stars" (Sidoti, *Daily Herald Suburban Chicago*, November 6, A6). The fact that Palin has not resumed a serious bid for the White House since, however, is telling. The discursive strategies used in the press to define her in the 2008 election also made it difficult for her to be taken seriously as a candidate in the future. This is yet another instance of how the discursive constructions of women candidates compound over time, serving to both advance and regress the cause of women in politics. Before examining discourse about Palin in the broader context of the women's movement, one more aspect of Palin the politician will be briefly addressed: press discourse of her platform.

Drill, Baby, Drill

Discourse regarding Palin's platform was more specific and wide ranging than that of Rankin's and Smith's and, therefore, was more similar to Woodhull's. Yet, unlike Woodhull whose platform was largely criticized in the press, Palin's platform was usually simply stated, indicative of the objectivity norm of the press of the time. Therefore, Palin's case illustrates the press has placed a greater emphasis on providing readers with more diverse and less-opinionated information about a woman candidate's platform, which is important for both the candidates and voters and illustrates an improved discursive strategy in this area.

One of the more recognizable tenants of Palin's platform was her own discursive strategy to frame herself as a reformer who was anti-establishment. The press also shared this discourse, noting Palin was "bluntly critical of her party's leadership" and that she advocated for transparent and responsive government (Yardley, *The New York Times*, August 30, 2008, A1). Palin was described as "a little-known conservative newcomer who relishes fighting the establishment" (Associated Press, *Alton Telegraph*, August 30, 2008, A1). Another story mentioned Palin's "populist mockery of Beltway elites and what she has called 'the permanent political establishment'" (Tanenhaus, *The New York Times*, November 6, 2008, P1). She was said to have a "growing reputation as a maverick for bucking her party's establishment and Alaska's powerful oil industry" (Quinn, *Hutchinson News*, August 30, 2008, A3). Considering Gallup reported in July 2008 that congressional approval was 14 percent, "the lowest congressional job approval rating in the 34-year Gallup Poll history of asking the question" (Saad 2008), Palin's platform as an outsider seemed to be to her benefit. However, "the permanent political establishment," including the media, also viewed this outsider status as inexperience, as was described already. As a result, Palin's anti establishment platform grew to include the media, which she relished criticizing: "I've learned quickly these past few days that if you're not a member in good standing of the Washington elite, then some in the media consider a candidate unqualified for that reason alone" (Bumiller, *The New York Times*, September 4, 2008, A1). Other stories noted that Palin had criticized journalists' questions and "jabbed at the news media" (Stelter, *The New York Times*, October 9, 2008, C3; Associated Press, *Orange Leader*, September 4, 2008, 6A). This was a discursive strategy on Palin's part to delegitimize their coverage of her in an effort to increase her credibility with voters. Yet the press, particularly *The New York Times*, questioned how anti establishment she really was and, in so many words, noted she was a flip-flopper on the subject of congressional earmarks (i.e. Yardley, *The New York Times*, August 30, 2008, A1; Zeleny, *The New York Times*, September 10, 2008, A20; Cooper, *The New York Times*, September 13, 2008, A1; Powell, *The New York Times*, October 22, 2008, A22). In other words, the press was telling voters that Palin's discourse was simplified and her actions in the past weren't reflective of what she was saying now. This was the most noticeable instance of the press discursively delegitimizing Palin's platform. Other coverage of her platform focused on simply telling voters where Palin stood.

For instance, another prominent aspect of Palin's platform was her advocacy of energy development, with "drill, baby, drill" becoming her recognizable catchphrase (i.e. "The '08 Campaign," *The New York Times*, November 4, 2008, A1). The press wrote that she promoted offshore oil exploration, mining, pipelines, nuclear plants, clean coal, and alternative energy (Bumiller, *The New York Times*, September 4, 2008, A1; Yardley, *The New York Times*, October 18, 2008, A11; Powell, *The New York Times*, October 22, 2008, A22). Other stories noted that Palin's platform was in line with other conservative ideals of the time, such as fiscal conservativeness, advocacy of gun rights, disapproval of same-sex marriage, and opposition of abortion (Yardley, *The New York Times*, August 30, 2008, A1; Phillips, *The New York Times*, September 8, 2008, A19). Unlike Rankin, Palin was not "running as a woman," and, unlike Smith, voters had a clearer idea as to what Palin was running on. Although Palin's platform received some scrutiny from the press, it was not nearly as scrutinized as Woodhull's platform was in news stories. Therefore, the press appears to be improving in discursive equality in this specific area. One last item worth noting is the press mentioning Palin was a member of Feminists for Life, an anti abortion group. This is noteworthy for the rare mention of feminism in discourse of Palin's campaign. However, as the next section illustrates, the women's movement was certainly a component of the 2008 election.

PALIN AND THE WOMEN'S MOVEMENT

The discourse surrounding Palin's connection to the women's movement was one of the more fascinating findings of this analysis, particularly the press coverage that exhibited similarities to Woodhull's coverage. Although there wasn't a strong women's movement in 2008 like there was during Woodhull's and Rankin's campaigns, a discursive theme still emerged that touched upon old-fashioned tensions and beliefs related to the women's movement. The subcategories within this theme include discourse regarding the relationship between Palin and Hillary Clinton, discourse regarding the women's voting bloc myth, and discourse regarding what women voters hoped Palin would do for them.

Palin and Clinton

The discursive strategy used to discuss the relationship between Palin and Clinton (and their respective supporters) was reminiscent of the contentious relationship between Victoria Woodhull and Susan B. Anthony nearly 140 years earlier. There clearly were Palin and Clinton factions during the campaign season even though the two women offered some praise for the other. Following Palin's addition to the Republican ticket, Clinton released a statement saying:

> We should all be proud of Gov. Sarah Palin's historic nomination, and I congratulate her and Sen. McCain. While their policies would take America in the wrong direction, Gov. Palin will add an important new voice to the debate. (Associated Press, *Alton Telegraph*, August 30, 2008, A7)

Clinton clearly knew that she was expected to release a comment on the matter due to her status as the nation's most prominent woman politician. With this statement, Clinton is acknowledging both Palin's role in the advancement of women in politics and the importance of women's political progress. However, Clinton is also using discourse that is careful not to offer too much legitimized support to Palin's campaign and that establishes clear boundaries between Clinton's views and Palin's. Palin was initially less cautious in her discourse about Clinton and offered praise for the former presidential contender, even while establishing a new Palin faction: "Hillary left 18 million cracks in the highest, hardest glass ceiling in America, but it turns out the women of America aren't finished yet, and we can shatter that glass ceiling once and for all" (Cooper, *The New York Times*, August 30, 2008, A1). This statement draws from the "18 million cracks" commentary that Clinton made when ending her presidential campaign, commentary that was included at the very beginning of this book. Through this discourse, Palin was making "an explicit appeal to the disappointed supporters" of Clinton by offering women a new way to make history through her (Cooper, *The New York Times*, August 30, 2008, A1).

Yet it soon became clear that there would be no official joining of the old Clinton and new Palin factions just as Anthony was not about to give in to the establishment of Woodhull's new political faction in 1872. Clinton supporter and Wisconsin Lieutenant Governor Barbara Lawton said, "Hillary Clinton supporters know that this is no change for women to have Sarah Palin on the ticket" (Wehrman, *Wisconsin State Journal*, August 30, 2008, A10). Similarly, a political pollster said she did not think Clinton supporters would back Palin due to the women's differences on issues. The pollster added that "I don't think before today I would have ever heard someone call her [Palin] a feminist" (Yardley, *The New York Times*, August 30, 2008, A1). It's interesting to note that this was another rare direct mention of feminism in the news stories about Palin analyzed. The rare usage of the term is illustrative of the negative connotations of the word during this time. Regardless, feminism and the women's movement were certainly in play during the 2008 election even though the specific terms weren't used, as evidenced by the discursive battle between the Clinton and Palin camps. This discourse is also indicative that the journalistic culture in the 2000s had similarities to the journalistic culture in the 1870s, with the press of both eras providing readers with partisan political entertainment.

Clinton supporters continued to make clear that they would not join Palin's faction and that they were insulted by any suggestion that the two women were peers. *The New York Times* wrote that "Mrs. Clinton's friends said she was galled that Ms. Palin might try to capitalize on a movement that Mrs. Clinton of New York built among women in the primaries" (Healy, September 1, 2008, A15). Again, the similarities to Anthony and Woodhull are striking. This commentary is the discursive equivalent to when Anthony shut off the convention lights on Woodhull so that Woodhull would stop trying to convert the base that Anthony had originally worked to establish. The *Times* story provided further comments from offended Clinton supporters that drove the point in further. Clinton's former political director said, "It is insulting to compare Hillary's lifetime of service and her commitment to progressive causes with that of a novice, right-wing governor." Like Clinton, Anthony also was not happy that a newcomer with so-called wild ideas was trying to steal the show from a seasoned veteran. Clinton advisers said that Clinton would take a more active role campaigning for Obama now that Palin was in the political mix and that Clinton "would focus her efforts especially on working women . . . in swing states" (Healy, *The New York Times*, September 1, 2008, A15). Similarly, in so many words, Anthony voiced her support for Woodhull's opponents rather than for Woodhull.

Another flare-up in the Clinton/Palin relationship occurred a few weeks later. Palin planned to attend a protest against Iran outside of the United Nations, which prompted Clinton to cancel her plans to attend (Bumiller, *The New York Times*, September 18, 2008, A24). A Clinton spokeswoman said the event "was never billed to us as a partisan political event," while a Palin spokesperson said "the danger of a nuclear Iran is greater than party or politics" (Bumiller, *The New York Times*, September 18, 2008, A24). The story further noted that Clinton "has been careful to avoid a potential showdown with Ms. Palin," even though it's evident that this was already happening via the discursive choices that Clinton and her supporters were making to delegitimize Palin's campaign. As for Palin, she stopped praising Clinton within a few weeks of campaigning when this type of discourse "received boos from Republican audiences" (Washington Post, *Cedar Rapids Gazette*, September 13, 2008, A2). Yet, lest Clinton and her supporters be seen as the only aggressors, it must be noted that Palin wasn't entirely innocent in the discursive feud. The press noted that Palin had previously criticized Clinton's "whining" about sexism:

> When I hear a statement like that coming from a woman candidate with any kind of perceived whine about that excess criticism or maybe a sharper microscope put on her, I think "Man, that doesn't do us any good, women in politics or women in general, trying to progress in this country," she [Palin] said earlier this year. (Washington Post, *Cedar Rapids Gazette*, September 13, 2008, A2)

This discourse is certainly ironic because Palin and her supporters would soon be calling out the media for sexist coverage as well, as will be discussed later in this chapter. Still, the discursive tension between the Palin and Clinton factions is indicative that women do not necessarily share the same views just because they are politically involved or because they belong to the same era's women's movement. Although this may seem like common sense, the following discussion illustrates that myths can be stronger than sense.

The Women's Bloc

The assumed existence of a women's voting bloc is a myth that formed in the years before suffrage (Freeman 2000). The myth was immediately dispelled after women received the right to vote and did not band together and vote the same way, as historians, politicians, and other men expected them to do. Yet the idea of a women's political bloc has continued to persist and is now a long-running historical myth, defined as "the acceptance as fact for which belief is strong and evidence is skimpy" (Freeman 2000, 2). Why does the belief continue despite the lack of evidence? As Freeman explains, "Myths don't just happen. They are created to serve a purpose, usually the legitimation of one's actions or the delegitimation of opponents . . . myths survive because their exponents want to believe them" (2).

During the 2008 presidential election, the belief in the women's bloc myth was on full discursive display. Certainly McCain, whose campaign was fumbling with fundraising and staffing issues, wanted to believe that adding a woman to the ticket would give him a boost with women voters. A story written by *The Washington Post* that appeared in the *Cedar Rapids Gazette* said as much: "The McCain campaign is nonetheless trying to use Palin's selection to lure female voters, especially independents and Democrats who backed Clinton in the Democratic primaries" (September 13, 2008, A2). The myth also percolated into discourse by other journalists and campaign officials. The selection of Palin as McCain's running mate was described in *The New York Times* as "an unabashed bid for [Clinton] supporters" (Baker, August 30, 2008, A1), thereby stating the expectation that voters would simply shift to another woman candidate. Clinton political advisers also lent credence to the myth by saying they "expected that a bloc of her female supporters would give Mr. McCain a second look because of Ms. Palin" (Healy, *The New York Times*, September 1, 2008, A15). Another *New York Times* story said "it was far from clear" if adding Palin to the ticket would attract Clinton supporters (Cooper, August 30, 2008, A1). Although this may seem like it is downplaying the myth, this discursive choice leaves room for the concept of the women's bloc to go either way, therefore still suggesting the possibility of its existence.

Discourse of the women's bloc continued throughout September, as Republicans were said to be "making a new appeal to women with the addition" of Palin (Healy, *The New York Times*, September 4, 2008, A22). This is reminiscent of the former Republican chairman who thought that Margaret Chase Smith's candidacy could potentially "bring us the suffragettes and the old maids" (*Greenfield Recorder Gazette*, April 11, 1964, 3). When put as bluntly as that, the discourse seems ridiculous. Yet versions of it continued in 2008 and were viewed as legitimate discourse. One story said the McCain/Palin camp "has been aggressively courting women and others who supported Mrs. Clinton's presidential candidacy" (Bumiller, *The New York Times*, September 18, 2008, A24). Kansas Senator Sam Brownback was among those who "believed Palin would help McCain court women voters, including disaffected supporters" of Clinton (Green, *Hutchinson News*, September 1, 2008, A13). An Associated Press story said Palin had a chance to present herself as "a strong-willed reformer and a solid conservative with appeal to women, including" Clinton supporters (Taylor, *Clearfield Progress*, September 3,

2008, A3). Days later, another Associated Press story noted "Palin will be counted on to help McCain win votes from white women, those so-called 'soccer moms' who make up an important group of swing voters" (Seewer, *Sandusky Register*, September 12, 2008, A8). Palin was also described as "a draw for female votes" (Espo, *Daily Sitka Sentinel*, September 16, 2008, A1). Notably, this discourse tapered off toward the end of the month, and it is likely not a coincidence that this coincided with polling results that found the selection of Palin as McCain's running mate (and the selection of Biden to Obama's ticket) "had little effect on the race" ("Poll," *Harrisonburg Daily News Record*, September 24, 2008, A5). Myth busted, but a myth that has existed for this long surely is not yet gone for good.

Even before the poll results, there was some resistance to the women's bloc concept. At least some women voters voiced their disagreement of its promotion by saying that the selection of Palin "could be seen as patronizing, a suggestion that women would vote based on sex rather than on positions" (Cooper, *The New York Times*, August 30, 2008, A1). Voter Mary Ann Mazzola was among those who wasn't swayed by the addition of a woman to McCain's ticket: "I'm for women and equality, but the thought of her a heartbeat away is too much," she said (Lambert, *The New York Times*, October 26, 2008, LI1). Yet even though real women voters said they weren't swayed by gender, a number of political officials continued promoting the bloc myth, as was discussed above. Some Democrats downplayed the myth with then-Massachusetts Senator John Kerry saying women "would not be 'seduced' by the Republican ticket" (Healy, *The New York Times*, September 1, 2008, A15), while Obama advisers disagreed with the argument that "Clinton supporters might be drawn to Ms. Palin on the basis of sex, given that Ms. Palin opposes abortion rights and other commonly held positions for Democrats" (Healy, *The New York Times*, September 1, 2008, A15). Yet even these discursive counterattacks to the bloc myth did not stop it from being touted early in the campaign season.

One could point to the candidacy of Rankin to argue that a women's bloc existed or that the idea has some merit, particularly since past news coverage of Rankin's campaign included discourse indicating as much, such as "every woman is said to have taken a vow to vote for her" (*The Sun*, October 12, 1916, 4). Yet one cannot get too caught up in the gender aspect of this discourse as Rankin had bigger factors in her corner: statewide (and some national) name recognition, an active statewide campaign, a political message that appealed to both genders, and evidence that she could produce political results for Montana through her role securing suffrage. If Jane Doe had run in that same election, she would not have won. Rankin won not simply because she was a woman but because she was a good politician who appealed to both male and female Montana voters. She could not have won without the male vote as well. Therefore, press hype of a women's bloc during Rankin's campaign greatly underestimates Rankin's political skill.

Putting aside the concept of the mythical women's bloc for a moment, the fact that Palin was being touted as a draw for women voters is problematic in itself because it suggests that only women would consider voting for another woman when this is clearly not true. The next section covers discourse (and the lack thereof) of what women voters did want in a political candidate.

Palin and the Third Wave

The final subcategory within this women's movement theme is notable for the limited discourse about what women (and men) thought of Palin's platform or what they wanted from her as a potential vice president. This contrasts with Woodhull's and Rankin's coverage, which included commentary from members of the women's movement about their candidacies. A few stories in the data touched upon Palin and the third wave. One *New York Times* story said McCain's selection of Palin as a running mate was among the "landmark moments in the debate about work/family balance" (Allen, September 21, 2008, C13), which is a prominent concern among feminists in the twenty-first century. Yet, on the other hand, the "landmark" commentary is also interesting because it is indicative that work/family balance is viewed as a women's issue that only women politicians can address. John McCain has seven children, two more than Palin, yet it was the selection of Palin that prompted the landmark moment in work/family balance? Again, by using this type of discursive strategy, men can continue to be "off the hook," so to speak, for addressing certain voter concerns. This discursive strategy also assumes that all women candidates will be interested in "women's issues," even though this certainly was not the case with Margaret Chase Smith.

An Associated Press story with the headline "Some Moms Are Asking: Would Palin Help Us As VP?" was the only in-depth story about women, Palin, and issues deemed to be women's. The story noted that "Palin is a working mother herself, something that women voters across the political spectrum have noted with genuine excitement" (*Harrisonburg Daily News Record*, October 7, 2008, B5). The journalist wrote that there were women who wanted to know how Palin felt about paid maternity leave, expanded family leave, flexible work hours, and health care. One Chicago female voter was particularly critical about Palin's lack of discourse about these issues: "Where is she on all of this? I just don't feel any empathy from her as a woman . . . I've heard her say nothing about fair pay, about family medical leave. I don't hear her coming out with any strong stance on any of these family issues" (*Harrisonburg Daily News Record*, October 7, 2008, B5). Again, what is interesting here is the expectation from a woman that a woman politician would take a clear interest in issues labeled as women's issues. Since this book did not examine McCain's campaign coverage, it's not clear to what extent McCain was also pressed about "women's" issues. However, it is still interesting that—nearly 100 years after Rankin's congressional victory—the expectation that a woman candidate should "run as a woman" still existed in 2008. Further evidence of this continued conceptualization of "woman candidate" is apparent in discourse from the MomsRising group, which expressed its concern that "Palin hasn't shared her positions on the hot-button issues concerning working women" (Associated Press, *Harrisonburg Daily News Record*, October 7, 2008, B5). Perhaps this group had already been told the positions of McCain and Obama, but one wonders if Biden was asked for his positions on issues concerning working women or if Palin's views were wanted simply because she was a woman. Other discourse centered on criticizing Palin for going back to work right after giving birth—with one Denver woman saying it sent a "wrong message" to other mothers—and for running for office at all since she had five children, including a pregnant teenaged daughter and a baby with special needs (Associated Press, *Harrisonburg Daily News Record*, October 7, 2008, B5). One questions whether a male candidate with the same family situation would have been told to not run for office. This type of discourse is tied to strong emotional beliefs about proper gender roles for men and women and serves as a legitimizing (and simplifying) tool to maintain separate spheres. Therefore, it is a difficult discourse to overcome since it is rooted in an emotional foundation. However, Palin and her supporters soon began fighting back against what they saw as sexist discourse against her. This direct attempt to delegitimize differing standards for women in politics is a newer discursive strategy that was not found in the prior case studies. This strategy is discussed next.

PALIN AND SEXISM

Although only a handful of articles in this analysis directly discussed Palin and sexism, the articles illuminated that this was a broader conversation at the time, hence why the subject is also addressed here. The fact that sexism was openly discussed at all in press stories is noteworthy and indicative that at least a segment of society wanted to see change in the discourse surrounding women in politics. This is important because there cannot be potential for change until concerns are raised about a particular issue. To return to the framework of Murray (2010), this is related to the double bind of silence or shame. This means that gendered discourse continues if women remain silent, yet if they speak up about gender bias, they are criticized, which places women politicians in another lose-lose situation. Therefore, Palin's press discourse is important because sources other than Palin herself were criticizing this double bind and indicating it needed to change, thus adding broader legitimacy to the argument.

In Palin's case, these concerns became apparent within a week of her addition to the Republican ticket. McCain campaign officials complained "that the news media has launched a sexist smear campaign against" Palin (Bumiller, *The New York Times*, September 4, 2008, A23). Former New York mayor and Republican presidential candidate Rudy Giuliani specifically criticized those "who have questioned whether Ms. Palin will have enough energy to focus on the vice presidency as the mother of five" (Bumiller, *The New York Times*, September 4, 2008, A23). In the same story, Giuliani is quoted as saying, "How dare they question whether Sarah Palin has enough time to spend with her children and be vice president . . . How dare they do that? When do they ever ask a man that question?" (Bumiller, *The New York Times*, September 4, 2008, A23). The following day, another story on the matter ran that quoted a Republican official saying the party "will not stand by while Sarah Palin is subjected to sexist attacks" (Herman, *Syracuse Post Standard*, September 5, 2008, A7). No specific examples were given, but the official said the party would not repeat the mistakes the Democrats made by not defending Clinton enough. Another direct reference to sexism appeared in October, when there was uproar over the cost of Palin's campaign trail clothing, an issue that will be discussed in more detail shortly. Those who defended Palin said "the issue was tainted with sexism, given that male politicians often spend thousands of dollars on suits" (Healy, *Indiana Gazette*, October 23, 2008, A9). The party wagons were circling in defense of Palin, a phenomenon that female politicians of the past no doubt would have found astounding since gendered stereotypes and news frames toward them were an embedded and legitimated discursive strategy. Clearly, some progress has been made in discourse about women in politics even though the accusations of sexism indicate there is still a ways to go toward discursive equality.

Just as interesting as the Republicans accusing the outside world of being sexist toward Palin was the criticism right back at the McCain campaign for also being sexist toward Palin. CNN anchor Campbell Brown "slammed the campaign for sequestering Gov. Sarah Palin" from the media and said the campaign needed to "stop treating Sarah Palin like she is a delicate flower who will wilt at any moment" (Seelye, *The New York Times*, September 25, 2008, A24). Brown called this "chauvinistic treatment" and further said, "The McCain campaign says that if she were a man, the media would not be treating her this way . . . So it's fair of me to ask, if she were a man, would they be coddling her this way? (Seelye, *The New York Times*, September 25, 2008, A24). Brown was not letting the McCain campaign simplify the sexist discourse and was pointing out that it was a two-way street. If the media are to change their discourse, politicians themselves also need to change theirs. Palin also took heat for contributing to her own sexist discourse. Diane Stafford of McClatchy criticized Palin for winking during the vice presidential debate, saying "many professional women could almost hear plywood being nailed on top of the glass ceiling" (Stafford, *Syracuse Post Standard*, October 19, 2008, D2). Stafford further said: "Can you imagine any woman being interviewed for a corporate job winking at her interviewers? In a professional setting, it would be tantamount to saying, 'I may not have the answer, but aren't I cute?'" (Stafford, *Syracuse Post Standard*, October 19, 2008, D2). At a time when men were discussing Palin's body and critics were dismissing her "as a Barbie doll, the female equivalent of an empty suit," Stafford did not think Palin's action was helpful to combating sexist discourse. She noted that women candidates faced a different standard than men and that women need to work harder to end sexist stereotypes. This discourse is interesting because it places responsibility on women in politics to end their own sexist discourse rather than also shining light on the role that men and even other women play in perpetuating sexist discourse. In other words, it is an oversimplification of the problem, as if sexist discourse will simply disappear if a woman political candidate behaves absolutely perfectly (whatever behaving perfectly even means). Essentially, women candidates are being told it's their own fault. Certainly this troublesome view has far-reaching consequences.

However, problematic as this is, there is one silver lining in the discourse about sexism in Palin's news coverage. Although it did not end gendered news framing or the double binds faced by Palin and women candidates overall, it is a remarkable shift that signals a desire for change and a frustration with the different standards for women candidates. This illustrates progress has occurred in recent history, when compared to the other historical cases in this study. This type of discourse is necessary to attract greater public and media attention to the problems of discursive gender inequality. Furthermore, this discourse is indicative of changes in social and journalistic cultures. The fact that journalists published metadiscourse—or "journalism about journalism, where audiences are drawn into debates regarding journalistic practice" (Thomas and Finneman 2013, 173)—indicates the press was more self-aware of gender bias and willing to quote sources pointing it out. Again, this awareness is important for there to be change. One specific discursive strategy that needs to change dates back to at least Rankin and the 1910s and continued with Palin in the 2000s: discourse regarding the appearance of women politicians.

PALIN'S APPEARANCE

Journalists during Rankin's era placed an emphasis on attractiveness, while journalists during Smith's era focused on clothing and age. Therefore, it is not surprising journalists during Palin's era included discourse on her attractiveness, clothing, and age, continuing a discursive strategy that has become all too embedded in discourse of women politicians and added to the celebritization of Palin.

The New York Times and Associated Press offered a fair share of discourse that centered on Palin's personal appearance. One *Times* story said that "Mr. Obama is suddenly not the freshest and most telegenic figure on the ballot" (Zeleny, September 10, 2008, A20), a comment referencing Palin. Another story discussing the plot of a new book said that it "features a gun-toting television judge with a librarian's sex appeal (can you say Sarah Palin?)" (Stolberg, *The New York Times*, October 19, 2008, ST1). After Palin gave a speech, the Associated Press wrote that Palin "waved at the adoring crowd like the beauty pageant contestant she once was" (*Bedford Gazette*, September 4, 2008, 5). Another story said that "Palin consistently draws large crowds and is considered an attractive and dynamic presence" (Italie, *Daily Sitka Sentinel*, October 31, 2008, 7). The AP also wrote a story headlined "Need Palin Hair for Halloween?" that included tips on how to look like her (*Daily Herald Suburban Chicago*, October 27, 2008, 5). Discursive evidence such as this makes it difficult for the press to defend its press coverage of women candidates and say they are objectively covered. By continuing to use discourse focused on women politicians' physical appearance, these women too often get the "Barbie doll" treatment referenced above where they are not treated seriously and instead are treated like objects. This kind of media treatment does nothing to enhance the democratic ideals that the press claims to uphold and instead legitimizes the trivialization of women candidates.

Journalists certainly weren't alone in this type of discourse as news stories also included quotes from prominent men regarding Palin's appearance. Alaska delegate Ralph Seekins said that Palin was "an attractive lady and that's disarming to a lot of people" (Johnson, *Indiana Gazette*, September 4, 2008, 12). When Palin appeared on "Saturday Night Live," actor Alec Baldwin told her, "You are way hotter in person" (Bosman, *The New York Times*, October 19, 2008, 25). Journalists have a choice of what discourse to include from sources in stories and what comments not to include. Neither of these comments were critical information that readers needed to know. By choosing to include these kinds of comments, journalists are legitimating the discursive emphasis on the appearance of women in politics, thereby prolonging the inequality in coverage of male and female politicians. It's noteworthy to mention that both men and women journalists wrote about Palin's appearance, which is indicative of how ingrained this discourse has become in journalistic culture.

What was most notable of the discourse surrounding Palin's appearance was the coverage of her clothing. *The New York Times* noted that Palin left a hotel "wearing a miniskirt and black go-go boots" (Bosman, October 19, 2008, 25). In the same story, the journalist reported on the red suit and "trademark glasses" that Palin wore during her appearance on "Saturday Night Live." A local *Cedar Rapids Gazette* story said that eye doctors across the country were "having a hard time keeping the Sarah Palin style specs in stock" ("All in Favor," October 1, 2008, E1). The story then went into detail about the price, style, and designer. Another story discussed Halloween clothing in case anyone wanted to dress like Palin for the holiday (Scott, *Altoona Mirror*, October 5, 2008, D1). This discourse is all indicative of the infotainment nature of journalism culture of the time and the celebritization of Palin.

The biggest stories about Palin's clothing came in late October, however. *The New York Times* wrote about a Republican National Committee disclosure that $150,000 was spent on clothing and accessories for Palin and her family (Nagourney, *The New York Times*, October 23, 2008, A23). Following this disclosure, "cable television, talk radio and even shows like 'Access Hollywood' seemed gripped with sartorial fever" over the $75,000 spent at Neiman Marcus and $50,000 spent at Saks Fifth Avenue (Healy, *Indiana Gazette*, October 23, 2008, A9). The story relaying this information was headlined "Palin's Wardrobe Could Hurt Image." Considering the above discourse and the fact that the press has a century's worth of experience focusing on the appearance of women politicians, it is beyond ironic that the media decided to express outrage over Palin's wardrobe. Although the story noted that the high-priced clothing was viewed as problematic due to the bad economy and Palin's stance of shunning elites, this is still a case of damned if you do and damned if you don't, or another double bind for women in politics. The press scrutinizes the appearance of women candidates, yet then criticized Palin when money was spent to maintain this scrutinized appearance. Palin's wardrobe was viewed as problematic, yet, as previously noted, there is a lack of discourse surrounding the thousands of dollars male politicians spend on suits. This legitimizes the differing standards between men and women and is far from the objective and fair ideals that the press claims to uphold. There needs to be equal emphasis on the appearance of men and women or the emphasis should be scrapped altogether.

Interestingly, Palin's age did not attract the same kind of critical discourse that was directed at Smith. Still, there were news stories that made passing references to it. *The New York Times* described Palin as "youthful," while an Associated Press story noted that, at age 44, Palin was three years younger than Obama and "a generation younger than McCain, 72" (Yardley, *The New York Times*, August 30, 2008, A1; Quinn, *Hutchinson News*, August 30, 2008, A1). Although American culture tends to favor youth, this type of commentary may not have helped Palin in light of the repeated discourse questioning if she was experienced enough to be vice president. Another story pointed out that

Palin was younger than two of McCain's seven children, serving to both point out his perceived old age and her perceived youth (Associated Press, *Alton Telegraph*, August 30, 2008, A1). Other stories in the sample simply noted that Palin was 44 and made no other comment regarding her age (i.e. Baker, *The New York Times*, August 30, 2008, A1; Bumiller, *The New York Times*, September 4, 2008, A1; Associated Press, *Orange Leader*, September 4, 2008, A6). Considering the criticism of Smith's "old" age and the coverage of Palin's "youth," one wonders what would be considered the "correct" age for a woman politician appearing on a presidential ticket. As noted in the Smith chapter, age is another one of the double binds for women in politics.

The fact that women politicians' appearance, clothing, and age have become so embedded into journalistic culture in the past century means this discourse won't end anytime soon, unfortunately. Yet this does not mean that efforts should cease to try to change it, for perhaps one day the discursive tide will turn. What should also warrant additional discussion for change is the discursive construction of candidates' families.

PALIN'S PERSONAL TRAITS

Discourse about Palin's personal traits and life included news coverage of her family and references to her as both tough and womanly at the same time. Both Smith and Palin received press coverage grappling with their perceived masculine and feminine personal attributes, although Palin faced far greater scrutiny over her personal life than Smith ever did.

Messy Drama

Like Woodhull, Palin faced intense press coverage that scrutinized her family and her career, again illustrating the similarities between the partisan and watchdog press eras. One news story, headlined "Frenzied Media," described the scrutiny this way:

> The *New York Post* and the *New York Daily News* were camped out in Alaska on Monday gathering every bit of gossip about Sarah Palin they can find. There's so much to cover. Right now, (baseball player) Alex Rodriguez could date an underage stripper, bulk up on steroids and assassinate his bookie and no one in New York would hear about it for eight years. (*Odessa American*, September 6, 2008, A2)

The Associated Press also reported on the mass interest in Palin, writing that "airplanes in Alaska were unloading reporters and political operatives sent to pore through her personal and public life" (*Bedford Gazette*, September 4, 2008 5). This 180-degree shift in journalistic practice from what Smith encountered 50 years earlier is striking. What is also worthwhile to note is that, while the coverage of Woodhull was sensational, it was more event-driven. Coverage came after her mother's police complaint, after her Wall Street firm launched/then closed, after her arrest, etc. With Palin, journalists were taking a proactive stance of searching out potential underlying problems, in line with the journalistic standards of the era that journalists needed to be watchdogs and vet candidates.

This vetting resulted in a plethora of newspaper articles that mentioned Palin's children, a discursive strategy aimed at understanding Palin's character via her family. *The New York Times* wrote that Palin opted not to have an abortion after discovering her baby had Down syndrome (Cooper, August 30, 2008, A1) and reminded readers of this again a few days later when noting "Ms. Palin, a mother of five (including one with Down syndrome)" opposed abortion (Kershaw, September 4, 2008, G1). Palin's daughter, Bristol, bore the brunt of the media coverage, however, after the "stunning disclosure" that the then-17-year-old was unmarried and pregnant (Taylor, *Clearfield Progress*, September 3, 2008, A3). *The New York Times* referred to this as "messy drama" (Bumiller, September 4, 2008, A1), while another *Times* story said Palin "added a quick qualification that might, in another era, have eliminated the potential for embarrassment: the 17-year-old girl was to be married to the 18-year-old father of the baby" (Kershaw, September 4, 2008, G1). The reference to "another era" is an interesting word choice since the above discourse indeed seems like it is from the days of Smith, Rankin, or Woodhull rather than from 2008 when teenage pregnancies were no longer a taboo as they once were. Yet the media continued to bring up the matter (i.e. Bumiller, *The New York Times*, September 2, 2008, A1; Espo, *Alamogordo Daily News*, September 2, 2008, A1; Associated Press, *Roswell Daily Record*, September 3, 2008, A1; Associated Press, *Bedford Gazette*, September 4, 2008, 5). The economic troubles plaguing the press during this time combined with journalists' allegiance to a watchdog role combined with a media shift to infotainment resulted in this explosion of personal coverage during Palin's era that Smith did not endure. In 2008, a candidate's family life was viewed as an open invitation for scrutiny not only to understand the politician's character but also due to the celebrity culture of the 2000s where little was private anymore. However, this certainly raises an ethical question as to how much scrutiny underage children should have to endure in an Internet era where no story ever truly goes away. This discursive emphasis on candidates' families is one the press should not take lightly as ethics must take precedence over sensation.

One other family matter also frequently appeared throughout Palin's coverage. The press carried a number of stories about a public state ethics investigation into whether Palin fired Alaska's public safety commissioner because he would not fire her ex-brother-in-law, a state trooper (i.e. Luo, *The New York Times*, August 30, A13; Wehrman, *Madison Wisconsin State Journal*, August 30, 2008, A10; Bumiller, *The New York Times*, September 2, 2008, A1; Espo, *Alamogordo Daily News*, September 2, 2008, A1; Associated Press, *Bedford Gazette*, September 4, 2008, 5; Associated Press, *The New York Times*, October 4, 2008, A17; MCT News Service, *Odessa American*, October 11, 2008, A7; Associated Press, *Kinston Free Press*, October 15, 2008, A3). Since this matter was related to Palin's conduct as a public official, why the press took an interest in this is clear. What is noteworthy, however, is how little coverage otherwise there was about Palin's governorship. There was so much emphasis on her inexperience that little depth was provided about her actual experience.

The above news discourse about the ethics investigation and candidates' families is more enlightening of journalistic practice of the time than indicative of gendered discourse. Yet it was so prominent in Palin's news coverage that it would be remiss not to mention it. Discourse about Palin's personality, on the other hand, had gendered overtones.

Lipstick and Pitbulls

As was the case with Smith's coverage, the press of 2008 found the masculine/ feminine balance of Palin to be fascinating. The double bind discursive strategy of referring to these women as both tough and womanly at the same time seems to be a discursive struggle between promoting idealized womanhood and illustrating the women's "masculine" qualities. A *Madison Wisconsin State Journal* story headlined "A Portrait of Sarah Barracuda" noted that Palin was "tenacious" as a high school basketball player and had also competed in beauty pageants (Wehrman, August 30, 2008, A10). A *New York Times* story told readers that a grizzly bear hide was draped over Palin's office sofa, that Palin hunted and fished, and that she went back to work three days after giving birth. The same story noted Palin had "warmth and charm" and was "a PTA mom who got involved" (Yardley, *The New York Times*, August 30, 2008, A1). Republican strategist Karl Rove referred to Palin as a "gun-packing, hockey-playing woman," while Obama once described Palin as "mother, governor, moose shooter" (Baker, *The New York Times*, August 30, 2008, A1; Zeleny, *The New York Times*, September 10, 2008, A20). However, the words most commonly associated with Palin in news discourse during the 2008 election were hockey mom, pitbull, and lipstick. A *New York Times* headline described Palin as "A Two-Year Governor, Social Conservative, 'Hockey Mom,'" and the story's lead said she was a self-described hockey mom (Cooper, August 30, 2008, A1). During the Republican convention, Palin said she was "just your average hockey mom," while "delegates waved signs that said, 'I love hockey moms'" (Bumiller, *The New York Times*, September 4, 2008, A1). Another story referred to Palin as "a self-styled 'hockey mom'" (Ohlemacher, *Indiana Gazette*, August 29, 2008, A12). The pitbull/lipstick discourse rose out of the hockey mom comments when Palin said "the difference between a hockey mom and a pitbull" was lipstick (Bumiller, *The New York Times*, September 4, 2008, A1), a discourse that the news services also touted (i.e. Associated Press, *Bedford Gazette*, September 4, 2008, 5; Herman, *Syracuse Post Standard*, September 5, 2008, A7; Espo, *Daily Sitka Sentinel*, September 16, 2008, A1). A month later, the phrase was still in journalistic use as an Associated Press story began with the phrase "long before she became a pitbull with lipstick" (Goldman, *Tribune-Democrat*, October 9, 2008, A8).

Palin herself advocated much of the above discourse, which the press then merely reported. So, this is more her discursive strategy rather than that of the press. It is important to note two points about this strategy. First, this type of discourse was not unique to Palin's vice presidential run; she had utilized it in the past. Second, this strategy was not the same as Smith's staged attempts to appear feminine in the press, such as the time she made blueberry muffins. Rather, this was Palin's real personality. Yet her decision to promote herself as a hockey mom and as a pitbull with lipstick merits the same discussion as the muffin episode. Is it legitimate for a female candidate to use gendered discourse when she feels it will favor her, but then for her to critique when *others* use gendered discourse about her? This is perhaps along the lines of what Smith was referring to when she said "too many women who militantly advocate the Equal Rights Amendment are not willing to give up their special feminine privileges" (*Salisbury Times*, April 11, 1964, 14). To be clear, this is not implying that Palin favored the Equal Rights Amendment. Smith's discourse is simply being used to raise the question of what should and should not be acceptable in terms of gendered discourse and if women indeed need to think about if they have their own double standards of acceptability. If one wants to advocate for true discursive equality, this likely means that women would need to give up using their gender to their advantage, not just stop those who use it to their disadvantage. Again, this is not a matter that will be resolved overnight, and there is not an easy answer to the question of what is true gender discursive equality. Yet these kinds of questions deserve further consideration in a conversation about women and women's history.

On that note, this study now shifts to discuss one final theme that was evident in Palin's news coverage: discourse about her historical relevance.

PALIN'S HISTORICAL RELEVANCE

Like Rankin and Smith, Palin's news coverage included the discursive
strategy of highlighting her history-making political role. In Palin's case,
this type of discourse was most prominent during the first two weeks of her
candidacy. An initial news story about the vice presidential announcement
noted that Palin was "the first woman on a Republican presidential ticket"
as well as "the first woman and the youngest person to hold the Alaska
governorship" (Wehrman, *Madison Wisconsin State Journal*, August 30,
2008, A10). A front-page *New York Times* headline blared "First Woman
on GOP Ticket" (Cooper, August 30, 2008, A1). A story in the *Orange
Leader* said Palin was "claiming her historic place on the Republican ticket"
(Associated Press, September 4, 2008, A6), while another journalist wrote
that "Palin gives voters a chance to make history, too, by electing the first
woman as vice president" (Kuhnhenn, *Ashtabula Star Beacon*, September 7,
2008, A2). Other journalists offered more creative discourse. The Associated
Press wrote in the lead of a story that Palin went from being a "small-town
mayor with a taste for mooseburgers to the governor's office and now—making
history—to John McCain's side as the first female running mate on a
Republican presidential ticket" (Quinn, *Hutchinson News*, August 30, 2008,
A1). Although some could argue that this is an American Dream discursive
strategy that illuminates how Palin started at the bottom and rose to the top,
the journalists' decision to include "with a taste for mooseburgers" is clearly
intended to make Palin seem unusual since this dining option is not common
in the mainland United States. As a result, it distracts from the seriousness
of her breaking a barrier for women in politics by making her resume seem
humorous or strange. In addition, the decision to include the phrase "to John
McCain's side" is noteworthy. The sentence would have been complete without this phrasing by simply saying she was making history as the first female
running mate. Instead, the inclusion of the McCain phrasing results in an
imagery of a little woman standing by her man. This observation may seem
nitpicky, but one questions if journalists wrote about Joe Biden "at Obama's
side." Perhaps so, but it seems unlikely.

Another story with gendered overtones described Palin as "the first
woman running mate on a Republican ticket in history, making her a draw
for female voters" (Espo, *Daily Sitka Sentinel*, September 16, 2008, A1).
The myth that women voters would automatically be in favor of Palin simply due to her gender is discussed in another section of this chapter, yet it's
worthwhile to briefly touch upon here again. The fact that women have had
such limited opportunities to break the glass ceiling of national politics in
the past 140 years has essentially led to a discourse that assumes women
will vote for anyone of their gender simply to make history. This was not

the case with Margaret Chase Smith or Geraldine Ferraro or Hillary Clinton, yet this type of discourse persists as if (a) men wouldn't vote for a woman candidate; only women would, and (b) women, if given the option, would only vote for a woman candidate regardless of the qualifications of the opposing male candidate. This discursive strategy is oversimplification, if not flat out inaccuracy, yet journalists and political candidates have kept the myth alive.

Another story with interesting historical discourse appeared in *The New York Times*. The journalist wrote that Palin's "presence on the ticket will allow Republicans to argue that Mr. Obama would not be the only one to break barriers if elected" and that a woman would be "next in line to the presidency for the first time" (Baker, August 30, 2008, A1). Not surprisingly, the newspaper published corrections a few days later that said the story "referred imprecisely to the historical precedence of Ms. Palin's candidacy" ("Corrections," September 3, 2008, A4). To be fair, the journalist mentioned Ferraro later in the story so he was at least somewhat aware of women's political history. Yet the discursive slip-up in one portion of the story, that Palin was "the first" female vice presidential candidate, indicated a lack of a firm grasp of this history, not only by the reporter but by others on the editorial staff who would have copy edited the story before it went to press. In addition, another correction said the *Times*

> misstated the historical precedence of her [Palin's] candidacy and that of Geraldine Ferraro. Numerous women over the years have run for president and vice president on minor party tickets. Ms. Palin and Ms. Ferraro are not the only women who have been on presidential tickets. ("Corrections," September 3, 2008, A4)

This type of discourse is important to illustrate that Palin was actually part of a long history of women in politics, not just a novelty too far outside the norm. Yet how many people caught this small correction and why couldn't it have appeared in more stories to put Palin's candidacy in broader context? The fact that *The New York Times* was even mixed up and had to run a correction provides a clue as to why. Evidently there has not been much improvement in education regarding women's political history in the past 100 years if even *The New York Times* is struggling to explain it, thereby implying other journalists were likely unaware as well. Also of interest is the fact that few stories mentioned Ferraro at all, and no stories in this data sample mentioned women who ran for the presidency/vice president on minority tickets. As previously noted and reinforced here, there is an evident lack of journalistic discourse and knowledge about the history of women's political progression, hence why this particular study is important.

Beyond journalists' discourse of Palin's historical achievement, there was limited commentary on the matter from other sources. As previously noted, the Associated Press quoted Hillary Clinton as saying, "We should all be proud of Gov. Sarah Palin's historic nomination" (*Alton Telegraph*, August 30, 2008, A7). A statement from Obama and Biden said the selection of Palin "is yet another encouraging sign that old barriers are falling in our politics" (Babington, *Tribune-Democrat*, August 30, 2008, C7). College freshman Billie Carey said that Palin "is breaking down a lot of barriers for women and girls in America. She has certainly shattered the glass ceiling" (Riley, *Lawrence Journal World*, September 12, 2008, A5). Beyond the fact this student seems oblivious that Ferraro came before Palin nearly 25 years prior and that the glass ceiling is primarily associated with the presidency, it's noteworthy that discourse from a voter is included at all since, throughout this study, journalists have predominantly maintained discursive control of the historical commentary. It's unknown if this is because they want to quickly make note of it and move on or if there's some other reason, yet the trend is certainly there.

Overall, Palin's historical discursive theme has more similarities to Smith's than to Rankin's. Discourse about the excitement over Rankin's history-making potential was evident throughout her campaign, whereas historical discourse about Palin and Smith was more prominent at the beginning of their campaigns. (Discourse about Smith as a historical figure also picked up again right before the Republican convention, however.) The difference from Rankin's discourse may be attributed to the hard shift toward objectivity in journalism by the mid-1900s or due to the fact that journalists quickly decided Smith and Palin would not win office and therefore did not think it worthwhile to make much further mention of them as historical figures. Future research that involves interviewing national political reporters may find it worthwhile to ask about this discursive trend.

DISCUSSION

A review of Palin's press coverage during her vice presidential run suggests that discourse about her campaign can be summarized by the following: She was an attractive, inexperienced celebrity with family drama who was incorrectly perceived to be a magic bullet to attract women voters. For those who lived during the 2008 campaign, this narrative should sound familiar. However, this is also an oversimplified discourse, for Palin's press coverage was not just about Sarah Palin but was also about the discursive construction of women politicians of the past and of the future.

Palin's press coverage had much in common with that of her predecessors. Like Woodhull, Palin faced intense press scrutiny over her family life and her political life due to an aggressive journalism culture. Personal family matters were splashed across newspaper pages in an effort to give the public an inside view of the candidates' character in what was a blatant attempt to delegitimize Woodhull's campaign and a masked attempt to provoke questions about Palin's. Yet, in Woodhull's case, an event preceded the critical discourse, whereas journalists in Palin's era actively sought out potential skeletons in her closet. This is indicative of the watchdog and infotainment journalism prominent in the late 2000s, which involved journalists both vetting candidates and treating them like celebrities. In either case, private affairs were viewed as fair game to be made public, a striking difference from the journalism of Smith's era in the early 1960s. Palin's coverage illustrates that even a journalistic discursive precedent set nearly 140 years earlier still had ramifications well into the future. The press of the late 2000s also took an interest in Palin's relationship with the women's movement, just as journalists did with Woodhull and Rankin. The discursive construction of a feud between the Clinton and Palin factions was eerily similar to the feud between Woodhull and Anthony in the 1870s and again was illustrative of the similarities in journalistic culture of both eras.

Despite evidence in the late nineteenth century that the concept of a women's bloc was a myth, the bloc myth continued to percolate more than a century later in Palin's news coverage. Both journalists and politicians used discourse to promote the belief that female supporters of Clinton would automatically switch to Palin simply because Palin was a woman. That this myth was again disproved in the 2000s illustrates yet again that women do not necessarily share the same views just because they are politically involved or because they belong to the same era's women's movement. Simply put, they will not vote for a woman simply because she is a woman. The fact that this belief continued into the 2000s is troublesome as it simplifies and trivializes women in politics, as well as women voters. Just as problematic, this discursive strategy removes men from the equation by suggesting that only women would vote for other women, thereby giving men "permission" to continue discursive inequality toward women politicians. Furthermore, a belief in the existence of a women's bloc, combined with the historical reality that many women like Rankin "ran as a woman" in order to win, perpetuates the assumption that women candidates in recent times will automatically take an interest in "women's" issues. Overall, this gendered discourse serves to continue separate spheres between men and women in politics, making it difficult to achieve discursive equality and fairer treatment of women politicians.

Although Palin's news coverage had much in common with Woodhull's, it also had similarities with Smith's. When candidates like Smith and Palin do not fully fit into the concept of idealized womanhood, the result is a discursive strategy piecing together their "male" attributes with their femininity. This is a double bind as women candidates try to "correctly" balance qualities of both genders to appear tough and competent but to also not spark backlash over their perceived deviation from acceptable gender norms. Both Smith and Palin actively contributed to this dual discursive construction, although in differing ways. This begged the question earlier in this analysis as to whether discursive equality lies not only in ending gendered discourse placing women at a disadvantage, but also ending gendered discourse aimed at giving women an advantage. It is easy to criticize the emphasis on the personal appearance of women politicians. Yet should Smith's muffin baking and Palin's construction of herself as a hockey mom receive the same level of scrutiny for using gender in political discourse? If one truly promotes discursive equality, then yes. However, these are not easy questions just as there are not easy solutions.

This analysis found that the most notable differences in Palin's news coverage, when compared to her predecessors, were discourse about her inexperience and discourse about sexism. Considering that all of these women were political pioneers, it is interesting that only Palin's coverage frequently constructed her as a novice for the position she sought. In Woodhull's case, the press was too busy criticizing her personal life and platform. In Smith's case, Smith had more than two decades of experience in Congress, along with a resume similar to Lyndon Johnson's, thereby leaving little room to criticize her political experience. This therefore makes Palin most comparable to Rankin. Rankin, however, had factors in her corner that Palin did not: prior name recognition among the targeted voters, evidence of producing results for those voters (suffrage in Montana), and a solid campaign strategy. Palin also was at a disadvantage due to the presumption among the press that Palin should be vetted for the presidency instead of the vice presidency, thereby comparing her resume to the qualifications for an office she wasn't seeking. The ramifications of this discourse were evident via the news stories that quoted voters repeating that Palin was inexperienced. Taking into account that Palin was previously unknown to most voters in the mainland United States, this voter discourse is telling about the significant role that the press plays in establishing attitudes toward women political candidates.

Perhaps the most important finding in Palin's coverage, however, was the criticism of sexist discourse toward Palin. This is a major step forward in the battle for discursive equality, as this type of discourse was missing in press coverage of the other women included in this study. The fact that a segment of society wants to see change in the discourse toward women in politics illustrates there is growing recognition of the problem of discursive inequality and a determination to address it. Furthermore, it's important to underline that journalists are choosing to include this type of discourse in their stories.

Even though the press has continued using gendered news strategies in the 2000s, journalists are at least more cognizant that gendered news coverage is increasingly considered to be problematic. Although change will not happen overnight, this finding is a hopeful sign for the future as it illustrates the beginning of delegitimizing gendered discursive strategies commonly used with women in politics.

The next chapter provides a final summary regarding how newspapers have discursively constructed pioneering women politicians throughout the past 140 years. The chapter also examines in further depth the similarities and differences in press coverage among the four women featured in this study, as well as make predictions for the future of women, media, and politics. First, however, a brief epilogue of Palin's story is provided:

Following the McCain/Palin defeat in November 2008, Palin resumed her work as governor of Alaska. However, speculation immediately began that she would either run for president in 2012, run for the U.S. Senate, and/or seek a television commentary position (Benet 2009). In 2009, Palin resigned from her position as governor and released an autobiography, *Going Rogue: An American Life*. In the book she wrote of the constant media attention and attacks on her family even after the campaign ended, noting that "every action we took—or didn't take—was fodder for the national media" (Palin 2009, 348). During and after the campaign, Alaska's state government was pummeled with Freedom of Information requests regarding Palin, while she personally faced a number of ethics complaints and lawsuits that she considered frivolous (Palin 2009). As Palin herself said, "my record, my administration's efforts, and my family's reputation were shot to hell" (Palin 2009, 373), a type of discourse that Woodhull no doubt felt herself after her presidential campaign. In 2010, Palin became a political contributor for Fox News and starred in a reality television show, *Sarah Palin's Alaska*. She did not run for president in 2012 but has been a vocal supporter and activist for Tea Party Republican candidates.

Chapter 6

From Woodhull to Palin and Moving Forward

A women and media scholar writing about Sarah Palin once wrote, "It's possible to hate her politics but sympathize with her media experiences" (Ross 2010, 108). Although this is phrased a bit abruptly, the point that one must look past partisanship and recognize the discursive inequality faced by women in politics in general is an important one. This book sought to go beyond partisan boundaries with Victoria Woodhull, a third-party candidate; Jeannette Rankin, a self-described Republican in name only; Margaret Chase Smith, a moderate Republican; and Sarah Palin, a conservative Republican, in order to illustrate that gendered news frames should be of broad concern to journalists, politicians, and the general public. This analysis focused on four major case studies throughout history in order to understand the trajectory of gendered news coverage of women politicians from 1872 to the present, although certainly other women politicians left out of this analysis have encountered problematic coverage as well. Similar to this study's findings for Rankin, Smith, and Palin, a study of Democratic vice presidential candidate Geraldine Ferraro's newspaper coverage found discourse lending credence to the (mythical) women's bloc, and nearly 30 percent of Ferraro's coverage included references to her appearance (Heith 2003). In her autobiography *My Story*, Ferraro wrote about a journalist who personally referred to her as "cute," a headline that asked "Will This Queens Housewife Be the Next Vice President?," the constant opinions about her wardrobe, and the press's "siege" on the extent of her foreign policy knowledge (Ferraro 1985, 182, 77, 322). As the first woman on a major party's presidential ticket, Ferraro wondered if future women running for national office would also "be judged by a standard different from that used for her male opponents" (Ferraro 1985, 322). Recent history has provided evidence that they indeed still are.

In addition to Palin, other women politicians in the 2000s continued to receive press coverage that treated them differently due to their gender. During the 2000 presidential election, Republican contender Elizabeth Dole received less newspaper coverage about her platform than her male opponents and more coverage about her personal traits, according to one study (Aday and Devitt 2001). Another study came to the same conclusion, pointing to the unbalanced focus on Dole's personality, appearance, and gender, while noting that the press suggested "implicitly, if not explicitly, that she was a novelty in the race rather than a strong contender with a good chance of winning" (Heldman, Carroll, and Olson 2005, 315). In the 2006 lead-up to Democrat Nancy Pelosi becoming speaker of the House, the press continued using gendered discursive strategies present in the 1870s, 1910s, and 1960s. For example, a *New York Times* story focused on Pelosi's appearance and age, alluded to the women's bloc concept, and utilized an angry woman frame (Steinhauer 2006). Just as Woodhull was referred to as a "lunatic" and treated as a political pariah by opponents to her candidacy in the 1870s, the *Times* story about Pelosi mentioned her perceived "personification of liberal lunacy" and quoted a Republican who noted he would have been "crucified" for saying he liked her (Steinhauer 2006, a20). Like Rankin, Smith, and Palin, Pelosi's appearance was emphasized in the press, with word choices such as "an Armani-clad elitist," "a signature lilac suit," and "wears expensive suits." Like Smith in the 1960s, Pelosi's age was emphasized, with the *Times* story noting Pelosi "shot a frown—the sort a grandmother gives when someone arrives at Christmas dinner in a wrinkled shirt" (Steinhauer 2006, a20). As was the case with Palin a few years later, there was recognition within the press that there was gendered discourse being used against Pelosi, but it continued nonetheless. One source, in the same breath that acknowledged Pelosi faced sexism, said Pelosi "is an attractive woman who dresses very well and is soft spoken, from a generation that has a certain kind of softness" (Steinhauer 2006, a20). This *one* story alone about Pelosi should be illustrative of how problematic the compounding of gendered discursive strategies over time has become.

However, the candidacies of Democrat Hillary Clinton, a serious contender for the presidency in 2008 and 2016, have generated perhaps the most attention to sexist news coverage of women politicians. From her physical appearance to her pantsuits to her age to her seemingly never good enough balance of masculinity and femininity, Clinton's candidacy in 2008 "raised numerous questions about the gendered nature of presidential politics" (Katz 2013, 207; see also Curnalia and Mermer 2014; Carlin and Winfrey 2009). Still, complaints from Clinton supporters about sexism "brought more derision than sympathy or outrage" (Carlin and Winfrey 2009, 327), an indication that mainstream society was not yet ready to acknowledge or change the differing standards for women in politics. Yet when Palin received her own gendered news coverage in the same election cycle, discourse about the need for change suddenly became an issue for both major political parties. By providing a plethora of evidence about the problematic state of gendered discourse toward women politicians, the goal of this book is to continue this conversation and serve as a catalyst for further discussion and, ultimately, change in order to enhance equality in discourse.

The remainder of this chapter provides summaries of the findings for the four women analyzed in this book and includes cross-comparisons of the main themes evident in their news coverage. In addition, practical and scholarly implications are discussed, as well as suggestions for future research.

CHAPTER SUMMARIES

This section returns to one of the original questions of this book: How have newspapers discursively constructed pioneering women politicians during four particular historical points between the 1870s and the 2000s as rooted and manifested in particular historical contexts? A brief review of the previous chapters is offered as a reminder.

In 1872, Woodhull became the first woman to run for president of the United States, with her third-party campaign serving as a direct challenge to gender norms during an era when women had limited rights and feminism was in its infancy. The partisan press was quick to not only dismiss her, but to also outright mock her and drag her name through the mud. Journalistic discourse frequently reminded readers that Woodhull was outside of the mainstream, that "the vast army of wives and mothers in this nation" (see page 29) did not support her, and that her candidacy was a joke. Her personal life was splashed across newspaper pages, and emotional word choices of comparing Woodhull to castor oil, Satan, a lunatic, and a deadbeat were all meant to delegitimize any ground she had gained as a pioneer. Yet even though Woodhull is largely forgotten today, her ardent challenge of gender norms during her time did attract some support and undoubtedly aided in the (albeit slow) evolution of attitudes toward women in politics. She did receive some praise in the press for championing women's rights, for discussing important political matters, and for attracting a fan base. Some journalists admitted that Woodhull and her ideas were likely more popular than publicly acknowledged and that others were too afraid to openly challenge the patriarchal status quo along with her. Although Woodhull had no chance of beating Civil War hero and incumbent President Ulysses S. Grant, her pioneering run and strong personality were essential to making waves during her era and to paving the way for future women politicians.

In 1916, Jeannette Rankin, the first woman to win an election to Congress, encountered a remarkably different set of historical circumstances that gave her advantages that Woodhull did not have. Rankin sought election at a time when the first wave of feminism was within grasp of its suffrage victory, when the nation was relatively stable, when journalists strove to be more objective, and when Western states touted their progressivism. Although Rankin vied for national office, she is the one case within this study that involved a state election (Montana) as opposed to a national election. Rankin's case provided an opportunity to examine not only a pioneering run but a successful one to understand how journalistic discourse may have varied. Indeed, significantly different from Woodhull, Rankin received overwhelmingly positive press coverage. There are a number of explanations for this difference, in addition to the contextual factors discussed above. Unlike Woodhull's case, the local and regional press set the initial tone for Rankin's news coverage, not the national press, and the frontier press in the West had a history of supporting reform and democratic government. The national press did not take much note of Rankin's campaign until it became evident she would win and, therefore, entered the discursive conversation after the regional press had established an agenda on the matter. Another important reason for the difference in journalistic discursive tone toward Rankin is that she took a different approach to her candidacy than Woodhull. Rankin relentlessly campaigned across her voting territory and had a platform that appealed to voters of her time. It is a bit oversimplified to say that Rankin ran as a woman since she discussed other issues and was genuinely interested in women's and children's issues that she felt were being ignored by the all-male Congress. Still, the fact remains she had a platform that fit with gender roles of her time. It is important to point out that ideas about gender roles had changed some since Woodhull's campaign, however. Whereas the press derided Woodhull's relationship with the women's movement of her era, the press of Rankin's era accepted her as a suffragist and praised her work on behalf of the cause. Significantly, the press highlighted Rankin's popularity, the widespread benefit of her winning the election, and her experience. This last factor is critical to note. Newspapers included discourse from both journalists and Rankin herself saying that she was qualified for the position and explaining why. Rankin was not merely in the race to make noise or to become a historical footnote; she seriously thought that she could win and that she had the qualifications to do so. She also benefited by not having a direct challenge from a male incumbent, a most fortunate stroke of luck. It is also noteworthy that much of the gendered journalistic discourse—that is, an emphasis on her appearance, her single status, her homemaking skills—appeared *after* Rankin won the election, a rarity and a gift that allowed her to be treated more like a politician than a *woman* politician during her campaign. Although her platform focused on gendered issues, Rankin won her election due in large part to her political skill, a historical context that eased gender barriers, and journalistic discourse that treated her like a serious candidate.

In 1964, Margaret Chase Smith became the first woman to receive a nomination for president at a major political party's convention. As was the case with Woodhull, Smith's candidacy came at a time when the political, journalistic, and feminist contexts of the era were not on her side. In the aftermath of the Kennedy assassination, voters most certainly were going to choose his heir apparent, and the number of women in Congress had declined from 20 to 14 between 1961 and 1963, indicating regression for women in politics (*Women in the U.S. Congress 2015* 2015). Journalistically, the male-dominated press corps may have embraced the standard of objectivity, yet this was also a time when the press supported the status quo and generally did not challenge authority. Although the press was more apt to use the discursive strategy of equalizing, or including multiple viewpoints in stories, the lack of depth or context in reporting resulted in oversimplified and stereotypical discourse regarding Smith's candidacy. This was enabled by the norm of rigid gender roles in the early 1960s, since the second wave of feminism did not pick up steam until later in the decade. Therefore, discourse in the press regarding Smith's candidacy emphasized stereotypical norms that women were too emotional to be president, that the presidency was a man's job, and that a woman president was something for the future not the present. Interestingly, much of the discourse of these arguments did not specifically mention Smith herself or her qualifications but simply emphasized that gender was the sole problem. In other words, no matter how qualified a woman may have been, her gender automatically made her not good enough to be president. This discursive strategy served to maintain a gender barrier and separate spheres between men and women. Although a number of male public officials lent positive discourse to Smith's candidacy, the discourse was generally surface level, and they likely did not consider her a serious challenger. Unlike Woodhull and Rankin, Smith was not running as a woman. On the other hand, press discourse indicated it was not clear why she was running at all. The fact that Smith herself used discourse to indicate she was not putting much effort into her campaign also did not help her candidacy. Therefore, her run may have hindered more than helped future women presidential candidates by illustrating that a woman candidate was not to be taken seriously.

In 2008, Sarah Palin became the first Republican vice presidential candidate during a turbulent time in journalism and politics. In the late 2000s, journalists prided themselves on their watchdog role of being skeptical of authority. At the same time, the industry increasingly focused on infotainment in the now 24-7 news cycle amid attempts to attract consumers as competition grew fierce and as revenues dwindled due to national economic woes. Both of these factors contributed to the intense press coverage of Palin's personal life and family. Journalists no longer waited for an event to happen as they had in the past. Rather, they proactively sought out a story, not only to get a scoop but to generate web clicks. From a political perspective, the approval rating of Congress hit all-time lows, with Republicans taking the brunt of the blame as the economy sank and the nation's wars in Iraq and Afghanistan grew increasingly unpopular. Discourse about Palin's candidacy noted she was reform-minded and anti-establishment, yet this also contributed to intense scrutiny in the press over her level of experience. Although Palin was running for vice president, much discourse centered upon whether she was ready to serve as *president* and lacked context about qualifications of prior vice presidential candidates. Despite this delegitimization of her political skills, journalistic discourse also framed Palin as a celebrity who attracted large crowds and rejuvenated the Republican Party. The combined discursive strategies served to suggest that Palin was best left as a cheerleader on the sidelines than a player in the game. This framing was enhanced with the emphasis on Palin's physical appearance and clothing. A number of journalists and male politicians also discursively continued the myth of the women's voting bloc, believing that Palin's gender alone would be enough to attract women voters. Palin did not run as a woman—her major issues were reform, energy, and the broad conservative platform. However, the discursive strategies noted above and the discourse from at least some women voters who expected her to address women's issues served to construct her as a woman candidate rather than a candidate. Although Palin's press coverage illustrates a compounding of the gendered discourses used on her predecessors, there was one significant difference: her news coverage included more discourse criticizing the differing standards for women politicians and directly used the "sexist" word. As a result, her news coverage provides hope for future women politicians that the status quo of gendered discourse is becoming increasingly unacceptable and that there is a call for change.

CASE COMPARISONS

With this broad overview of the four cases now complete, we turn next to the final major question of this study: How were the media discourses of these women different from or similar to each other? To answer this, each of the 10 themes found among the four cases are cross-compared here, with discussion included as to the practical implications of each.

Political

It is not surprising that the one candidate in this analysis who won her race was discursively constructed in the press as a good politician. Rankin campaigned hard, had a platform that appealed to voters, had a prior record of public service, and was qualified for the position she sought, all of which were factors mentioned in the press throughout her campaign. In contrast, neither Woodhull nor Smith were considered to be serious contenders for the presidency, not only due to gender norms of their times but also due to their lack of skill as presidential politicians. Neither woman seriously sought to reach mainstream voters. The little news coverage there was about Smith's platform indicated her political priorities were more in line with constituents of her time than Woodhull's were, yet voters also had a better idea as to why Woodhull was running than they did Smith. Smith may have had a long record of service in Congress, but there was no press coverage indicating she used it to her advantage or touted her experience. Interestingly, there was no press scrutiny over Smith's political record, either, as there was with Palin. Journalists, politicians, and voters frequently questioned Palin's political qualifications, although this was usually framed in relation to the presidency even though she was a vice presidential candidate. The case of Palin is unique since she was the only candidate in this analysis who was a running mate. Therefore, she was expected to follow the campaign strategy and message of McCain and, as was discussed in the press, her campaign appearances were controlled. This added discursive ammunition to the fire that she was not ready for primetime, so to speak. Like Woodhull, Palin was also framed as a "polarizing figure" in politics (Lambert, *The New York Times*, October 26, 2008, LI1).

The practical implications of this: Journalists should not underestimate the power of their words in discourse about political candidates. How they frame their stories matters as discursive strategies can legitimize or delegitimize political campaigns. This is not to suggest that every candidate, qualified or not, must be praised in the press. However, if the press wants to provide a fair and balanced overview of candidates, it must further examine if it is picking winners and losers through its discursive choices or if it is providing information to let the public do so.

Personal Traits

Personal coverage of women in politics has varied throughout history, depending upon the journalistic culture of the era. It is evident that Woodhull's and Palin's candidacies occurred during more aggressive periods in journalism culture while Smith and Rankin ran for national office during more passive journalistic times. Both Woodhull and Palin encountered scrutinizing coverage of their personal lives and families, although Woodhull's coverage tended to occur after a specific event, whereas journalists sought out details about Palin's personal life. Neither Rankin nor Smith encountered much press interest in their personal lives during their campaigns. Interestingly, much of Rankin's news coverage about her personally came *after* she won the election. Yet Woodhull, Rankin, and Palin, who were in their 30s and early 40s, all received discursive constructions in the press related to their sexuality. The three also had news coverage that, consciously or not (and some more direct than others), compared how they aligned with idealized womanhood.

The practical implications of this: Journalistic emphasis on candidates' personal lives is not likely to end in the foreseeable future since personal character and family life are now viewed as critical components for judging how candidates may perform as government officials. Yet there must be more ethical consideration for how underage children of candidates are treated in the press, particularly due to changes in journalistic culture that mean stories now live on the Internet forever rather than end after the local broadcast or when the day's paper is tossed out. The 24-7 news cycle also should not be viewed as an automatic free pass for sensational discourse reminiscent of the yellow journalism era. Continued sexualization of female candidates and unrealistic standards of womanhood do greater damage to women as a whole than just to particular political races, and discourse in these areas must be significantly critiqued.

Women's Movement

A clear similarity among all four cases was the complicated relationship that these women had with the broader women's movement of their eras. Woodhull was accepted into the mainstream Anthony/Stanton movement for a time, but their falling out over issue differences became fodder in the press. Likewise, Rankin had close ties to the women's movement in the 1910s, yet (secretly, in her case) had disagreements with leadership who did not support her political ambition. Smith and Palin did not publicize or maintain connections to the formal women's movement, yet also had complicated relationships with feminism. Smith steered clear of feminism as much as possible and insisted she was not a woman politician, a woman senator, or a feminist, to the point this was mentioned in her obituary. Yet she also said in her presidential campaign announcement that she was running to challenge male dominance in the White House and to pave the way for future women since prior women politicians had paved the way for her. News coverage about Palin, meanwhile, was like a trip back in time to the days of Woodhull, as evidenced by the press interest in the strained relations between the Palin and Clinton camps. In regard to feminism, Palin herself has said she favors equal opportunity but doesn't subscribe to the "radical mantras" of feminism (Palin 2009, 29). During the campaign season, some women questioned why Palin did not talk more about women's issues, yet Palin also formed her own faction of feminism with her appeals to "hockey moms" (Bumiller, *The New York Times*, September 4, 2008, A1). Clearly the complicated relationship between women politicians and feminism has a long history that is not likely to end anytime soon.

Another similarity among the cases, to varying degrees, was the concept of a women's bloc. This was less evident in Woodhull's coverage, although Woodhull did criticize the "disgraceful treatment" she received from fellow women, which indicates she expected women to show her more support (New York *Sun*, August 24, 1872, 4). A news story also emphasized that Woodhull did not have the support of the "vast army of wives and mothers in this nation," thereby suggesting there was a woman's bloc against her (*The New Northwest*, June 7, 1872, 2). With Rankin's news coverage, there were also hints of the women's bloc concept, as a few news stories noted "women voters stood solidly by" her and that she was firmly favored by women (*Washington Court House Herald* (Ohio), November 8, 1916). It may be that there wasn't much direct commentary about this in Woodhull's and Rankin's coverage because, in the days before suffrage, it was an assumed fact that a women's bloc existed and there was not yet contrary evidence. Ironically, press promotion of the bloc increased in the decades after suffrage despite the contrary evidence of its existence. Smith received news coverage that told readers her candidacy "brought expressions of mild or strong disapproval from many of her sex" (*Pasadena Independent*, January 29, 1964, 9). The story was headlined "Smith Divides Women," as if Smith was only vying for the women's vote and male voters were irrelevant. Ironically, discourse supporting the women's bloc concept was most prevalent in Palin's news coverage despite nearly a century's worth of evidence illustrating there is not a bloc. Yet Palin was frequently framed as a catalyst for securing women voters.

The practical implications of this: Politicians and the press must stop promoting the myth that a women's bloc exists. If it did, half of the nation's government officials would be women. Rankin won her election because she had a political strategy and message that appealed to both genders, not just women. Journalistic stories should include interviews with both men and women reacting to candidates because, by only writing about women's reactions to women candidates, men are left out of the conversation and essentially told they aren't expected to support women.

Furthermore, it should be noted that the press played a significant role throughout history in creating the negative connotation that now exists regarding the word "feminism" (Hesford 2013). This is unlikely to be undone. Yet the press must consider its historical lack of objectivity in this area and the resulting repression of the women's movement. The press cannot promote itself as the watchdog of democracy while also discursively delegitimizing the equality of half of the nation's population. Women candidates should not need to gingerly balance their support of women's rights or new opportunities for fear that the press will discursively construct them as radicals. Further attention to word choices when discussing feminism and the women's movement would help create a more equalized discourse.

Platform/Issues

There are various ways that one could analyze politicians' platforms. This cross-analysis is most interested in the extent that women candidates incorporated "women's issues" into their platforms and the reaction to their platforms. Woodhull was noted for flinging "a very broad banner to the breeze" (*Boston Post*, June 6, 1872, 1), meaning she had a broad platform, which included economic and taxation proposals. However, the press mostly focused on her advocacy of free love, or the right of individuals (particularly women) to determine their personal lives without government interference or public scorn. Yet public scorn is what Woodhull received for her platform. Since Woodhull's "women's issues" plank was viewed as outside of gender norms, it became a hindrance to her campaign. Rankin, on the other hand, received positive reaction to her platform, which focused primarily on "women's issues" of children, family, and health and was in line with gender and progressive political norms of her era. Like Woodhull, Rankin was said to be interested in economic issues, yet this received limited attention in the press. As a result, like Woodhull, Rankin was primarily framed as a one- or two-dimensional politician. Yet, when compared to Smith, at least news coverage provided some idea of their political beliefs. Journalists covering Smith said they were unsure why she was even running and said she didn't seem to know herself. Some stories noted Smith's interest in foreign policy and staying tough on Communism, but either she provided few details of her views or the press opted not to include them. Brief discourse noted her views on the Equal Rights Amendment, yet women's issues were not a component of her press coverage. As for Palin, news coverage provided voters with a broader idea of her political stances than they did with the prior three women. Palin did not "run as a woman" since her platform focused on reform, energy, and the broad conservative platform. Yet news coverage indicated that women voters wanted to know more about where Palin stood on "women's issues." Although there was discourse about Palin's interest in special needs children, her anti abortion stance, and the fact that she was a working mother, this "women's issues" discourse was limited.

The above findings suggest that women in politics face a tricky balance. As the previous section noted, feminism has long been a contentious subject in this country and its mere mention can alienate voters. Yet women running for public office are often noted for advancing the women's movement, and voters who feel male-dominated political culture has not adequately addressed "women's issues" see women candidates as their hope for change. This, however, serves to reinforce separate spheres of men's and women's politics.

The practical implications of this: Journalists should stop labeling issues as "women's" or "men's" and simply inquire and write about "issues." Women's interests are as diverse as men's, which means there should not be an assumption that every woman candidate will be interested in "women's issues." Male candidates should also be asked about legislation regarding children, education, health, and home, and voters and the press should hold them accountable if they feel public concerns are not being addressed rather than wait for women candidates to handle them.

The Masculine/Feminine Double Bind

Press discourse that emphasized both masculine and feminine characteristics of the woman candidate emerged as a theme in both Smith's and Palin's press coverage. There was a hint of this framing in Rankin's coverage when a story noted "her femininity, her sweetness, and her direct, but not aggressive, talks" (*Boston Post*, November 11, 1916, 4), as if the writer wanted to indicate Rankin had the "male" capability to take charge but also reassure readers that Rankin was still predominantly feminine. However, this theme did not become noticeably apparent until Smith's coverage in 1964. Since Smith had such a "male" resume due to her longtime service in Congress, both the press and Smith herself seemed to feel that she needed to be feminized. Smith's experience with generals and admirals was juxtaposed against her past as a teacher, even though she was a teacher for less than a year. Another article noted she was a defense expert "but also is a great lover of flowers" (*Ogden Standard Examiner*, July 12, 1964, 55). The most blatant use of this strategy occurred when Smith brought blueberry muffins to a press luncheon. As for Palin, her past as both a beauty pageant contestant and a basketball player nicknamed "Barracuda" were noted, as well as her love of hunting and guns and her "warmth and charm" (Yardley, *The New York Times*, August 30, 2008, A1). Palin also constructed herself as a hockey mom who was like a pitbull wearing lipstick, thereby framing herself as both masculine and feminine as well.

Why this discursive strategy was not more present in the first two case studies is unclear. Perhaps both Woodhull's and Rankin's ties to the women's movement and their push for women's issues made them so solidly feminine—and the concept of separate spheres was so entrenched—that no gendered overlap was deemed necessary. Perhaps they also were not viewed as a serious threat to male dominance. Woodhull's campaign was viewed as a joke and Rankin was just one of many members of Congress. Smith and Palin, on the other hand, were vying for the biggest leadership roles in the nation, thereby serving as a greater challenge to gender roles. This meant needing to illustrate they could take on the job, while also not coming off as threatening to male voters. In the previous chapter, the question was raised as to whether it is legitimate for a female candidate to use gendered discourse when she feels it will favor her, but then for her to critique when others use gendered discourse against her. This chapter raises the question as to why female candidates and the press must create masculine/feminine constructions in the first place. Entrenched gender norms leave women politicians in a double bind of needing to present themselves as competent while still "[doing] their gender right" (Butler 1990, 273). In other words, strong women are viewed as "Satan" in Woodhull's case or "bitch" in more contemporary times if they are too "manly," yet women who are overly feminine are considered weak. Achieving the "correct" balance is socially made to be impossible. These are discursive strategies to maintain separate spheres between men and women in order to keep men in positions of power and must be recognized as such.

The practical implications of this: Journalists, politicians, and the public must stop discursively rewarding men for certain behaviors and punishing women for the same behaviors (and vice versa). This includes paying attention to adjectives used to describe women in leadership and discontinuing assumptions that gender is a determinant of competence in particular fields. Journalists unsure of how to change this discursive strategy could consider mentally substituting a male candidate's name in a story about a female candidate to gauge whether a man would have been framed the same way.

The Age Double Bind

Journalistic emphasis on a woman politician's age did not exist in the early decades of women in politics and was instead a later development. What is ironic is there was no journalistic discourse about this in the one case where age truly mattered. Woodhull was only 34 years old on Election Day 1872 and did not meet the constitutionally mandated age of 35 to serve as president. Yet either because the press did not know her age or journalists did not take her candidacy seriously enough to even bring it up, Woodhull did not receive any press coverage about her age in the stories analyzed. Rankin's age also was not an issue. Although a few stories mentioned she was young or romantically available, the fact that she was 36 was not of interest to journalists in the 1910s. This trend drastically changed with Smith in 1964 when the media's emphasis on her age got to a point that Smith publicly complained about it. News stories referred to her as a "white-haired widow," "the oldest of the candidates at 66," and "a gray-haired 66-year-old veteran," to name a few examples (*Provo Daily Herald*, January 28, 1964, 2; *Arkansas City Daily Traveler*, February 5, 1964, 12; *Salina Journal*, January 27, 1964). Smith said her age was "referred to almost daily" in the press, yet male candidates' ages weren't (*Des Moines Register*, February 11, 1964, 10). She also pointed out that other male national leaders were older than her. Why the press focused so much on Smith's age but not Rankin's or Woodhull's is unclear and can only be speculated upon. Regardless of the reason, the double bind of age was now part of discourse related to women in politics. Although reporters may also include the ages of men in their stories, women writers have pointed out there are differing standards of age for men and women in U.S. society, as the "social convention [is] that aging enhances a man but progressively destroys a woman" (Sontag 1972, 29). As Murray (2010b) wrote, women past the age of motherhood face stereotypes about menopause, purported weakness, unattractiveness, or being "past their prime" (18). Older men, on the other hand, are considered distinguished and experienced. On the other end of the spectrum, younger women "are assumed to be inexperienced, unviable, and are expected to be at home raising children" (Murray 2010b, 17), assumptions that younger men with children do not face. This double bind also applied to Palin. She did not receive as much direct attention to her age as Smith did, yet Palin did receive frequent journalistic discourse pointing to her political inexperience and to her family life that served as references to her age. Stories that directly mentioned her age noted she was younger than two of McCain's children, a generation younger than McCain, and "youthful" (Associated Press, *Alton Telegraph*, August 30, 2008, A1; Quinn, *Hutchinson News*, August 30, 2008 A1; Yardley, *The New York Times*, August 30, 2008, A1). One wonders if there even is a "correct" age for woman politicians as this seems to have become a discursive strategy to delegitimize them without directly stating their gender is the problem.

The practical implications of this: Journalists writing about the age of women politicians should consider whether they are using the same discursive strategy for male politicians and ask themselves: Would I be making an issue out of this if the candidate were male? Am I being consistent in my references to all of the candidates' ages? Am I personally keeping in mind the historical context that presidents have ranged in age from 42 (Theodore Roosevelt) to nearly 70 (Ronald Reagan) at the time they took office? In addition, do not automatically assume that someone younger is less prepared than someone older, or that someone older is less mentally or physically fit to perform the job than someone younger. Although age may appear to be an objective fact to include in stories, reporters should be cognizant that differing societal interpretations of age do exist based on gender.

Appearance

The journalistic emphasis on women candidates' appearance has increased throughout history, with this type of discourse gaining momentum in the 1910s and still considered relevant a century later. Woodhull received little journalistic discourse about her appearance, but Rankin's hair and physical appearance were considered newsworthy in 1916, although more so after her victory. Smith's coverage was unique in that she did not campaign often, so there were few potential opportunities for news comment on her appearance. However, when she did campaign, journalists described her clothing and, as previously mentioned in the age theme, her hair color was noted as well. Journalists also made metaphorical references to clothing in discourse about Smith by writing that she threw her "bonnet in the presidential ring" and stuffed votes "into her handbag" (*Independent Press Telegram*, February 2, 1964, W4; *Provo Daily Herald*, January 28, 1964, 12). Smith assumes a good share of the blame for the bonnet discourse since she acted this out for the cameras and thereby promoted her own gendered discourse while apparently trying to appear to be affable. Nevertheless, other commentary about her appearance was a clear journalistic choice. By the time Palin sought national office, the press was still interested in physical appearance and clothing. The press compared Palin's appearance to "a librarian's sex appeal" and noted that she "waved at the adoring crowd like the beauty pageant contestant she once was" (Stolberg, *The New York Times*, October 19, 2008, ST1; *Bedford Gazette*, September 4, 2008, 5). Although journalists weren't the only sources who referenced Palin's appearance, they made the choice to include this type of discourse from others as well. Yet, ironically, there was also outrage in the press over the cost of Palin's campaign clothing. For a century, the press has considered the appearance of women politicians to be important. Yet when the candidate sought to maintain that expectation, there was uproar over it. This is another example of the double bind that women politicians face. If they dress or look too casual, they are letting themselves go and are visually unappealing. Yet if they try to live up to public expectations, they risk being considered frivolous or elitist. Meanwhile, male candidates spend thousands of dollars on suits with little to no commentary about their appearance, as was pointed out in Palin's news coverage.

The practical implications of this: Of the assorted gendered discursive strategies, this should be the easiest one to address since it involves simple deletion of text. Journalists need to ask themselves the following: What news value is there in writing about a candidate's appearance? If I am mentioning a woman's appearance, is there a specific reason I need to do so or am I merely contributing to gender stereotypes? Am I using the same discursive strategy with male politicians? In order to achieve discursive equality, journalists must either increase the amount of attention to male appearance to make it equitable to women's or greatly decrease the amount of women's appearance coverage so it is more in line with men's.

Historical Relevance

Similar to the above theme, a discursive emphasis on the historical relevance of these pioneering women began with Rankin and continued to the present. The fact that Woodhull was so widely disliked by the press of her era that her candidacy was constructed as a joke undoubtedly contributed to a lack of interest in emphasizing her role in history. The press in the 1910s, however, applauded Rankin's political ambition and viewed her historical run as progress and "another step forward" when noting she would be the first woman elected to Congress (*The Enterprise*, October 12, 1916, 1). Discourse about the excitement over Rankin's history-making potential was evident throughout her campaign, whereas historical "first woman" discourse about Smith and Palin was more prominent at the beginning of their campaigns (and at the very end for Smith). The difference from Rankin may be due to the fact that journalists quickly decided Smith and Palin would not win office and therefore did not think it worthwhile to make much further mention of them as historical figures.

The practical implications of this: Mentioning that a woman candidate is "the first" is not problematic in and of itself. However, without additional context, this discourse lends itself to a construction of inexperience or "otherness" that can serve as a disadvantage (see also Falk 2010; Murray 2010b). Notably few stories in the Rankin, Smith, or Palin samples referenced prior women's history. Quoted sources in Smith's and Palin's coverage were clearly unaware of women's political history as well. If women candidates are to become more normative, journalists should provide greater context about the state of women in politics rather than treating a particular race as an isolated, novel event. For example, Palin's nomination came on the heels of cabinet gains during the Bush administration, Pelosi's selection as speaker, Clinton's run for the presidency, and increasing numbers of women in Congress. Yet, beyond a few mentions of Geraldine Ferraro (none of which questioned why it took a generation for another woman vice presidential candidate), Palin (and Rankin and Smith) was primarily a lone historical dot on the map. Until women reach a discursive equality with men where their gender is not viewed as a novelty in their political race, providing more context about women's history in stories will balance out the novelty and provide more equal footing for women.

Celebrity

The political and personal news coverage of these women made them all public figures, although the extent of their celebrity varied. Woodhull made a name for herself even before her presidential campaign with her opening of a Wall Street firm. Her public status grew with press coverage of her testimony before Congress, her involvement with the women's movement, and her family troubles. During the six months prior to Election Day 1872, Woodhull was referred to as "the only advocate of woman suffrage of any political importance" and "the irrepressible champion of women's rights" (*The New Northwest*, June 7, 1872, 2; New York *Sun*, July 17, 1872, 3). Yet even though she was said to attract crowds, the press often ridiculed her supporters, and Woodhull was predominantly constructed as "the notorious Woodhull woman," "Mrs. Satan," and "a fit subject for a lunatic asylum" (*The Hickman Courier*, May 25, 1872, 1; *Harper's Weekly*, February 1872; *The Daily Phoenix*, September 25, 1872, 3). Therefore, while Woodhull may have had the attention of "the entire press of the nation" (*The New Northwest*, May 3, 1872, 1), her celebrity status had negative connotations, which certainly impacted her campaign. Rankin, too, had built up a prior status as a public figure due to her campaigning across Montana and the nation on behalf of suffrage. Yet unlike Woodhull, she enjoyed a positive celebrity status that included discourse about her endorsements, large crowds, and "phenomenal" ovations (*The Glasgow Courier*, November 3, 1916, 1). As for Smith, her lack of campaigning meant she did not generate a celebrity frame. Smith herself noted she received a warm reception in New Hampshire, but she did not capitalize on that interest and wage a more aggressive campaign. While opponents spoke at large rallies, she "quickly made the rounds at colleges and small gatherings" and was "received more like a favorite aunt," thereby limiting her public figure status and leading to discourse indicating she was not a serious contender (*Salisbury Times*, April 15, 1964, 1; *The New York Times*, April 19, 1964, 81). National newcomer Palin, on the other hand, received celebrity framing with similarities to both Woodhull and Rankin. Although described as "polarizing" to some voters (Lambert, *The New York Times*, October 26, 2008, LI1), Palin was also framed as a Republican Party star who attracted large crowds. She contributed to her own fame by appearing on shows like "Saturday Night Live." Overall, the extent that a woman politician makes herself publicly available influences her level of celebrity, and journalistic discourse about her public and personal persona influences whether that celebrity is favorable or unfavorable.

The practical implications of this: Journalists must be aware that the adjectives used to describe women politicians and their supporters/opponents play a role in legitimating or delegitimizing campaigns. This is not to say that this type of discourse should never be used. However, the power of this discourse should not be underestimated. How "celebritized" a woman is may also distract from her platform, resulting in a popularity contest as opposed to a political contest.

Sexism

Although there were references to sexism in Rankin's and Smith's news coverage, Palin's coverage was the first case in this analysis that included discourse indicating sexism was a problem that must be addressed. In Rankin's case, comments about male congressmen potentially not liking her presence or refusing to seat her were included in a few news articles, yet there was no discourse condemning this. In Smith's case, a voter alluded to sexism by saying women needed to be twice as good as a man to be considered equals. Smith herself tried to counter gendered discourse by saying women "are people just as much as men are" and "are no more and no less capable" (*Lowell Sun*, June 28, 1964, 76). Yet, in Palin's case, sexism became a widespread conversation among journalists and politicians who noted this was not fair.

The practical implications of this: The sexism discourse in Palin's coverage is a remarkable shift that indicates frustration with the different standards for women politicians nearly 150 years after Woodhull. This type of discourse is necessary in order for there to be change. This means that journalists will likely face increasing scrutiny over their work and whether they are delegitimizing women in politics through gendered discourse. As a result, journalists must commit to recognizing the problem and illustrating a willingness to change as well. What this means for women candidates and the public is the potential for a broadened democracy that does not exclude or trivialize half of the nation's population.

MOVING FORWARD

As was said at the start of this chapter and found throughout this analysis, gendered media coverage of women in politics crosses party lines, journalistic eras, and historical times, and thereby has become engrained in American society. Nearly 150 years after Woodhull's foray into national politics and a century after Rankin's first national political victory for women, the press continues to use gendered discursive strategies in its coverage. This is indicative that the press may not be the agent of change some believe it to be, but is rather a more conservative defender of the status quo, at least in terms of gender roles and norms. Although there was a progressive boost during Rankin's era, overall, gendered coverage of women politicians has compounded over time rather than steadily becoming more equalized. Do journalists and voters today believe that women politicians should be treated with the same gendered discourse used with women in the late 1800s and early 1900s? While it's easy to say no to that question, it will take effort on behalf of journalists, politicians, and voters for discursive change to happen.

In her autobiography, Geraldine Ferraro wrote, "The country is never going to be ready for anything new until people are put in the position of experiencing it" (322). Since the 1800s, women have challenged gender and political norms in order to reach the state of women and politics today. Along the way, these women met great resistance, yet now once controversial ideas such as property rights, congressional representation, and voting are commonplace. Back in 1964, voters frequently indicated that a woman president was an ambition for the future. Fifty years later, the future is now here. Are voters today going to continue passing the buck to the future or is it time to stop talking about the glass ceiling for women and shatter it once and for all? Certainly the potential for the latter is there. From a journalistic perspective, there is now greater awareness among the media and journalism students regarding gendered news coverage, which indicates that improvement in discourse is possible. From a feminist perspective, the third wave of feminism has pushed for inclusion. Gender norms in the nation have loosened to the point that gay marriage is legal and transgenderism is gaining more attention. The increasing flexibility in gender norms has also provided women more opportunity to partake in male-characterized endeavors. From a political perspective, the 2008 presidential election featured both major political parties supporting female candidates with Clinton and Palin. In addition, other women politicians are gaining an increasing percentage of public offices. Overall, from the contexts of journalism, feminism, and political cultures, the United States is positioned for the election of a woman president.

To be clear, the purpose of this study is not to indicate that any woman should fill the presidency for the sake of doing so. That strategy clearly did not work in Smith's era, and not just anyone should occupy the world's most powerful position. Rather, the point is to promote a more democratic discourse and nation, for as feminist Gloria Steinem once noted, the automatic elimination of half of the population for the presidency drastically limits the talent pool (Schnall 2013). Gendered discursive strategies serve to delegitimize women candidates, giving them an unfair disadvantage in the political arena and cementing old-fashioned stereotypes best left in the past.

From a political perspective, Murray (2010a) suggested that women seek out experience in "male areas," such as foreign affairs and defense, and frame themselves as candidates of change in order to better position themselves for the White House. Yet, as this study found, women candidates will also be expected to address "women's issues" and to maintain that rocky balance of feminine masculinity since these discursive strategies will not change overnight. Rankin's political victory in 1916 illustrates that an aggressive campaign strategy to meet and speak with voters, a clear platform with widespread support, and recognized experience in public service are also important factors for success. Politicians and public relations practitioners who frame political discourse must also understand that they play a role in the enhancement or negation of gendered discourse.

From a journalistic perspective, enhanced training of college journalists in the area of media and diversity is essential for discursive change (as is diversity training for male and female students overall) in order to change negative gendered stereotypes of women and girls. This is not to say that current journalists should be let off the hook until the next generation arrives, although it is certainly easier to incorporate new skills at the beginning of a career than at the middle or the end when habits are already formed. Newsrooms should consider bringing in diversity trainers or planning diversity sessions at state conventions. In addition, political reporters should review their past stories to analyze whether they are incorporating gendered discursive strategies in their work and whether they could provide more fair and balanced reporting on women politicians.

To be clear, the suggestions are not intended to be viewed as silver bullets that will solve discursive inequality. Although this study has made a number of suggestions for journalistic improvement, one must keep in mind that this is certainly easier said than done and that potential change will be slow. Although journalists do have agency to write their own stories, industry standards and norms at the organizational level can make it difficult to change the broader culture. Editors demand certain stories, and copy editors assert their own influence via story editing and headline choices. News organizations also tend to follow the pack and report on the same stories as the competition so as to not be scooped. The discursive themes in this study from 1872 that were still present in 2008 serve as evidence of how engrained gendered norms are in the journalism industry. The industry's leadership also continues to be largely male-dominated, thereby making it challenging to disrupt the hegemonic status quo even though more women are working in the industry today. Although this study did not analyze the economics of journalism and discursive inequality, objectification of women has a long history of commercialization in this country, which is another factor in the complexity of changing journalistic culture. In addition, going back to the circular process noted by Richardson (2007), journalism is influenced by political discourse which is influenced by journalistic discourse, creating a circular pattern of its own engrained discourse that feeds upon the other and can be difficult to change. From a scholarly perspective, this study has illustrated that media coverage of women politicians has not been a straight line of progress throughout U.S. history. Rather, depending on journalistic and gender norms, discourse has both progressed and regressed across time. One would think an emphasis on a woman's appearance would have been left on the women's pages in the early and mid-twentieth century, yet Palin's appearance still drew attention in 2008. Although Rankin received news coverage that legitimized her candidacy, thereby improving upon Woodhull's coverage, Smith and Palin found their candidacies largely delegitimized. Therefore, this research joins other scholarly works that have critiqued or debunked "progressive history" as a framework for historical writing (i.e. Butterfield 1965; Foucault 1977). In this study, there was no upward straight line of progress to more equality in discourse for women politicians between the 1800s to the 2000s. Rather, the historical-diachronic approach utilized in this study helped illuminate that discursive inequality for women political candidates was a process of building upon prior cases and ebbing and flowing across time. In addition, this study does not follow the "Great Man" theory of history, or for the purposes of this study, "Great Women" history. Rather, these four cases illustrate the historical continuities and disruptions of media discourses on political women. The results indicate that media discourse not only mirrors the social expectation of women at a particular historical time, but also helps construct an image of women politicians as novelties who are defined and confined by their gender. The women featured in this study had differing political platforms, personalities, and historical contexts, yet this study overall provides support for the argument of Ross (2010) that women interested in political careers are typically framed "as women first and then, maybe, as politicians" (99). Similarly, this study also lends support in its own way to the prior work of Finneman and Thomas (2014), who found that first ladies are in a state of permanent conjuncture, stuck between tradition and modernity. Women politicians, too, are stuck between modern standards for women and "idealized womanhood," a societal concept that clings to separate spheres and gendered roles for women.

This book also has provided additional support for the need to utilize a historical-diachronic approach to research, as evidenced in part by the lack of historical context and knowledge on the behalf of the press throughout this analysis. In the case of this study, with very few exceptions, news coverage treated each pioneering political woman as an isolated case. This neglect of historical reference to earlier women pioneers not only served to construct each pioneer as outside the norm, thereby serving as a delegitimizing strategy, but also served to limit journalists' understanding of the implications of gendered news frames over time. In the case of research overall, the isolation of a particular case also results in a narrow understanding of a particular issue, which would likely benefit from a more longitudinal approach.

Regarding gendered discourse in particular, this study has lent further support to the framework of gender stereotypes, gendered news frames, and double binds as outlined by Murray (2010b). However, this study offers optimism that the "silence or shame" double bind included in that framework may finally be cracking. The increasing inclusion of discourse in media texts from various sources critiquing the gendered news frames utilized for women candidates indicates a greater awareness on the part of the press and the public about the implications of these frames. This awareness is necessary in order for changes in discourse to occur, and this study hopes to provide additional context to spur further discussion and research.

From a future research perspective, certainly a next step after this study would be to add race as a concept of analysis in addition to gender. A longitudinal examination of women of color pioneering politicians would illustrate the challenges that these women face that are similar and different to the white women featured in this study. This would allow for a greater understanding of the discursive inequality faced by women as a whole as opposed to one segment of the female population. There are a number of other potential studies related to women, media, and politics that would be useful to conduct as well. For example, what exactly does discursive gender equality entail, as defined by journalists, feminists, and politicians? What does media fairness to politicians of both genders mean? Future research could also involve a longitudinal examination of opinion page content about women in politics to better gauge the opinions of the letter-writing public and the "official" stances of newspapers via editorials. This content would provide additional clarity not only about attitudes toward women politicians but also about attitudes toward women overall during particular times. Another relevant longitudinal research approach would be to analyze news coverage of women in state government positions in order to understand how gendered discursive strategies may vary from the national level.

As far as varying platforms, this study focused on news coverage in mainstream newspapers due to the consistency of the platform across time. However, other types of media are certainly important to analyze since newspapers are just one form of mass communication. For example, an analysis of posts and comments on the social media sites of women politicians would provide insight into the state of gendered discourse, as well as further examination of official campaign public relations materials. Beyond women politicians, analysis of other high-level women in politics is also pertinent. Although first ladies and candidates' wives are not directly considered women politicians, research has found that they, too, encounter much of the same gendered discursive strategies in media (i.e. Finneman and Thomas 2014; Burns 2008; Anderson 2005; Winfield and Friedman 2003). Therefore, it is important to also draw attention to this discourse to further understand the discursive constructions of women in politics and the resulting implications.

Watson (2003) once wrote that the election of a woman president in the United States would likely not mean the end of inequality for women in politics. Equality would not be considered accomplished until women had proportional representation in government and until gender was an unimportant factor for both voters and the media. Watson is quite right, and this study was an effort to bring continued awareness to that inequality. Although Katz (2013) predicts gendered discourse in presidential elections will likely remain for decades to come, this inequality does not have to continue. Yet it will take journalists, politicians, and voters to implement change.

Appendix

Methodology

The analysis of all four cases featured in this book focused specifically on news and feature stories to understand how reporters discursively construct women politicians. In order to find newspaper articles to analyze, the researcher used the Historical New York Times, Chronicling America, and Newspaperarchive.com databases. *The New York Times* served as a control throughout this analysis to see how this particular outlet—known as the media's agenda setter since the mid-1910s (Cose 1989)—covered women politicians across a nearly 140-year time frame. However, because *The New York Times* is not necessarily representative of other newspapers in America, the other databases provided a variety of newspaper stories to analyze in order to provide more context in understanding newspaper coverage of each of these women.

Chronicling America is a website supported by the National Endowment for the Humanities and the Library of Congress. The site contains more than 8 million pages of newspaper content from across the United States between 1836 and 1922. State universities, libraries, and historical societies across the country receive funding to select state and local newspapers from their resources and digitize them for the national database. However, because this database ends at 1922, only articles for Woodhull and Rankin were searched here. Still, the national scope of the database makes it a valuable historical resource.

Newspaperarchive.com describes itself as "the largest historical newspaper database online" with more than 145 million pages of content from all 50 states from 1607 to the present. The number of newspapers in the system per state varies from one Hawaiian newspaper to 266 Iowan newspapers. Still, every state is represented. Although there may be some duplication with Chronicling America, past personal research using both databases found they

181

do have original content compared to the other, making it useful to search both. Newspaperarchive.com is also useful because, like *The New York Times*, it includes data from all of the election years under consideration in this study. This study solely analyzed mainstream newspaper coverage to maintain consistency due to the existence of the medium throughout this entire analysis.

To find data, each woman's name was searched in The Historical New York Times and Newspaperarchive.com databases. Depending upon cultural mores of the time, searches included terms such as "Victoria Woodhull," "Mrs. Woodhull," "Jeannette Rankin," and "Miss Rankin AND Montana" since it was common to refer to women by courtesy titles in the past. "Margaret Chase Smith" and "Sarah Palin" were the sole search terms used for their respective searches due to the originality of their names and to journalistic custom of the eras to refer to sources by first and last name on first reference, thus ensuring a comprehensive search.

Because each of these women's political careers, campaigns, and results differ, the time frames for the data searches also differed. Woodhull received her presidential nomination in May 1872 and lost the election in November. Therefore, newspaper coverage about her from May 1, 1872, to November 7, 1872, was analyzed. The election was on November 5, so this allowed for collection of reaction from the press in the days after her defeat. Rankin ran for Congress in Montana in 1916 and won in the fall general election. Therefore, the newspaper coverage analyzed spanned from January 1, 1916, to November 12, 1916. Smith announced her presidential aspirations on January 27, 1964. Data collection concluded July 18, 1964, two days after the Republican national convention where she lost her bid. As for Palin, data collection ranged from August 29, 2008, when her vice presidential selection was announced, to November 6, 2008, two days after McCain and Palin lost the election.

Census sampling, or examination of all database articles, was used in Woodhull's and Rankin's cases since this approach provides "the most valid discussion of a population" (Riffe, Lacy, and Fico 1998, 84) and the number of results was manageable. However, the large number of search results for Smith and Palin resulted in more selective sampling.

In Smith's case, there were 121 total results from The Historical New York Times. NewspaperArchive.com returned 9,996 results, so sampling was utilized. The articles were sorted in chronological order and then every 20th result was pulled. Therefore, the discursive analysis involved examination of 621 newspaper articles included in the Historical New York Times and NewspaperArchive.com databases. However, some of the pulled data needed to be discarded since it was not news story content. Examples of discarded data include opinion pieces, standalone photos, and TV listings. This left

416 articles from NewspaperArchive.com and 117 from *The New York Times*, for a combined total of 533 news articles from 38 states textually analyzed for this case. It is noteworthy to mention that none of May Craig's articles were included in the database results. Craig, the Washington correspondent for the Guy Gannett newspapers in Maine, often wrote about Smith (Wallace 1995), and analysis of her work would be worthwhile in future study.

The Palin news analysis involved examination of newspaper articles included in the Historical New York Times and NewspaperArchive.com databases. Originally, there were 584 total results from *The New York Times* for the time frame examined, so sampling was utilized. The articles were sorted in chronological order, and the first five stories were collected in order to analyze the initial discourse of the Palin campaign. From there, every fifth result was pulled for a total of 120 articles. However, some of the pulled data needed to be discarded since it was not news story content. Examples of discarded data include opinion pieces and standalone photos. This left 83 *New York Times* articles for analysis. NewspaperArchive.com returned 5,095 results for the time frame under review, so sampling was again utilized. The articles were sorted in chronological order and then every 20th result was pulled for a total of 254 articles. Again, some of the pulled data needed to be discarded either because it was not news story content or because access to the article was denied. Examples of discarded data include opinion pieces and standalone photos. This left 145 articles from this database, for a combined total of 228 news articles from 20 states and Washington, D.C., textually analyzed for this particular chapter.

This book incorporates historical-diachronic analysis, which involved explaining the political, journalistic, and feminist cultures of each woman's era within each chapter in order to contextualize and interpret the data results. This included discussing the key political players in each race, the major issues of the era, and the background of how each woman entered her pioneering race. Journalistically, this included examining extent of advocacy, power distance to government officials, and market orientation. From a feminist perspective, this involved discussing the state of feminism at the time and the women's relationship to the women's movement.

As far as the data itself, the researcher followed the framework of Carvalho (2008), who noted that key questions to ask include: "How are things said and what are the possible implications of that? [and] What is absent from a particular text (factual data, arguments, points of view, etc.)?" (166). After taking "a long preliminary soak" in the data to establish familiarity and context (Hall 1975, 15), the researcher studied each woman's news coverage individually to determine emerging themes for that particular woman and compared and contrasted these themes to those established in the other women's coverage. Finally, the researcher considered what themes apply to the data as a whole.

Each text was read closely multiple times in chronological order by the researcher, who kept a memo throughout the analysis to take notes of patterns throughout the texts. Primarily using the textual analysis strategies advocated by Carvalho (2008, 167), this meant examining the following in each text:

Newspaper Name and State. This data was collected to determine the scope of coverage.

Layout and Structural Organization. This involved examining the prominence of each text (i.e. what page the story ran on, if the text was a story or a brief, and whether there was an accompanying visual) to determine the level of attention for each woman. A brief was defined as an article about the woman with a handful of paragraphs or less, or as an article that may have been about another topic but included a handful of paragraphs or less about the woman. A story was defined as more than a handful of paragraphs about the woman.

Objects. This involved analyzing the text to determine key topics or themes in each article, prompting the researcher to use a constant-comparative approach to compare "each incident to other incidents in order to decide in which categories they belong" (Lindlof and Taylor 2002, 219).

Actors. Data was collected to identify who was discussing the woman in each article: the politician herself, the journalist, a political opponent, a political supporter, or another source. This helped determine who had primary framing power with each politician.

Discursive Strategies. This involved examining particular word choices and excluded language. Carvalho (2008) describes this as selection and composition, meaning analysis of which facts, opinions, and judgments are the media highlighting and how high up in the story do they appear. This may include utilizing the following micro level discursive strategies used by Kwon, Clarke, and Wodak (2014):

1. Equalizing: The extent that multiple viewpoints are included.
2. Simplifying: Reducing the complexity of competing definitions by narrowing down understanding and making the issue "felt" at an emotional level.
3. Legitimating: Justifying underlying assumptions and building up the credibility of particular views. (283)

Ideological Standpoints. Carvalho (2008) views ideology as an "overarching aspect of the text" (170), although she notes that this can be difficult to determine in news texts. For the purpose of this study, this involved noting any word choices used to describe feminism, the woman's movement, women's rights, or other synonyms related to these concepts.

Table A.1 Case Comparisons of News Coverage

Politician	Woodhull	Rankin	Smith	Palin
# Articles analyzed*	279	256	533	228
Dates examined	May 1–Nov. 7, 1872	Jun. 1–Nov. 11, 1916	Jan. 27–July 18, 1964	Aug. 29–Nov. 6, 2008
Brief vs. story**	75% briefs	87% briefs	85% briefs	56% briefs
	25% stories	13% stories	15% stories	44% stories
Framing power***	79% journalists	85% journalists	74% journalists	38% journalists
	14% Woodhull or supporters	14.5% Rankin or supporters	21 % Smith or supporters	39% Palin or supporters
	7% opponents	0.4% opponents	5% opponents	16% opponents
				7% other outside neutral sources
% with woman's picture	0%	13%	5%	25%
% on front page	25%	25%	30%	15%

*All of the search results for Woodhull and Rankin were analyzed. Sampling was utilized with Smith and Palin due to the large number of search results. Although the fewest number of articles were analyzed with Palin, just as much content or more was analyzed when compared to the other women due to the greater length of Palin's articles.

**A brief was defined as an article about the woman with a handful of paragraphs or less, or as an article that may have been about another topic but included a handful of paragraphs or less about the woman. A story was defined as more than a handful of paragraphs about the woman.

***Framing power was determined by evaluating each article about the woman and determining which source(s) were discussing her: the journalist, the woman herself, her supporters, or those who opposed her candidacy. "Opponents" does not necessarily mean her direct election challengers, as the term also includes anyone who voiced opposition to her.

The next step in the process was the contextual analysis of comparing each woman's results to the context of her time and how they informed each other. Finally, the historical-diachronic approach required examination over time of media discourse "to produce a history of media constructions of a given social issue" (Carvalho 2008, 172). Therefore, the researcher used a constant comparative approach throughout the entire analysis to compare each woman's coverage to her predecessors and to generate broader themes to see how media discourse of women politicians has or has not changed over time.

Because "women's relations with power can be seen first and foremost in language" (Perrot 1992, 160), discourse analysis is an appropriate method due to both the historical nature of this study and the goal to analyze media constructions of these four women. As Appleby, Hunt, and Jacobs (1994) write, "to interrogate a text is to open up the fullness of meaning within" (267). As McKee (2003) points out,

> we interpret texts . . . to try and obtain a sense of the ways in which, in particular cultures at particular times, people make sense of the world around them. And, importantly, by seeing the variety of ways in which it is possible to interpret reality, we also understand our own cultures better. (1)

Discourse analysis of newspaper stories is important because "most of our social and political knowledge and beliefs about the world derive from the dozens of news reports we read or see every day" (van Dijk 2002, 110). Therefore, how the media portrayed these women likely influenced public perceptions of them—and, potentially, influenced perceptions of acceptable roles for women overall. Discourse analysis of newspaper articles provides insight into the dominant views of the role of women in a particular time frame via reporters' word choices and framing choices for their news stories about women. Indeed, Zelizer (2011) notes that "the accounts provided by journalists constitute an important source of information about practices, issues, and events of a given time period" (358). Scott believed "traditional language posits a hierarchical order that consistently over time has resulted in the subjugation of women" (Iggers 2005, 131).

Limitations to this methodology included restrictions on which newspapers were archived in the databases. Although these databases are among the best available for historical newspaper research, time and financial constraints of archivists limit how many newspapers have been scanned into the system to date. In addition, this study only examined four cases even though hundreds of women have sought national office. However, as explained throughout the book, the selected cases are believed to provide a representative sample and critical insight into women politicians' press coverage.

Data References

WOODHULL 1872

"A Call on Horace Greeley." 1872. *The New Northwest*, June 7, 2.

"A Greeley 'Reformer.'" 1872. *The New York Times*, September 14, 11.

"Another Set of Candidates." 1872. *Newport Daily News*, May 13, 2.

"A Piebald Presidency." 1872. *New York Herald*, May 11, 10.

"A Pitiable Spectacle." 1872. *The Centre Reporter*, May 24, 3.

"Arrest of Victoria Woodhull, Tennie C. Claflin and Col. Blood." *The New York Times*, November 3, 1.

"Budget of Fun." 1872. *The Ottawa Free Trader*, June 22, 7.

"Campaign Notes." 1872. *Holmes County Republican*, June 6, 2.

"Chips and Things." 1872. *The Athens Post*, May 17, 3.

"Col. Tennie Claflin & Co." 1872. *The Sun*, July 17, 3.

"Glimpses of Gotham." 1872. *The Charleston Daily News*, May 14, 1.

"Glimpses of Gotham." 1872. *The Charleston Daily News*, May 18, 1.

"Here's Your Tickets." 1872. *Bloomington Daily Leader*, May 13, 2.

"Home News." 1872. *Knoxville Daily Chronicle*, November 5, 1.

"Items." *The Holt County Sentinel*, June 7, 2.

"Lady Reformers on the Alert." *New York Herald*, May 11, 10.

"Latest By Telegraph." 1872. *Knoxville Daily Chronicle*, May 12, 1.

"Latest News Items." 1872. *The Emporia News*, September 6, 2.

"Lecture Season." 1872. *Public Ledger*, October 2, 2.

"Mrs. Woodhull's Acceptance." 1872. *Boston Post*, June 6, 1.

"Mrs. Woodhull on a Rampage." 1872. *Boston Post*, May 7, 2.

"News." 1872. *The Columbian*, May 17, 2.

"News of the Week." 1872. *Eaton Weekly Democrat*, May 23, 4.

"News of the Week." 1872. *The Andrew County Republican*, May 24, 4.

"News of the Week." 1872. *Eaton Weekly Democrat*, September 5, 4.

"News Summary." *The Jasper Weekly Courier*, May 24, 2.

"News Summary." 1872. *The True Northerner*, May 24, 2.

"New York." 1872. *Memphis Daily Appeal*, August 28, 1.

"New York City." 1872. *The Wheeling Daily Intelligencer*, August 28, 1.

"Notes and Comments." 1872. *Vermont Watchman and State Journal*, November 6, 1872, 2.

"On Their Feet Again." 1872. *Kokomo Howard County Republican*, November 1, 2.

"Our New York Letter." 1872. *Lamoille Newsdealer*, May 22, 2.

"Political." 1872. *Nashville Union and American*, May 12, 1.

"Political." 1872. *Orleans County Monitor*, May 20, 2.

"Poor Women!" 1872. *Nashville Union and American*, August 28, 1.

Stanton, Elizabeth Cady. 1872. "Woman Suffrage Organization." *The New Northwest*, May 3, 1.

"Sympathy." 1872. *The Elk County Advocate*, November 7, 2.

"Telegraphic." 1872. *The Daily Phoenix*, May 12, 3.

"Telegraphic." 1872. *Washington Standard*, June 22, 2.

"The Dolly Vardens." 1872. *Nashville Union and American*, May 18, 1.

"The Free Love Brokers." 1872. *The Orangeburg News*, May 18, 1.

"The Highly Colored Ticket for the Presidency: The Free Love Communist Candidates in the Field." 1872. *The New Northwest*, June 7, 4.

"The Mother-in-Law Bill." 1872. *The Charleston Daily News*, July 16, 3.

"The National Woman Suffrage Association Are Opposed to Mr. Greeley." 1872. *The New York Times*, May 10, 8.

"The New York Convention." 1872. *The New Northwest*, May 31, 2.

"The Widow Woodhull Furious." 1872. *Evening Star*, May 9, 1.

"The Women's Nomination." 1872. *The Hickman Courier*, May 25, 1.

"The Woodhull." 1872. *The Wheeling Daily Intelligencer*, November 4, 1.

"The Woodhull-Claflin Case." 1872. *The Daily State Journal*, November 5, 1.

"The Woodhull Claflin Party in Trouble." 1872. *The Elk County Advocate*, November 7, 2.

"The Woodhull's Debts." 1872. *The New York Times*, August 28, 2.

"Untitled." 1872a. *Sunbury American*, May 11, 2.

"Untitled." 1872b. *Memphis Daily Appeal*, May 12, 2.

"Untitled." 1872c. *Boston Post*, May 13, 2.

"Untitled." 1872d. *The Cairo Daily Bulletin*, May 15, 2.

"Untitled." 1872e. *The Donaldsonville Chief*, May 18, 2.

"Untitled." 1872f. *Memphis Daily Appeal*, May 21, 2.

"Untitled." 1872g. *The Wichita City Eagle*, May 24, 2.

"Untitled." 1872h. *The Weekly Louisianan*, May 25, 1.

"Untitled." 1872i. *Western Reserve Chronicle*, May 29, 2.

"Untitled." 1872j. *The Tiffin Tribune*, May 30, 1.

"Untitled." 1872k. *The Democratic Press*, June 6, 4.

"Untitled." 1872l. *The Wheeling Daily Intelligencer*, July 12, 1.

"Untitled." 1872m. *The Opelousas Courier*, July 13, 1.

"Untitled." 1872n. *The Pacific Commercial Advertiser*, August 17, 4.

"Untitled." 1872o. *The Hickman Courier*, August 31, 4.

"Untitled." 1872p. *The Daily Phoenix*, September 25, 3.
"Untitled." 1872q. *Dixon Sun*, November 6, 5.
"Victoria on the Rampage." 1872. *The Sun*, August 24, 4.
"Wolves! Wolves! Wolves!" 1872. *Nashville Union and American*, June 27, 4.
"Women Going Wrong." 1872. *The Arizona Sentinel*, June 29, 2.
"Woodhull and Douglass." 1872. *The Sun*, May 11, 1.

RANKIN 1916

"A Divided Congress." 1916. *Rogue River Courier*, November 9, 2.
"A Woman in the House." 1916. *The Washington Times*, November 9, 6.
"Bitter Campaign On In Montana." 1916. *Bismarck Daily Tribune*, November 5, 14.
"Congress to Have Woman Member." 1916. *The Daily Gate City and Constitution-Democrat*, November 10, 2.
"Congresswoman is Well Known Here." 1916. *The Washington Times*, November 11, 14.
"Congresswoman No. 1 Good Cook and Seamstress." 1916. *The Topeka State Journal*, November 11, 5.
"Congresswoman Nominated in Montana." 1916. *New Castle News*, September 14, 5.
"Country Watches Jeannette Rankin." 1916. *The Glasgow Courier*, September 22, 1.
"Democrats Have House and Senate." 1916. *Mohave County Miner*, November 11, 1.
"Democrats Lose Full Control of the Lower House." 1916. *Daily Capital Journal*, November 10, 2.
"Democrats May Not Control House." 1916. *Bisbee Daily Review*, November 10, 2.
"Democrats Tied in House, Three Districts Missing." 1916. *The Evening World*, November 10, 1.
"Edwards Leads in Montana Count." 1916. *Bakersfield Californian*, August 31, 2.
"First Congress Woman Makes Own Clothes and Cooks Well." 1916. *Indianapolis Star*, November 11, 3.
"First Congresswoman Said to be Splendid Cook." 1916. *Indiana Evening Gazette*, November 11, 1.
"First Congresswoman Trims Her Own Hats, Makes Her Clothes, and Can Cook, Too." 1916. *Hammond Lake County Times*, November 11, 1.
"First Congresswoman Trims Her Own Hats, Makes Her Clothes, and Can Cook, Too." 1916. *Newark Advocate*, November 11, 5.
"First Woman to Congress." 1916. *Richmond Times-Dispatch*, November 11, 1.
"First Woman Wins Seat in Congress." 1916. *The Oklahoma City Times*, November 11, 1.
"For Congress." 1916. *Anaconda Standard*, October 31, 6.
"Girl Enters Race for Lower House." 1916. *Tulsa Daily World*, August 30, 1916, 5.
"Good Government Club Banquet at the Butte." 1916. *Anaconda Standard*, July 12, 9.
"Hughes Will Carry Montana." *Bismarck Daily Tribune*, October 4, 1.
"Introducing Jeannette." 1916. *The Washington Times*, November 11, 1.

"Is First Congress Woman." 1916. *The Daily Gate City and Constitution-Democrat,* November 11, 1.

"Is First Woman in Congress." 1916. *Boston Post,* November 11, 1.

"Jeannette Rankin for Congress." 1916. *The Enterprise,* October 12, 1.

"Jeannette Rankin is Some Chicken." 1916. *Fort Wayne News,* November 11, 3.

"Jeannette Rankin Out for Congress." 1916. *The Glasgow Courier,* August 18, 12.

"Jeannette Rankin Out for Congress." 1916. *The Glasgow Courier,* August 23, 12.

"Jeannette Rankin Teas." 1916. *The Glasgow Courier,* September 29, 1.

"Let People Know." 1916. *The Topeka State Journal,* November 2, 3.

"Majorities in Congress Have Been Cut Down." 1916. *Arizona Republican,* November 10, 1.

"Malta Items." 1916. *The Glasgow Courier,* October 6, 1916, 5.

"Miss Jeannette Rankin." 1916. *Logansport Times,* October 20, 4.

"Miss Jeannette Rankin Is Given Big Reception." 1916. *Anaconda Standard,* August 3, 3.

"Miss Rankin at Deer Lodge." 1916. *Anaconda Standard,* September 3, 9.

"Miss Rankin Boosted by Miller." 1916. *Daily Inter Lake,* September 27, 1.

"Miss Rankin Elected." 1916. *Harrisburg Telegraph,* November 11, 11.

"Miss Rankin Elected: Montana Woman Will Be the First to Sit in Congress." 1916. *The New York Times,* November 11, 2.

"Miss Rankin is Coming Saturday." 1916. *Cut Bank Pioneer Press,* September 15, 1.

"Miss Rankin Lays Congress Plans." 1916. *New York Tribune,* November 11, 1.

"Miss Rankin Talks at Havre On Why Woman for Congress." 1916. *Anaconda Standard,* August 16, 14.

"Miss Rankin's Campaign for Congressional Nomination." 1916. *Anaconda Standard,* August 12, 9.

"Montana." 1916. *New Castle News,* November 7, 1916, 5.

"Montana." 1916. *Logansport Pharos Reporter,* November 7, 1916, 5.

"Montana." 1916. *East Liverpool Evening Review,* November 7, 1916, 4.

"Montana." 1916. *Marysville Evening Tribune,* November 8, 1916, 1.

"Montana." 1916. *Washington Court House Herald,* November 8, 5.

"Montana Elects Woman to Congress." 1916. *New York Tribune,* November 10, 1.

"Montana Has First Woman in Congress." 1916. *Boston Post,* November 11, 4.

"Montana May Elect a Woman to Congress." 1916. *Stevens Point Daily Journal,* October 22, 3.

"Montana to Elect a Congresswoman." 1916. *The Sun,* October 12, 4.

"Montana Will Elect a Woman to Next Congress." 1916. *Syracuse Herald,* October 15, 10.

"Montana Woman is Out for Congress." 1916. *Evening Independent,* July 14, 15.

"Montana Woman is Out for Congress." 1916. *The Ogden Standard,* July 17, 4.

"Montana Woman is Out for Congress." 1916. *Grand Forks Herald,* July 17, 10.

"Montana Woman is Out for Congress." 1916. *The Topeka State Journal,* July 19, 7.

"Montana Woman Still in Lead for Congress." 1916. *Boston Evening Globe,* November 10, 7.

"Not One But Both." 1916. *Anaconda Standard,* November 4, 6.

"Republicans Draft Platform to Meet the New Time in Montana." 1916. *Cut Bank Pioneer Press*, September 15, 1.
"Sees Hughes Majority in Electoral College." 1916. *The Washington Times*, October 21, 8.
"Sentiment for Miss Rankin Still Growing." 1916. *The Glasgow Courier*, November 3, 1.
"Seven Men in Race Against Her." 1916. *The Daily Ardmoreite*, August 24, 3.
"Suffragists Rejoice as Miss Rankin Wins in Mont." 1916. *Harrisburg Telegraph*, November 9, 9.
"The House Beautiful." 1916. *The New York Times*, October 13, 10.
"The Lady from Mont." 1916. *The Washington Times*, November 11, 1.
"Three Women Running for Congress." 1916. *Norwich Bulletin*, November 7, 1.
"T.R. Indorses [sic] Woman." 1916. *Grand Forks Herald*, November 4, 3.
"Untitled." 1916a. *Anaconda Standard*, October 8, 4.
"Untitled." 1916b. *The Butler Weekly Times*, July 13, 3.
"Untitled." 1916c. *The Daily Gate City and Constitution-Democrat*, October 20, 1916, 3.
"Untitled." 1916d. *The Daily Gate City and Constitution-Democrat*, November 6, 4.
"Untitled." 1916e. *The Holt County Sentinel*, November 10, 1.
"Untitled." 1916f. *Williston Graphic*, September 28, 4.
"Victory Certain." 1916. *Daily Inter Lake*, October 18, 2.
"Wilson in California." 1916. *The New York Times*, November 9, 1.
"Woman Congressman." 1916. *The Bennington Evening Banner*, November 9, 1.
"Woman Going to Congress Hard Fighter." 1916. *Des Moines Daily News*, November 11, 1.
"Woman Leading in Montana Primaries." 1916. *Boston Daily Globe*, September 1, 1.
"Woman Leads State Ticket." 1916. *Evening Star*, September 1, 3.
"Woman Likely to Sit in Next Congress." 1916. *Fort Wayne News*, October 26, 8.
"Woman's Election Predicted." 1916. *Evening Star*, November 5, 14.
"Woman Voters Fail to Follow Leaders." 1916. *The New York Times*, November 10, 5.
"Women May Swing Vote in Two States." 1916. *The New York Times*, November 5, 2.
"Wonder Woman is Miss Jeannette Rankin." 1916. *Evening Public Ledger*, November 11, 6.
"Would Sit in House of Representatives." 1916. *The Evening Herald*, October 25, 4.

SMITH 1964

"A Chic Lady Who Fights: Margaret Chase Smith." 1964. *The New York Times*, January 28, 17.
Associated Press. "Candidate List in N.H. Growing." 1964. *Daily Journal*, January 28, 1.
Associated Press. "Cloud of Indecision Hovers Over New Hampshire Primary." 1964. *Reno Evening Gazette*, March 9, 1.

Associated Press. "Cow Palace Capsules." 1964. *North Adams Transcript*, July 17, 4.

Associated Press. "Goldwater Heads for New Hampshire Today." 1964. *Centralia Evening Sentinel*, March 2, 2.

Associated Press. "Goldwater Flying Mrs. Smith to N.H." 1964. *Berkshire Eagle*, January 30, 30.

Associated Press. "Goldwater Says Sen. Chase to Get Surprising Vote." 1964. *North Adams Transcript*, January 29, 8.

Associated Press. "Make Pleas for Oregon Votes." 1964. *Lock Haven Express*, May 14, 20.

Associated Press. "Margaret Chase Smith Into Race." 1964. *Arkansas City Daily Traveler*, January 27, 1.

Associated Press. "Margaret Smith Joins the Race." 1964. *Salina Journal*, January 27, 2.

Associated Press. "Mrs. Smith Beats Sun to the Voters." 1964. *The New York Times*, February 12, 21.

Associated Press. "Mrs. Smith Gets Warm Reception." 1964. *Phoenix Arizona Republic*, February 11, 11.

Associated Press. "Mrs. Smith on Oregon Ballot." 1964. *The New York Times*, March 6, 40.

Associated Press. "Mrs. Smith Setting Precedent." 1964. *Freeport Journal Standard*, July 15, 1.

Associated Press. "Mrs. Smith: The Pros Treat Her With Respect." 1964. *Des Moines Register*, January 28, 5.

Associated Press. "N.H. Votes for Lodge." 1964. *Hutchinson News*, March 11, 1.

Associated Press. "Oklahoman Keeps Affairs in Order for First Lady Member of Senate." 1964. *Ada Evening News*, February 9, 12.

Associated Press. "Republican Hopefuls in Last Oregon Campaign." 1964. *Appleton Post Crescent*, May 14, 2.

Associated Press. "Rocky Aims Barbs at Goldwater." 1964. *Joplin Globe*, February 15, 2.

Associated Press. "Senator Cotton Calls on Mrs. Smith at Dartmouth." 1964. *The New York Times*, February 13, 18.

Associated Press. "Sen. Smith Becomes Presidential Candidate." 1964. *Rocky Mount Evening Telegram*, January 27, 1.

Associated Press. "Sen. Smith Expected to Seek Nomination." 1964. *High Point Enterprise*, January 27, 2.

Associated Press. "Sen. Smith Opens Campaign." 1964. *Biddeford Journal*, February 10, 1, 8.

Associated Press. "Sen. Smith Said After U.S. Vice Presidency." *Greenfield Recorder Gazette*, April 11, 3.

Associated Press. "Six-Way GOP Primary Fight Boils Toward Showdown." 1964. *Baytown Sun*, May 14, 1.

Associated Press. "Smith Buttons Collector's Items." 1964. *Portsmouth Herald*, July 18, 6.

Associated Press. "Smith Divides Women." 1964. *Pasadena Independent*, January 29, 9.

Associated Press. "Solon Hoping Extremism Not an Issue." 1964. *San Antonio Express and News*, July 18, 6.

Associated Press. "Some GOP Leaders Disturbed Goldwater May Head Party." 1964. *The News*, June 8, 19.

Associated Press. "Takes Firm Issue." 1964. *Monroe News Star*, February 6, 1.

Associated Press. "Upsets Invited by Indecision." 1964. *San Antonio Light*, March 9, 3.

Associated Press. "Warm Welcome for Mrs. Smith." 1964. *Des Moines Register*, February 11, 10.

Associated Press. "Women Not Unanimous on Sen. Smith's Entry." 1964. *Fitchburg Sentinel*, January 29, 25.

"Barkis is Willing: School May Yield GOP Candidate." 1964. *Lowell Sun*, February 5, 35.

Bell, Jack. "New Hampshire Primary Voting Could Surprise." 1964. *Madison Wisconsin State Journal*, March 8, 6B.

Bell, Jack. "Lodge Looms as Threat." 1964. *Burlington Daily Times News*, March 9, 1.

"Candidate Smith Gets Little Support From Her Own Sex." 1964. *Salina Journal*, January 31, 1964, 5.

Carlton, Mary Ellis. "Ballots and Bonnets: Should the Next President Be a Woman?" 1964. *Independent Press Telegram*, February 2, W4.

Carocci, Vincent. "Blatt Wonders If Senator Smith is Serious Candidate." 1964. *Somerset Daily American*, January 30, 2.

Christensen, Jennie. "Outlook Seen Bright for Women in Politics." 1964. *Logan Herald Journal*, June 25, 2.

Conway, William. "Barry Wins Illinois Test." *Huron Daily Plainsman*, April 15, 1.

Conway, William. "Goldwater Wins GOP Primary Race in Illinois." 1964. *Salisbury Times*, April 15, 1.

Davis, J.W. "Republicans Working Against 'Better Deal' Johnson." 1964. *Petersburg Progress Index*, March 22, 3.

Fenton, John. "New Hampshire Campaign Heads for Climax Tuesday." 1964. *The New York Times*, March 8, 1.

Fenton, John. "Senator Smith on Campaign Trail." 1964. *The New York Times*, February 11, 1.

Hawkins, Lewis. "All GOP Leaders on Oregon Ballot." 1964. *Oneonta Star*, February 29, 1.

Herman, Pat. "Untitled." *Salisbury Times*, April 11, 14.

Hinton, Pat. "Woman Who Never Lost an Election Seeks Presidency." 1964. *Altoona Mirror*, January 30, 21.

Hunter, Marjorie. "Margaret Chase Smith Seeks Presidency: Moved to Run, She Says, by Reasons Not to Do So." 1964. *The New York Times*, January 28, 1.

Kent, John. "Would You Vote for a Woman as President?" 1964. *Lowell Sun*, June 28, 76.

Klein, Jerry. "Who's Who at the GOP Convention?" 1964. *Ogden Standard Examiner*, July 12, 55.

Lewine, Frances. "Women in Government Bewail Slow Progress." 1964. *Cedar Rapids Gazette*, February 3, 15.

"Margaret Chase Smith." 1964. *Biddeford Journal*, February 25, 8.

"Margaret Smith Stays in Race 'to the Finish.'" 1964. *The New York Times*, July 7, 24.

Marlow, James. "Campaign Looks Odd to Writer." 1964. *Ada Evening News*, April 16, 10.

Marlow, James. "GOP is All Mixed Up on Candidates." 1964. *Arkansas City Daily Traveler*, February 5, 12.

Marlow, James. "New Hampshire Presidential Race Exhibits an Almost Dreamy Quality." 1964. *Joplin News Herald*, February 13, 5.

Marlow, James. "New Hampshire Primary Has Almost Dreamy Pace So Far." 1964. *Alton Evening Telegraph*, February 13, 9.

Marlow, James. "N.H. Primary Race Seems Unreal." 1964. *Kingsport Times*, February 13, 8.

Marlow, James. "Who Will Win New Hampshire?" 1964. *Sandusky Register*, February 13, 18.

Mohr, Charles. "Goldwater Fears Unclear Primary: Doubts Wide Margin for Any New Hampshire Hopeful." 1964. *The New York Times*, January 29, 16.

"Mrs. Smith Says Her Age Is No Bar to Presidency." 1964. *The New York Times*, February 7, 14.

"Mrs. Smith Winds Up New Hampshire Trip." 1964. *The New York Times*, February 16, 48.

"Mrs. Smith Puts Bonnet in Ring." 1964. *Tyrone Daily Herald*, January 28, 1.

Phelps, Robert. "Rockefeller Opens California Drive: Wife Accompanies Him on Trip to San Francisco." 1964. *The New York Times*, January 29, 17.

Posner, Michael. 1964. "Mrs. Smith Assured of Maine's 14 Votes." 1964. *Provo Daily Herald*, January 28, 12.

Robbins, Cordelia. "World in a Spin." 1964. *Elyria Chronicle Telegram*, February 17, 2.

Stahl, Judith. "Senator Loves Being Treated Like a Lady." 1964. *Burlington Daily Times News*, March 12, 8C.

"Teenage Forum." 1964. *Lebanon Daily News*, February 7, 11.

Thomas, Helen. "Lady Orator to Deliver GOP Talk." 1964. *Cedar Rapids Gazette*, July 12, 1964 7C.

UPI. "Barry, Rock Step Up Pace." 1964. *Billings Gazette*, February 17, 9.

UPI. "'Courageous Leadership' Asked by Senator Smith." 1964. *The New York Times*, June 15, 32.

UPI. "Lady Assured 14 Votes." 1964. *Huron Daily Plainsman*, January 28, 1.

UPI. "Margaret Chase Smith Out to Remove Sign." 1964. *Santa Fe New Mexican*, January 28, 2.

UPI. "Mrs. Smith Dwells on Feminism." 1964. *Berkshire Eagle*, February 11, 3.

UPI. "Mrs. Smith May Seek Presidency." 1964. *New Castle News*, January 27, 1.

UPI. "New Hampshire Gets Ready for 'Big Two.'" 1964. *Western Kansas Press*, February 18, 2.

UPI. "Official Vote is Released." 1964. *Danville Bee*, March 14, 9.
UPI. "Race Entered by Mrs. Smith." 1964. *Statesville Record and Landmark*, January 28, 1.
UPI. "Sen. Smith in GOP Race." 1964. *Amarillo Daily News*, January 28, 2.
Wehrwein, Austin. "Mrs. Smith Ran Well in Suburbs: Illinois Showing Surprising in Some Goldwater Areas." 1964. *The New York Times*, April 19, 81.
Wilson, Richard. "Mrs. Smith's Bonnet in Ring." 1964. *Des Moines Register*, January 28, 1.
Wicker, Tom. "Splintered Vote Likely in Primary." 1964. *The New York Times*, March 9, 1.

PALIN 2008

Allen, Eugenie. "Start Me Up: Profiles of Seven Women Who Successfully Returned to the Work Force." 2008. *The New York Times*, September 21, C13.
"All in Favor Say Eye – Glasses That Is." *Cedar Rapids Gazette*, October 1, E1.
Associated Press. "Claiming Place on GOP Ticket, Palin Mocks Obama." 2008. *Orange Leader*, September 4, 6A.
Associated Press. "Court Will Hear Appeal in Palin Investigation." 2008. *The New York Times*, October 4, A17.
Associated Press. "GOP Praises McCain, Defends Palin at RNC." 2008. *Roswell Daily Record*, September 3, A1, A9.
Associated Press. "McCain Taps Palin for VP." 2008. *Alton Telegraph*, August 30, A1, A7.
Associated Press. "Need Palin Hair for Halloween?" 2008. *Daily Herald Suburban Chicago*, October 27, 5.
Associated Press. "Palin Casts Herself as Washington Outsider." 2008. *Bedford Gazette*, September 4, 5.
Associated Press. "Palin Has Checkered Ethics Past." 2008. *Kinston Free Press*, October 15, A3.
Associated Press. "Palin Seeks to Defend Qualifications." 2008. *Indiana Gazette*, September 12, A13.
Associated Press. "Palin Still Excites GOP, but Her Luster Dims a Bit." 2008. *Amarillo Globe News*, September 30, B4.
Associated Press. "Some Moms Are Asking: Would Palin Help Us As VP?" 2008. *Harrisonburg Daily News Record*, October 7, B5.
Associated Press. "Tonight at 8: Biden vs. Palin." 2008. *Daily Herald Suburban Chicago*, October 2, 13.
Babington, Charles. "Mixed Signals." 2008. *Tribune-Democrat*, August 30, C7.
Baker, Peter. "A Bold Move, With Risks." 2008. *The New York Times*, August 30, A1.
Bosman, Julie. "On 'SNL,' Fey as Palin, and Palin as Palin." 2008. *The New York Times*, October 19, 25.

Bumiller, Elisabeth. "Palin Disclosures Spotlight McCain's Screening Process: Daughter's Pregnancy One of Several Revelations." 2008. *The New York Times*, September 2, A1.

Bumiller, Elisabeth, and Jeff Zeleny. "With Themes Set, Both Campaigns Begin a 60-Day Dash to Election Day." 2008. *The New York Times*, September 6, A13.

Bumiller, Elisabeth, and Michael Cooper. "On Center Stage, Palin Electrifies Convention: McCain Selected as Nominee of G.O.P." 2008. *The New York Times*, September 4, A1, A23.

Bumiller, Elisabeth, and Patrick Healy. "Palin Plans to Visit U.N. and Join Protest of Iran." 2008. *The New York Times*, September 18, A24.

Cole, Jean. "Looking for Sign? McCain Signs in Demand." 2008. *Athens News Courier*, September 9, A1, A4.

Cooper, Michael, and Elizabeth Bumiller. "Alaskan is McCain's Choice." 2008. *The New York Times*, August 30, A1.

Cooper, Michael, and Jim Rutenberg. "McCain Barbs Stirring Outcry As Distortions: Backlash Focuses on 2 Attacks on Obama." 2008. *The New York Times*, September 13, A1.

"Corrections: Business Day." 2008. *The New York Times*, September 3, A4.

Espo, David. "GOP Convention Opens with Appeal for Aid." 2008. *Alamogordo Daily News*, September 2, A1.

Espo, David. "McCain Campaign Limits Palin Access." 2008. *Daily Sitka Sentinel*, September 16, A1.

Faher, Mike. "Palin Rally Expected to Fill War Memorial." 2008. *Tribune-Democrat*, October 10, A1, A2.

"Frenzied Media." 2008. *Odessa American*, September 6, A2.

Goldman, Adam. "Palin's Tenacity Showed on the Court." 2008. *Tribune-Democrat*, October 9, A8.

Green, Chris. "Brownback Supportive of VP Pick." 2008. *Hutchinson News*, September 1, A13.

Healy, Patrick. "Campaign Diary: The Podium View." 2008. *The New York Times*, November 2, AR1.

Healy, Patrick. "McCain's Pick May Foster Bigger Campaign Role for Clinton." 2008. *The New York Times*, September 1, A15.

Healy, Patrick. "Two Conventions With No Shortage of Contrasts." 2008. *The New York Times*, September 4, A22.

Healy, Patrick, and Michael Luo. "Palin's Wardrobe Could Hurt Image." 2008. *Indiana Gazette*, October 23, A9.

Herman, Ken. "The Best and Worst of the GOP Convention in St. Paul." 2008. *Syracuse Post Standard*, September 5, A7.

Italie, Hillel, and Anne Sutton. "Palin May Not Be Able to Cash In on Veep Fame." 2008. *Daily Sitka Sentinel*, October 31, 7.

Johnson, Glen. "Palin's Speech Boosts GOP." 2008. *Indiana Gazette*, September 4, 12.

Kershaw, Sarah. "Now, the Bad News on Teenage Marriage." 2008. *The New York Times*, September 4, G1.

Kuhnhenn, Jim. "Historic Race Alters Landscape, Breaks Mold." 2008. *Ashtabula Star Beacon*, September 7, A1, A2.

Lambert, Bruce. "Economy Is No. 1 Concern, But Agreement Stops There." 2008. *The New York Times*, October 26, LI1, 6.

Luo, Michael. "Investigators Are Looking at Governor About Firing." 2008. *The New York Times*, August 30, A13.

"McCain, Palin to Spend Next Few Weeks on Trail." 2008. *Syracuse Post Standard*, September 11, A9.

MCT News Service. "Troopergate Report: Palin Abused Power." 2008. *Odessa American*, October 11, A7.

Nagourney, Adam. "A Onetime McCain Insider Is Now Offering Advice (Unwanted) From the Outside." 2008. *The New York Times*, October 23, A23.

Nagourney, Adam, and Elizabeth Bumiller. "McCain Leaps Into a Thicket." 2008. *The New York Times*, September 26, A1.

Nagourney, Adam, and Jeff Zeleny. "Obama Raises Level of Attack As Party Frets: New TV Ads Against Energized G.O.P." 2008. *The New York Times*, September 12, A1.

Ohlemacher, Stephen. "Obama Accepts Nomination." 2008. *Indiana Gazette*, August 29, A12.

"On nytimes.com: A Convention Concludes." 2008. *The New York Times*, September 5, A4.

Phillips, Kate. "As a Matter of Faith, Biden Says Life Begins at Conception." 2008. *The New York Times*, September 8, A19.

"Poll: Hillary Voters Not Coming to Obama." 2008. *Harrisonburg Daily News Record*, September 24, 2008, A5.

Powell, Michael, and Jo Becker. "Palin's Hand Seen in Battle Over Mine in Alaska." 2008. *The New York Times*, October 22, A22.

Quinn, Steve, and Calvin Woodward. "Meet Sarah Palin: Making History and Unknown." 2008. *Hutchinson News*, August 30, A1, A3.

Riley, Robert. "What is Your Opinion of Sarah Palin?" 2008. *Lawrence Journal World*, September 12, A5.

Scott, Megan. "Talking Heads: A Barometer of an Election?" 2008. *Altoona Mirror*, October 5, D1.

Seelye, Katharine Q. "Beyond Roe, Palin Has No Regrets on Court Rulings." 2008. *The New York Times*, October 2, A26.

Seelye, Katharine Q. "Seeking Sarah Palin." 2008. *The New York Times*, September 25, A24.

Seewer, John. "Obama Notches Slight Lead in Ohio." 2008. *Sandusky Register*, September 12, A8,

Sidoti, Liz. "Wounded GOP Seeks Remedy." 2008. *Daily Herald Suburban Chicago*, November 6, A6.

Stafford, Diane. "Let's Not Wink at Careless Gesture." 2008. *Syracuse Post Standard*, October 19, D2.

Stelter, Brian. "Hannity Renews Contract, Cementing Fox News Role." 2008. *The New York Times*, October 9, C3.

Stelter, Brian. "Record Audience for Debate." 2008. *The New York Times*, October 4, A15.

Stelter, Brian. "SNL's Goals: Funny and Evenhanded." 2008. *The New York Times*, September 17, E2.

Stelter, Brian. "The Other Tina Fey." 2008. *The New York Times*, October 11, A13.

Stolberg, Sheryl Gay. "Free to Be His Own Buckley: A Choice That Breaks with Pups Legacy." 2008. *The New York Times*, October 19, ST1.

Tanenhaus, Sam. "A Once-United G.O.P. Emerges, in Identity Crisis." 2008. *The New York Times*, November 6, P1.

Taylor, Andrew. "Palin Takes Center Stage As Questions Swirl." 2008. *Clearfield Progress*, September 3, A3.

"The '08 Campaign: A Sea Change for Politics as We Know It." 2008. *The New York Times*, November 4, A1.

"The Mayor, My Friend." 2008. *The New York Times*, September 29, A17.

Toney, Lauren. "Palin's Visit Fires Up GOP." 2008. *Roswell Daily Record*, October 21, A1, A6.

Washington Post. "GOP's Palin Says Obama Regrets Bypassing Clinton." 2008. *Cedar Rapids Gazette*, September 13, A2.

Wehrman, Jessica. "A Portrait of 'Sarah Barracuda.' " 2008. *Madison Wisconsin State Journal*, August 30, A1, A10.

Yardley, William. "An Outsider Who Charms: Sarah Heath Palin." 2008. *The New York Times*, August 30, A1.

Yardley, William. "Whale Protection Bolstered as Palin Objects." 2008. *The New York Times*, October 18, A11.

Zeleny, Jeff. "Feeling a Challenge, Obama Sharpens His Silver Tongue." 2008. *The New York Times*, September 10, A20.

References

The 2000s in America. 2013a. Edited by Craig Belanger. Vol. 1. Ipswich, MA: Salem Press.

The 2000s in America. 2013b. Edited by Craig Belanger. Vol. 2. Ipswich, MA: Salem Press.

"The 2006 Elections: Alaska." 2006. *The New York Times*, November 9, P13.

Aday, Sean, and James Devitt. 2001. "Style Over Substance: Newspaper Coverage of Elizabeth Dole's Presidential Bid." *The Harvard International Journal of Press/ Politics* 6 (2):52–73.

Alexander, Paul. 2008. *Man of the People, Revised and Updated: The Maverick Life and Career of John McCain*. Hoboken, N.J.: John Wiley & Sons.

Almond, Gabriel. 1956. "Comparative Political Systems." *The Journal of Politics* 18 (3):391–409.

Andersen, Kristi. 1996. *After Suffrage: Women in Partisan and Electoral Politics Before the New Deal*. Chicago, IL: University of Chicago Press.

Anderson, Karrin Vasby. 2005. "The First Lady: A Site of 'American Womanhood'." In *Leading Ladies of the White House: Communication Strategies of Notable Twentieth-Century First Ladies*, edited by Molly Meijer Wertheimer, 1–15. Lanham, MD: Rowman & Littlefield Publishers.

Anderson, Karrin Vasby, and Kristina Horn Sheeler. 2005. *Governing Codes: Gender, Metaphor, and Political Identity*. Lanham, MD: Lexington Books.

Anderson, Kathryn. 2002. "Introduction." In *Jeannette Rankin: America's Conscience*, edited by Norma Smith, 5–22. Helena, MT: Montana Historical Society Press.

Anthony, Katharine. 1954. *Susan B. Anthony: Her Personal History and Her Era*. New York, N.Y.: Russell and Russell.

Appleby, Joyce, Lynn Hunt, and Margaret Jacobs. 1994. *Telling the Truth About History*. New York, N.Y.: W.W. Norton & Co.

Associated Press. 1950a. "Clubwomen Laud Senator Smith." *Portland Press Herald* June 3, 1.

————. 1950b. "Senator Margaret Chase Smith Delivers Blistering Attack." *Norwich Sun* June 2, 1.

————. 1950c. "Woman Senator Blasts Tactics in Red Inquiry." *Bradford Era*, June 2, 1.

————. 1989. "President Awards Lucille Ball Freedom Award Posthumously." *Galveston Daily News*, July 7, 4A.

Baker, Paula. 1984. "The Domestication of Politics: Women and American Political Society, 1780–1920." *American Historical Review* 89 (June):620–647.

Balz, Dan, and Haynes Johnson. 2009. *The Battle for America 2008*. New York, N.Y.: Viking.

Banning, Stephen A. 1998. "The Professionalization of Journalism." *Journalism History* 24 (4):157–164.

Barber, James. 2009. *The Presidential Character: Predicting Performance in the White House*. 4th ed. New York, N.Y.: Pearson.

Barnhurst, Kevin G., and Diana Mutz. 1997. "American Journalism and the Decline in Event-Centered Reporting." *Journal of Communication* 47 (4):27.

Barnhurst, Kevin, and John Nerone. 2009. "Journalism History." In *The Handbook of Journalism Studies*, edited by Karin Wahl-Jorgensen and Thomas Hanitzsch, 17–28. New York, N.Y.: Routledge.

Barry, Kathleen. 1988. *Susan B. Anthony: A Biography of a Singular Feminist*. New York, N.Y.: New York University Press.

Beasley, Maurine, and Sheila Gibbons. 2003. *Taking Their Place: A Documentary History of Women and Journalism*. 2nd ed. State College, PA: Strata Publishing.

Bell, Allan. 1998. "The Discourse Structure of News Stories." In *Approaches to Media Discourse*, edited by Allan Bell and Peter Garrett, 64–104. Oxford: Blackwell.

Benet, Lorenzo. 2009. *Trailblazer: An Intimate Biography of Sarah Palin*. New York, N.Y.: Threshold Editions.

Blake, Aaron. 2014. "Yes, Politics Is Still Dominated by Old, White Men. Here's Why." *Washington Post*, September 3. From: http://tinyurl.com/ncd9dap.

Braden, Maria. 1996. *Women Politicians and the Media*. Lexington, KY: University Press of Kentucky.

Bradley, Patricia. 2005. *Women and the Press: The Struggle for Equality*. Evanston, IL: Northwestern University Press.

Brands, H.W. 2010. *American Dreams: The United States Since 1945*. New York, N.Y.: Penguin Press.

Bronstein, Carolyn. 2005. "Representing the Third Wave: Mainstream Print Media Framing of a New Feminist Movement." *Journalism & Mass Communication Quarterly* 82 (4):783–803.

Bulkeley, Christy. 2002. "A Pioneering Generation Marked the Path For Women Journalists." *Nieman Reports* 56 (1):60.

Bunting III, Josiah. 2004. *Ulysses S. Grant*. New York, N.Y.: Times Books.

Burns, Lisa. 2008. *First Ladies and the Fourth Estate*. DeKalb, IL: Northern Illinois University Press.

Butler, Judith. 1990. "Performative Acts and Gender Constitution: An Essay in Phenomenology and Feminist Theory." In *Performing Feminisms: Feminist Critical Theory and Theater*, edited by Sue-Ellen Case, 270–282. Baltimore, MD: Johns Hopkins University Press.

Butterfield, Herbert. 1965. *The Whig Interpretation of History*. New York, N.Y.: W.W. Norton & Co.

Byerly, Carolyn M., and Karen Ross. 2006. *Women and Media: A Critical Introduction*. Malden, MA: Blackwell Publishing.

Carlin, Diana B., and Kelly L. Winfrey. 2009. "Have You Come a Long Way, Baby? Hillary Clinton, Sarah Palin, and Sexism in 2008 Campaign Coverage." *Communication Studies* 60 (4):326–343. doi: 10.1080/10510970903109904.

Caro, Robert. 2002. *The Years of Lyndon Johnson: Master of the Senate*. New York, N.Y.: Knopf.

———. 2012. *The Years of Lyndon Johnson: The Passage of Power*. New York, N.Y.: Knopf.

Carr, David, and Brian Stelter. 2008. "Campaigns in a Web 2.0 World." *The New York Times*, Nov. 3, B1, B11.

Carvalho, Anabela. 2008. "Media(ted) Discourse and Society." *Journalism Studies* 9 (2):161–177. doi: 10.1080/14616700701848162.

Census Bureau. n.d. Resident Population and Apportionment of the U.S. House of Representatives. http://www.census.gov/dmd/www/resapport/states/montana.pdf.

Chafe, William H. 1972. *The American Woman: Her Changing Social, Economic, and Political Roles, 1920–1970*. New York. N.Y.: Oxford University Press.

———. 2000. "The Road to Equality: 1962–Today." In *No Small Courage: A History of Women in the United States*, edited by Nancy Cott, 529–586. Oxford, UK: Oxford University Press.

Chamberlin, Hope. 1973. *A Minority of Members: Women in the U.S. Congress*. New York, N.Y.: Praeger Publishers.

Chambers, Deborah, Linda Steiner, and Carole Fleming. 2004. *Women and Journalism*. London: Routledge.

Chozick, Amy. 2015. Hillary Clinton Announces 2016 Presidential Bid. *The New York Times*, http://www.nytimes.com/2015/04/13/us/politics/hillary-clinton-2016-presidential-campaign.html?_r=1.

Cooper Jr., John Milton. 2009. *Woodrow Wilson: A Biography*. New York, N.Y.: Alfred Knopf.

Cose, Ellis. 1989. *The Press*. New York, N.Y.: William Morrow and Co.

Cott, Nancy. 1987. *The Grounding of Modern Feminism*. New Haven, CT: Yale University Press.

Cott, Nancy F., Gerda Lerner, Kathryn Kish Sklar, Ellen Carol DuBois, and Nancy A. Hewitt. 2003. "Considering the State of U.S. Women's History." *Journal of Women's History* 15 (1):145–163.

Curnalia, Rebecca M. L., and Dorian L. Mermer. 2014. "The 'Ice Queen' Melted and It Won Her the Primary: Evidence of Gender Stereotypes and the Double Bind in News Frames of Hillary Clinton's 'Emotional Moment.'" *Qualitative Research Reports in Communication* 15 (1):26–32. doi: 10.1080/17459435.2014.955589.

Curran, James. 2005. "What Democracy Requires of the Media." In *The Institutions of American Democracy: The Press*, edited by Geneva Overholser and Kathleen Hall Jamieson, 120–140. Oxford, UK: Oxford University Press.

Daly, Christopher. 2012. *Covering America: A Narrative History of a Nation's Journalism.* Amherst, MA: University of Massachusetts Press.

"Democratic Congressmen Elected." 1916. *Boston Post*, November 9, 10.

Deutsch, Sarah Jane. 2000. "From Ballots to Breadlines: 1920–1940." In *No Small Courage: A History of Women in the United States*, edited by Nancy Cott, 413–472. Oxford, UK: Oxford University Press.

Dicken-Garcia, Hazel. 1989. *Journalistic Standards in Nineteenth-Century America.* Madison, WI: University of Wisconsin Press.

DuBois, Ellen, Mari Jo Buhle, Temma Kaplan, Gerda Lerner, and Carroll Smith-Rosenberg. 1980. "Politics and Culture in Women's History: A Symposium." *Feminist Studies* 6 (1):26–64.

Edwards, Rebecca. 1997. *Angels in the Machinery: Gender in American Party Politics from the Civil War to the Progressive Era.* New York, N.Y.: Oxford University Press.

Esser, Frank, and Andrea Umbricht. 2014. "The Evolution of Objective and Interpretative Journalism in the Western Press: Comparing Six News Systems since the 1960s." *Journalism & Mass Communication Quarterly* 91 (2):229–249. doi: 10.1177/1077699014527459.

Fahrney, Ralph. 1936. *Horace Greeley and the Tribune.* Cedar Rapids, IA: Torch Press.

Fairclough, Norman. 2001. *Language and Power.* 2nd ed. Essex, UK: Pearson Education Limited.

Fairclough, Norman, Jane Mulderring, and Ruth Wodak. 2011. "Critical Discourse Analysis." In *Discourse Studies: A Multidisciplinary Introduction*, edited by Teun A. Van Dijk, 357–378. London: Sage.

Falk, Erika. 2010. *Women for President: Media Bias in Nine Campaigns.* Urbana, IL: University of Illinois Press.

———. 2013. "Clinton and the Playing-the-Gender-Card Metaphor in Campaign News." *Feminist Media Studies* 13 (2):192–207.

Fermaglich, Kirsten, and Lisa Fine. 2013. "Introduction." In *Betty Friedan: The Feminine Mystique: A Norton Critical Edition*, edited by Kirsten Fermaglich and Lisa Fine, xi–xx. New York, N.Y.: W.W. Norton and Co.

Ferraro, Gerladine. 1985. *Ferraro: My Story.* New York, N.Y.: Bantam Books.

Fink, Katherine, and Michael Schudson. 2014. "The Rise of Contextual Journalism, 1950s–2000s." *Journalism* 15 (1):3–20. doi: 10.1177/1464884913479015.

Finneman, Teri, and Ryan J. Thomas. 2014. "First Ladies in Permanent Conjuncture: Grace Coolidge and 'Great' American Womanhood in the New York Times." *Women's Studies in Communication* 37 (2):220–236.

Formisano, Ronald P. 2001. "The Concept of Political Culture." *Journal of Interdisciplinary History* 31 (3):393–426.

Foucault, Michel. 1977. *Language, Counter-Memory, Practice: Selected Essays and Interviews.* Ithaca, N.Y.: Cornell University Press.

Freeman, Jo. 2000. *A Room at a Time: How Women Entered Party Politics*. Lanham, MD: Rowman and Littlefield.

Gabriel, Mary. 1998. *Notorious Victoria: The Life of Victoria Woodhull, Uncensored*. Chapel Hill, N.C.: Algonquin Books.

Gaddis, John. 2002. *The Landscape of History: How Historians Map the Past*. New York, N.Y.: Oxford University Press.

Garrett, Peter, and Allan Bell. 1998. "Media and Discourse: A Critical Overview." In *Approaches to Media Discourse*, edited by Allan Bell and Peter Garrett, 1–20. Oxford: Blackwell.

George, Alexander L., and Andrew Bennett. 2005. *Case Studies and Theory Development in the Social Sciences*. Cambridge, MA: MIT Press.

Gertzog, Irwin. 1995. *Congressional Women: Their Recruitment, Integration, and Behavior*. 2nd ed. New York, N.Y.: Praeger.

Giardina, Carol. 2010. *Freedom for Women: Forging the Women's Liberation Movement, 1953–1970*. Gainesville, FL: University Press of Florida.

Gill, Rosalind. 2007. *Gender and the Media*. Cambridge, UK: Polity Press.

Ginzberg, Lori. 2009. *Elizabeth Cady Stanton: An American Life*. New York, N.Y.: Hill and Wang.

Goodwin, Doris Kearns. 1976. *Lyndon Johnson and the American Dream*. New York, N.Y.: Harper and Row.

Graham Jr., Frank. 1964. *Margaret Chase Smith*. New York, N.Y.: John Day Co.

Greene, John. 2010. *America in the Sixties*. Syracuse, N.Y.: Syracuse University Press.

Guba, Egon G., and Yvonna S. Lincoln. 1998. "Competing Paradigms in Qualitative Research." In *The Landscape of Qualitative Research*, edited by Norman K. Denzin and Yvonna S. Lincoln, 195–220. London, UK: Sage.

Gustafson, Melanie S., Kristie Miller, and Elisabeth Israels Perry. 1999. *We Have Come to Stay: American Women and Political Parties, 1880–1960*. Albuquerque, N.M.: University of New Mexico Press.

Hachten, William. 2005. *The Troubles of Journalism*. 3rd ed. Mahwah, N.J.: Lawrence Erlbaum Associates.

Hall, Stuart. 1975. "Introduction." In *Paper Voices: The Popular Press and Social Change, 1935–1965*, edited by Anthony Charles H. Smith, Elizabeth Immirzi, and Trevor Blackwell, 11–24. Totowa, N.J.: Rowman and Littlefield.

Hanitzsch, Thomas. 2007. "Deconstructing Journalism Culture: Toward a Universal Theory." *Communication Theory* 17 (4):367–385. doi: 10.1111/j.1468-2885.2007.00303.x.

Hardt, Hanno. 1998. *Interactions: Critical Studies in Communication, Media & Journalism*. Lanham, MD: Rowman & Littlefield.

Hartmann, Susan. 1989. *From Margin to Mainstream: American Women and Politics Since 1960*. New York, N.Y.: Knopf.

Havel, James T. 1996. *U.S. Presidential Candidates and the Elections: A Biographical and Historical Guide*. New York, N.Y.: Simon and Schuster Macmillan.

Haydu, Jeffrey. 1998. "Making Use of the Past: Time Periods as Cases to Compare and as Sequences of Problem Solving." *American Journal of Sociology* 104 (2):339–371.

Heith, Diane. 2003. "The Lipstick Watch: Media Coverage, Gender, and Presidential Campaigns." In *Anticipating Madam President*, edited by Robert P. Watson and Ann Gordon, 123–130. Boulder, CO: Lynne Rienner Publishers.

Heldman, Caroline, Susan J. Carroll, and Stephanie Olson. 2005. "'She Brought Only a Skirt': Print Media Coverage of Elizabeth Dole's Bid for the Republican Presidential Nomination." *Political Communication* 22 (3):315–335. doi: 10.1080/10584600591006564.

Hesford, Victoria. 2013. *Feeling Women's Liberation*. Durham, N.C.: Duke University Press.

Hesseltine, William. 1935. *Ulysses S. Grant: Politician*. New York, N.Y.: Frederick Ungar Publishing.

Hill, Jeff. 2006. *Defining Moments: Women's Suffrage*. Detroit, MI: Omnigraphics.

Howe, Daniel Walker. 1991. "The Evangelical Movement and Political Culture in the North During the Second Party System." *The Journal of American History* 77 (4):1216–1239. doi: 10.2307/2078260.

Husband, Julie, and Jim O'Loughlin. 2004. *Daily Life in the Industrial United States, 1870–1900*. Westport, CT: Greenwood Press.

Hyde, Grant. 1912. *Newspaper Reporting and Correspondence*. New York, N.Y.: D. Appleton and Co.

Iggers, Georg. 2005. *Historiography in the 20th Century: From Scientific Objectivity to the Postmodern Challenge*. Middletown, CT: Wesleyan University Press.

Ingersoll, L.D. 1873. *The Life of Horace Greeley: Founder of the New York Tribune*. New York, N.Y.: Union Publishing.

Iverson, Peter. 1997. *Barry Goldwater Native Arizonan*. Norman, OK: University of Oklahoma Press.

Jamieson, Kathleen Hall. 1995. *Beyond the Double Bind: Women and Leadership*. Oxford, UK: Oxford University Press.

Jeansonne, Glen. 2006. *A Time of Paradox: America Since 1890*. Lanham, MD: Rowman & Littlefield.

Jorgensen, Marianne W., and Louise J. Phillips. 2004. *Discourse Analysis as Theory and Method*. London: Sage.

Kahn, Kim. 1996. *The Political Consequences of Being a Woman*. New York, N.Y.: Columbia University Press.

Kantor, Jodi. 2012. *The Obamas*. New York, N.Y.: Little, Brown & Co.

Kaplan, Richard L. 2002. *Politics and the American Press: The Rise of Objectivity, 1865–1920*. Cambridge, UK: Cambridge University Press.

Katz, Jackson. 2013. *Leading Men: Presidential Campaigns and the Politics of Manhood*. Northampton, MA: Interlink Books.

Kerber, Linda. 1988. "Separate Spheres, Female Worlds, Woman's Place: The Rhetoric of Women's History." *Journal of American History* 75 (1):9–39.

Kimball, Bruce. 1992. *The "True Professional Ideal" in America: A History*. Cambridge, MA: Blackwell.

Kolodzy, Janet. 2006. *Convergence Journalism: Writing and Reporting Across the News Media*. Lanham, MD: Rowman & Littlefield Publishers.

Kraditor, Aileen S. 1965. *The Ideas of the Women's Suffrage Movement, 1890–1920*. New York, N.Y.: Columbia University Press.

Krolokke, Charlotte, and Anne Scott Sorensen. 2006. *Gender Communication Theories and Analyses: From Silence to Performance*. Thousand Oaks, CA: Sage.

Kwon, Winston, Ian Clarke, and Ruth Wodak. 2014. "Micro-Level Discursive Strategies for Constructing Shared Views around Strategic Issues in Team Meetings." *Journal of Management Studies* 51 (2):265–290. doi: 10.1111/joms.12036.

Lansford, Tom. 2012. *9/11 and the Wars in Afghanistan and Iraq: A Chronology and Reference Guide*. Santa Barbara, CA: ABC-CLIO.

Larsen, Jonathan Z. 2001. "Forty Years on a Roller Coaster." *Columbia Journalism Review* 40 (4):40.

Lawrence, Regina G., and Melody Rose. 2010. *Hillary Clinton's Race for the White House: Gender Politics and the Media on the Campaign Trail*. Boulder, CO: Lynne Rienner Publishers.

Lerner, Gerda. 1975. "Placing Women in History: Definitions and Challenges." *Feminist Studies* 3 (1/2):5–14.

Lindlof, Thomas R., and Bryan C. Taylor. 2002. *Qualitative Communication Research Methods*. 2nd ed. Thousand Oaks, CA: Sage.

Lorber, Judith. 2012. "Third-Wave Feminism." In *Gender Inequality: Feminist Theories and Politics*, edited by Judith Lorber, 304–307. New York, N.Y.: Oxford University Press.

"Luncheon for Miss Rankin." 1913. *Omaha Daily Bee*, June 12, 8.

Maihafer, Harry. 1998. *The General and the Journalists*. Washington, D.C.: Brassey's.

Malone, Michael, and Richard Roeder. 1976. *Montana: A History of Two Centuries*. Seattle, WA: University of Washington Press.

Marshall, Jon. 2011. *Watergate's Legacy and the Press: The Investigative Impulse*. Evanston, IL: Northwestern University Press.

Matthews, Donald. 1960. *U.S. Senators and Their World*. New York, N.Y.: Vintage Books.

"May Out Talk the Males." 1913. *The Ocala Evening Star*, May 9, 1.

McCabe, Janet. 2012. "States of Confusion: Sarah Palin and the Politics of U.S. Mothering." *Feminist Media Studies* 12 (1):149–153. doi: http://dx.doi.org/10.108 0/14680777.2011.640009.

McDowell, Edwin. 1964. *Barry Goldwater: Portrait of an Arizonan*. Chicago, IL: Henry Regnery Co.

McFadden, Robert. 1973. "Ex-Rep. Jeannette Rankin Dies; First Woman in Congress, 92." *The New York Times*, May 20, 65.

McFeely, William. 1981. *Grant: A Biography*. New York, N.Y.: W.W. Norton & Co.

McKee, Alan. 2003. *Textual Analysis: A Beginner's Guide*. London, UK: Sage.

McMillian, John. 2011. *Smoking Typewriters: The Sixties Underground Press and the Rise of Alternative Media in America*. Oxford, UK: Oxford University Press.

Mead, Rebecca. 2004. *How the Vote Was Won: Woman Suffrage in the Western United States, 1868–1914*. New York, N.Y.: New York University Press.

Meiner, Ruth. 1952. "Sen. Smith First Woman to Seek Veep Office." *Logansport Pharos Tribune*, July 11, 6.

Meyer, Philip. 2004. *The Vanishing Newspaper: Saving Journalism in the Information Age*. Columbia, MO: University of Missouri Press.

Miller, Carl. 1962. *Modern Journalism*. New York, N.Y.: Holt, Rinehart and Winston.

"Miss Rankin Gains Good Support in North." 1914. *The Missoulian*, March 23, 3.

"Miss Rankin Probably Defeated in Democratic Landslide in Montana." 1916. *New Castle News* November 9, 1.

Moeller, Susan D. 2004. "Follow the Leader." *American Journalism Review* 26 (2):16–18.

Morrison, John, and Catherine Morrison. 1997. *Mavericks: The Lives and Battles of Montana's Political Legends*. Moscow, ID: University of Idaho Press.

Mott, Frank Luther. 1962. *American Journalism: A History, 1690–1960*. 3rd ed. New York, N.Y.: Macmillan.

"Mrs. Clyde Smith Enters Primary to Succeed Husband in House." 1940. *Daily Kennebec Journal*, April 13, 1, 3.

"Mrs. Woodhull and Her Critics." 1871. *The New York Times*, May 22, 5.

Murray, Rainbow. 2010a. "Conclusion: A New Comparative Framework." In *Cracking the Highest Glass Ceiling: A Global Comparison of Women's Campaigns for Executive Office*, edited by Rainbow Murray, 223–248. Santa Barbara, CA: Praeger.

———. 2010b. "Introduction: Gender Stereotypes and Media Coverage of Women Candidates." In *Cracking the Highest Glass Ceiling: A Global Comparison of Women's Campaigns for Executive Office*, edited by Rainbow Murray, 1–28. Santa Barbara, CA: Praeger.

Neukom, Lisetta. 1916. "Wonder Woman is Miss Jeannette Rankin." *Evening Public Ledger*, November 11, 6.

Palin, Sarah. 2009. *Going Rogue: An American Life*. New York, N.Y.: HarperCollins.

Patterson, Thomas E. 1994. "Legitimate Beef: The Presidency and a Carnivorous Press." *Media Studies Journal* 8 (2):21–26.

Perrot, Michelle. 1992. "Women, Power and History." In *Writing Women's History*, edited by Michelle Perrot, 160–174. Oxford, UK: Blackwell.

Ragin, Charles. 1987. *The Comparative Method: Moving Beyond Qualitative and Quantitative Strategies*. Berkeley, CA: University of California Press.

Rhodan, Maya. 2014. "Senator Says Male Colleague Told Her 'You're Even Pretty When You're Fat.'" *Time*, August 27. From: http://tinyurl.com/o9nksbm.

Richardson, John E. 2007. *Analysing Newspapers: An Approach from Critical Discourse Analysis*. New York, N.Y.: Palgrave Macmillan Basingstoke.

———. 2010. "Language and Journalism: An Expanding Research Agenda." In *Language and Journalism*, edited by John E. Richardson, 1–9. New York, N.Y.: Routledge.

Riffe, Daniel, Stephen Lacy, and Frederick G. Fico. 1998. *Analyzing Media Messages: Using Quantitative Content Analysis in Research*. Mahwah, N.J.: Lawrence Erlbaum Associates.

Ross, Charles. 1911. *The Writing of News: A Handbook*. New York, N.Y.: Holt and Co.

Ross, Karen. 2010. *Gendered Media: Women, Men, and Identity Politics*. Lanham, MD: Rowman & Littlefield.

Rutenbeck, Jeffrey B. 1995. "Newspaper Trends in the 1870s: Proliferation, Popularization, and Political Independence." *Journalism & Mass Communication Quarterly* 72 (2):361–375.

Ryfe, David M. 2006. "News, Culture and Public Life." *Journalism Studies* 7 (1):60–77. doi: 10.1080/14616700500450343.

Rymph, Catherine E. 2006. *Republican Women: Feminism and Conservatism from Suffrage through the Rise of the New Right.* Chapel Hill, N.C.: University of North Carolina Press.

Saad, Lydia. 2008. "Congressional Approval Hits Record-Low 14%." *Gallup*, http://www.gallup.com/poll/108856/congressional-approval-hits-recordlow-14.aspx.

Sabato, Larry. 2000. *Feeding Frenzy: How Attack Journalism Has Transformed American Politics.* New York, N.Y.: The Free Press.

Sanders, Elizabeth. 2004. "Economic Regulation in the Progressive Era." In *The American Congress: The Building of Democracy*, edited by Julian Zelizer, 337–355. Boston, MA: Houghton Mifflin Company.

Schmidt, Patricia. 2005. "Vibrating to an Iron String: Margaret Chase Smith and Her Construction of Gender at the Century's Mid-Point." In *Of Place and Gender: Women in Maine History*, edited by Marli Weiner, 371–398. Orono, ME: The University of Maine Press.

Schnall, Marianne. 2013. *What Will It Take to Make a Woman President?* Berkeley, CA: Seal Press.

Schudson, Michael. 1978. *Discovering the News: A Social History of American Newspapers.* New York, N.Y.: Basic Books.

———. 2001. "The Objectivity Norm in American Journalism." *Journalism* 2 (2):149–170.

Severo, Richard. 1995. "Margaret Chase Smith is Dead at 97; Maine Republican Made History Twice." *The New York Times*, May 30.

Sherman, Janann. 2000. *No Place for a Woman.* New Brunswick, N.J.: Rutgers University Press.

Sloan, Wm. David. 2011. *The Media in America: A History.* 8th ed. Northport, AL: Vision Press.

Smith, Aaron. 2009. "Mass Layoffs Hit Seven-Year High." *CNN*, http://money.cnn.com/2009/01/28/news/economy/mass_layoffs/.

Smith, Jean Edward. 2001. *Grant.* New York, N.Y.: Simon & Schuster.

Smith, Karen Manners. 2000. "New Paths to Power: 1890–1920." In *No Small Courage: A History of Women in the United States*, edited by Nancy Cott, 353–412. Oxford, UK: Oxford University Press.

Smith, Margaret Chase. 1952. No Place for a Woman? *The Ladies Home Journal*, 50.

Smith, Norma. 2002. *Jeannette Rankin: America's Conscience.* Helena, MT: Montana Historical Society Press.

Snay, Mitchell. 2011. *Horace Greeley and the Politics of Reform in Nineteenth Century America.* Lanham, MD: Rowman & Littlefield Publishers.

Sonderman, Jeff. 2012. "600 Newspaper Layoffs in One Day Is, Unfortunately, Not a Record." *Poynter*, http://www.poynter.org/news/mediawire/177145/600-newspaper-layoffs-in-one-day-is-unfortunately-not-a-record/.

Sontag, Susan. 1972. The Double Standard of Aging. *The Saturday Review*, September 23, 29–38.

Startt, James. 2004. *Woodrow Wilson and the Press: Prelude to the Presidency.* New York, N.Y.: Palgrave Macmillan.

Steinhauer, Jennifer. 2006. "With the House in the Balance, Pelosi Serves as a Focal Point for Both Parties." *The New York Times*, October 30, A20.

Stepp, Carl Sessions. 2014. *State of the American Newspaper: Then and Now* (September) 1999 [cited November 13, 2014]. Available from http://ajrarchive.org/Article.asp?id=3192.

"Suffragists Plan Counter Activity." 1913. *The Washington Times*, April 18, 6.

Swain, Carol. 1997. "Women and Blacks in Congress: 1870–1996." In *Congress Reconsidered*, edited by Lawrence Dodd and Bruce Oppenheimer. Washington, D.C.: CQ Press.

Swanborn, Peter. 2010. *Case Study Research: What, Why and How?* London, UK: Sage.

The Project for Excellence in Journalism. 2009. The State of the News Media 2009: Newspapers. http://www.stateofthemedia.org/2009/a-year-in-the-news/newspapers/.

Thomas, Ryan J., and Teri Finneman. 2013. "Who Watches the Watchdogs?" *Journalism Studies* 15 (2):172–186. doi: 10.1080/1461670x.2013.806068.

"To Our Subscribers." 1872. *Woodhull & Claflin's Weekly*, January 13, 8.

"Transcript: Hillary Clinton Endorses Barack Obama." 2008. *The New York Times*, June 7.

Underhill, Lois Beachy. 1995. *The Woman Who Ran for President: The Many Lives of Victoria Woodhull*. New York, N.Y.: Penguin Books.

"Untitled." 1870. *Delaware Gazette*, May 13, 2.

"Untitled." 1872a. *Woodhull & Claflin's Weekly*, January 20, 11.

"Untitled." 1872b. *The Opelousas Courier*, July 13, 1.

Van Deusen, Glyndon. 1953. *Horace Greeley: Nineteenth Century Crusader.* Philadelphia, PA: University of Pennsylvania Press.

van Dijk, Teun A. 2002. "The Interdisciplinary Study of News as Discourse." In *A Handbook of Qualitative Methods for Mass Communication Research*, edited by Klaus Bruhn Jensen and Nicholas W. Jankowski, 108–120. London, UK: Routledge.

"Victoria C. Woodhull." 1872. *Woodhull & Claflin's Weekly*, January 27, 15.

"Victoria Martin, Suffragist, Dies." 1927. *The New York Times*, June 11, 19.

Volle, Jeffrey. 2010. *The Political Legacies of Barry Goldwater and George McGovern: Shifting Party Paradigms.* New York, N.Y.: Palgrave MacMillan.

Vos, Tim P. 2011. "'Homo Journalisticus': Journalism Education's Role in Articulating the Objectivity Norm." *Journalism* 13 (4):435–449. doi: 10.1177/1464884911431374.

Vos, Tim P., and Teri Finneman. 2014. "Legitimizing News Judgments: The Early Historical Construction of Journalism's Gatekeeping Role." In *Association for Education in Journalism and Mass Communication History Division*. Montreal, Canada.

"Wall Street Aroused." 1870. *The New York Times*, February 6, 8.

Wallace, Patricia Ward. 1995. *Politics of Conscience: A Biography of Margaret Chase Smith.* Westport, CT: Praeger.

Ware, Susan. 1981. *Beyond Suffrage: Women in the New Deal.* Cambridge, MA: Harvard University Press.

Watson, Robert P. 2003. "Introduction: The White House as Ultimate Prize." In *Anticipating Madam President,* edited by Robert P. Watson and Ann Gordon, 1–20. Boulder, CO: Lynne Rienner Publishers.

Weatherford, Doris. 2012. *Women in American Politics: History and Milestones.* Los Angeles, CA: CQ Press.

Weaver, David, Randal Beam, Bonnie Brownlee, Paul Voakes, and G. Cleveland Wilhoit. 2007. *The American Journalist in the 21st Century.* Mahwah, N.J.: Lawrence Erlbaum Associates.

Weiner, Marli. 2005. *Of Place and Gender: Women in Maine History.* Orono, ME: The University of Maine Press.

"Where Tribute is Due." 1914. *The Suffrage Daily News,* September 26, 2.

White, Theodore. 1965. *The Making of the President 1964.* New York, N.Y.: Antheneum Publishers.

Winfield, Betty Houchin, and Barbara Friedman. 2003. "Gender Politics: News Coverage of the Candidates' Wives in Campaign 2000." *Journalism & Mass Communication Quarterly* 80 (3):548–566.

Witt, Linda, Glenna Matthews, and Karen M. Paget. 1995. *Running as a Woman: Gender and Power in American Politics.* New York, N.Y.: Simon and Schuster.

Wodak, Ruth. 2001. "The Discourse-Historical Approach." In *Methods of Critical Discourse Analysis,* edited by Ruth Wodak and Michael Meyer, 63–94. London: Sage.

Woloch, Nancy. 2002. *Women and the American Experience: A Concise History.* 2nd ed. New York, N.Y.: McGraw Hill.

"Woman M.C. Votes Against the War." 1917. *Rogue River Courier,* April 6, 1.

"Woman's Rights." 1870. *Memphis Daily Appeal,* May 21, 4.

"The Women Going Wrong." 1872. *Arizona Sentinel,* June 29, 2.

Women in Elective Office 2014. 2014. Center for American Women and Politics 2014 [cited October 26, 2014]. Available from http://www.cawp.rutgers.edu/fast_facts/ levels_of_office/documents/elective.pdf.

"Women in the Stock Market." 1870. *Charleston Daily News,* February 9, 1.

Women in the U.S. Congress 2015. 2014. Center for American Women and Politics 2015 [cited February 20, 2015, 2014]. Available from http://www.cawp.rutgers. edu/fast_facts/levels_of_office/documents/cong.pdf.

Women Presidential and Vice Presidential Candidates. 2014. Center for American Women and Politics 2012 [cited October 26, 2014]. Available from http://www. cawp.rutgers.edu/fast_facts/levels_of_office/documents/prescand.pdf.

Yardley, William. 2006. "Novice Stands Her Ground on Veterans' Turf in Alaska." *The New York Times,* October 29, 25.

Zelizer, Barbie. 2011. "Journalism in the Service of Communication." *Journal of Communication* 61 (1):1–21.

Zelizer, Julian. 2007. "Without Restraint: Scandal and Politics in America." In *The Columbia History of Post-World War II America,* edited by Mark Carnes, 226–254. New York, N.Y.: Columbia University Press.

Index

About the Author

Dr. Teri Finneman is an award-winning journalism scholar and former political reporter who received her Ph.D. from the Missouri School of Journalism. Finneman's research focuses on news coverage of first ladies and women politicians, although she also conducts research related to media ethics, media history, and oral history. She is a co-author of *A Companion to First Ladies, Cross Cultural Journalism: Communicating Strategically About Diversity,* and *Swinging for the Fences: Black Baseball in Minnesota.* Finneman teaches journalism at South Dakota State University. Follow her on Twitter @finnemte.

CPSIA information can be obtained at www.ICGtesting.com
Printed in the USA
BVOW04*0102181115

427068BV00002BA/2/P